AMRITA PRITAM

Amrita Pritam was a prominent Punjabi poet, novelist and essayist who captured the realities of everyday life in the India of the early 1900s and presented the unique voices of the women of the Indian subcontinent. This book offers a comprehensive understanding of the writer's work by situating it in the context of not just Punjabi literature but Indian literature, while showcasing its continued relevance in contemporary times.

With a career spanning over six decades, Amrita produced more than 100 books of poetry, fiction, biographies, essays, collections of folk songs and autobiographies; many of which were translated into several Indian and foreign languages. This volume includes critical essays on her works as well as a selection of her poems and stories in translation including, 'To Waris Shah' ('Ajj Aakhaan Waris Shah nu'), *The Skeleton (Pinjar)* and *Village No. 36 (Chak No. 36)* and excerpts from other prominent writings to give readers a glimpse into Amrita's rich literary oeuvre as well as her legacy in a post-colonial India which is still grappling with many of the same taboos around gender, national and religious identity and women's sexuality. It discusses the diversity of themes and sociocultural realities in her works, focussing especially on Punjab, agency of her women protagonists, national and communal identities and the testimonies of the traumas which the cataclysmic 1947 Partition of India brought on women. A writer who consistently subverted the existing social, political and patriarchal structures of her times, both in her life and in her writings, this book encapsulates the relevance of her writings and her voice in our times.

Part of the 'Writer in Context' series, this book will be useful for scholars and researchers of Indian literature, Hindi literature, Punjabi literature, English literature, Postcolonial Studies, Cultural Studies, Global South Studies and Translation Studies.

Hina Nandrajog is Associate Professor in the Department of English and currently serving as Officiating Principal, Vivekananda College, University of Delhi. She is an academic, scholar, critic, teacher and translator. Her areas of interest are the Partition of India in 1947 from a historical and literary perspective, the idea of diversity and multi-linguality in India and translation. She is an avid translator from Punjabi and Hindi into English and has won several awards.

Prem Kumari Srivastava is Professor of English with University of Delhi at Maharaja Agrasen College. With several publications including 11 books (authored and edited), many research papers, book chapters, review articles, translations and creative writing: poems and stories, her research displays an overarching focus on the 'other': the popular, the indigenous, the non-urban and gender within Cultural Studies. Her recent publications are *Tribal Literature and Oral Expressions in India* (2021) and *Indian Popular Fiction: New Genres, Novel Spaces* (2021).

WRITER IN CONTEXT

Series Editor: **Sukrita Paul Kumar**, *critic, poet and academic*; **Chandana Dutta**, *academic, translator and editor*

The 'Writer in Context' Series has been conceptualized to facilitate a comprehensive understanding of Indian writers from different languages. This is in light of the fact that Indian literature in English translation is being read and even taught extensively across the world with more and more scholars engaging in research. Each volume of the Series presents an author from the post-Independence, multilingual, Indian literature from within her/his socio-literary tradition. Every volume has been designed to showcase the writer'soeuvre along with her/his cultural context, literary tradition, critical reception and contemporary resonance. The Series, it is hoped, will serve as a significant creative and critical resource to address a glaring gap in knowledge regarding the context and tradition of Indian writing in different languages.

Sukrita Paul Kumar and Chandana Dutta are steering the project as Series Editors with Vandana R. Singh as the Managing Editor.

So far, twelve volumes have been planned covering writers from different parts and traditions of India. The intent is to facilitate a better understanding of Indian writers and their writings for the serious academic, the curious researcher as well as the keen lay reader.

Krishna Sobti
A Counter Archive
Edited by Sukrita Paul Kumar and Rekha Sethi

Joginder Paul
The Writerly Writer
Edited by Chandana Dutta

Indira Goswami
Margins and Beyond
Edited by Namrata Pathak and Dibyajyoti Sarma

Amrita Pritam
The Writer Provocateur
Edited by Hina Nandrajog and Prem Kumari Srivastava

Mahasweta Devi
Writer, Activist, Visionary
Edited by Radha Chakravarty

For more information about this series, please visit: www.routledge.com/Writer-In-Context/book-series/WIC

AMRITA PRITAM

The Writer Provocateur

Edited by
Hina Nandrajog and
Prem Kumari Srivastava

Routledge
Taylor & Francis Group
LONDON AND NEW YORK

First published 2023
by Routledge
4 Park Square, Milton Park, Abingdon, Oxon OX14 4RN

and by Routledge
605 Third Avenue, New York, NY 10158

Routledge is an imprint of the Taylor & Francis Group, an informa business

© 2023 selection and editorial matter, Hina Nandrajog and Prem Kumari Srivastava; individual chapters, the contributors

British Library Cataloguing-in-Publication Data
A catalogue record for this book is available from the British Library

Library of Congress Cataloging-in-Publication Data
A catalog record has been requested for this book

ISBN: 978-0-367-69968-0 (hbk)
ISBN: 978-1-032-10295-5 (pbk)
ISBN: 978-1-003-21465-6 (ebk)

DOI: 10.4324/9781003214656

Typeset in Sabon
by Deanta Global Publishing Services, Chennai, India

Dear Prem

You danced your way out of this life
In sync with the music of the Universe

Your laughter lingers in our ears while
Your joyful spirit spreads cheer out there!

Dedicated to the memory of Professor Prem Kumari Srivastava

Figure 1 Amrita wielding a pen

Figure 2 The poem 'Main Tainu Pher Milangi' in original Punjabi in the author's hand. Sketch of a tree by Imroz that forms the word 'Amrita' in Gurumukhi

CONTENTS

PHOTOGRAPHS

PREFACE TO THE SERIES

The conceptualisation and making of the 'Writer in Context' series must in itself be seen in the context of a historical evolution of literary studies in English in India. It was as late as the mid-1980s of the 20th century, decades after the independence of India, that the angst to redefine English literary studies in the universities manifested itself in thoughtful discussions amongst scholars. In 1986 the Kenyan writer Ngugi wa Thiong'o published his well-known book *Decolonizing the Mind* that had a widespread appeal amongst the academia and people in general who were struggling to shed their deep-set colonial hangover. Soon after, English departments of the Indian universities and the Centres of South Asian Studies abroad began to incorporate Indian literatures in translation into their syllabi. This encouraged more translations of Indian literatures into English, even though translation studies never picked up as a popular academic discipline. Other than the translations of a few critical texts from Indian languages, the creation of appropriate critical material for an understanding of the comprehensive context of the writers remained minimal. There still remains an impending need to place Indian writers within the context of their own literary as well as sociocultural linguistic traditions. Each language in India has a well-developed tradition of creative writing and the writings of each writer require to be understood from within that tradition even if she/he may be writing against the tide. Readers, translators, editors, and publishers ought to be able to acknowledge and identify these writings from within their own intimate contexts. Familiarity with the oeuvre of the writers, with their times as well as the knowledge of their critical reception by the discerning readers of their own language, facilitates an understanding of certain otherwise inaccessible nuances of their creative writings. Apart from getting an insight into the distinctive nature of the specific writer, this would also add to the sense of the fascinating diversity in Indian literatures.

Each volume in this series is designed to provide a few extracts from the creative and other prose writings by the author in focus, followed by the English translations of selected critical essays on the author's works. For better insights into the writer's art and craft, self-reflexive essays and articles by the author about the creative process and her/his comments on the writerly environment are also included. Much of this material may be available as scattered correspondence, conversations, notes and essays that lie untranslated and locked – as it were – in different *bhashas*. A discreet selection of such material has also been included in each of the volumes in this series.

In the making of this series, there has been an ongoing exchange of ideas amongst the editors of different volumes. It is indeed intriguing that while the writers selected belong to more or less the same times, the contexts vary; and, even when literary conventions may be similar in some languages, the author stands out as unique. At times the context itself creates the writer but many a time the writer creates her/his own context. The enquiry into the dialectic between the writer and the context lends a significant dimension to the volume. While the distinctive nature of each volume is dictated by the uniqueness of the author, all the volumes in the series conform to the shared concept of presenting an author from within the literary context of her/his language and culture.

It is hoped that the 'Writer in Context' series will make it easier for the scholar to, first, examine the creative interventions of the writer in her/his own language and then help study the author in relation to the others, thus mapping the literary currents and cross-currents in the subcontinent. The series presents fiction writers from different Indian languages of the post-Independence era in their specific contexts, through critical material in translation and in the English original. This generation of 'modern' writers, whether in Malayalam or Urdu, Assamese or Hindi, or for that matter in any other Indian language, evolved with a heightened consciousness of change and resurgence fanned by modernism, postmodernism, progressivism and other literary trends and fashions, while rooted in tradition. Highly protective of their autonomy as writers, they were freely experimental in form, content and even the use of language. The volumes as a whole offer a vision of the strands of divergence as well as confluence in Indian literature.

The Writer in Context series would be a substantial intervention, we believe, in making the Indian writers more critically accessible and the scholarship on Indian literature more meaningful. While the series would be a creative attempt at contextualising Indian writers, these volumes will facilitate the study of the diverse and multilingual Indian literature. The intent is to present Indian writers and their writings from within their socio-literary context to the serious academic, the curious researcher as well as the keen lay reader.

Sukrita Paul Kumar and Chandana Dutta
Series Editors

PREFACE

This book is dedicated to the life and words of one of the most charismatic figures of the Indian literary landscape – Amrita Pritam (1919–2005). She has captured the imagination of the masses for over half a century with her writings; and even more so for a life led on her own terms. Her vast body of work is a veritable feast of myriad forms of creativity and has provoked and inspired scholars and critics to decode her feminism and humanism stemming from her passionate belief in the autonomy of the self. Her life lived by these principles has imbued her with a larger-than-life persona in public imagination.

The volume has been arranged thematically, offering a glimpse into the diverse genres of Amrita Pritam's creative writings – poems, novels, stories and prose – to sample the flavours of Amrita's rich palette, though a disclaimer is required that this is by no means representative of all her dimensions. The volume further analyses different aspects of her writings that have often been overshadowed by the radical life she led. It explores the thematics of her work and seeks recurrent motifs in her writings that emerge from the very essence of her being. Having dominated half a century of Punjabi literature and counted among major Indian writers, the legacy she has left behind is a lasting one. Its echoes reverberate not just in literature but in film, theatre and television, too. This makes her a significant presence on the contemporary register leading to her ever-increasing global importance as a writer. In all, this volume, as part of the 'Writer in Context' series will be of immense value to scholars and critics of Literary Studies, Cultural Studies, Film Studies, Gender Studies and South Asian Studies.

Hina Nandrajog and Prem Kumari Srivastava

ACKNOWLEDGEMENTS

A page to acknowledge and thank all the people who have guided and helped us on this beautiful journey seems inadequate to express the gratitude in our hearts. We merely mention them knowing that we all share a common bond in our admiration and love for Amrita Pritam.

We are beholden to Sukrita Paul Kumar, a close friend and mentor, for reaching out to us to be a part of the project 'Writer in Context' series and to Chandana Dutta, the other series editor. The volume would not have been possible but for their unstinting guidance and support. We thank Vandana R. Singh, and all our co-conspirators in the Writer in Context series for regular intellectual exchanges and discussions.

Several scholars in Punjabi language and literature helped to conceptualise the volume and guided us to researchers on Amrita Pritam; we thank Prof. Rawail Singh, Dr Mohanjit Singh, Dr Amia Kunwar, Prof. Surjit Patar, Dr Vanita, Dr Dhanwant Kaur, Prof. Surjit Singh, Dr Arvinder Kaur, Mr Surinder Sharma, Dr Gurpreet Kaur Brar and Dr Parveen Kumar. Dr Paul Kaur and Ms Nirupama Dutt enriched the volume immensely with their advice; we also thank them for sharing their research and some photos. We thank noted actor and poet Ms Deepti Naval for sharing her experience of 'becoming Amrita' on stage, and well-known theatre director Mr Salim Arif for his interview and permission to translate excerpts from his play *Main Tumhe Phir Miloongi*. We express our gratitude for their generosity in sharing sources and material.

The contributors and the translators for the volume merit a heartfelt thanks for their adherence to timelines and openness to suggestions and for submitting endless revisions.

We thank:

- Mala Dayal for permission to reprint an extract from Amrita Pritam's novel *Pinjar*'s translation in English by Khushwant Singh as *The Skeleton*, Delhi: Dynamic Publishers, 2021, p. 17–20.
- Ms Nirupama Dutt for permission to print her English translations of:
  - "I Call to Waris Shah" of the poem "Ajj Aakhaan Waris Shah nu" https://scroll.in/article/847004/when-amrita-pritam-called-out

-to-waris-shah-in-a-heartrending-ode-while-fleeing-the-partition
-riots

- "I Will Meet You Yet Again" of the poem "Main Tainu Pher Milangi" https://scroll.in/article/815278/the-story-of-amrita-pritams-final-love-poem, and
- "The Shah's Harlot" of the short story "Shah di Kanjari" https://scroll.in/article/875515/on-baisakhi-two-classic-short-stories-that-capture-the-spirit-of-punjab
- Lt. Col. Jasbir Bhullar for permission to translate and print the following:
  - Jasbir Bhullar, "Sahan de Hisse di Maulsari de Baare", *Sahan de Hisse di Maulsari*, ed. Jasbir Bhullar, Chandigarh: Punjab Sahit Akademi and Amritsar: Lok Sahit Prakashan, 2001, p. 11–12.
  - Mohan Bhandari, "Aavaaz de kahaan hai", *Saahaan de Hisse di Maulsari*, ed. Jasbir Bhullar, Chandigarh: Punjab Sahit Akademi & Amritsar: Lok Sahit Prakashan, 2001, p. 62–74.
- Mr Satish Sharma of Shilalekh Publishers for his generous support and guidance, and permission to print, and translate and print, the following extracts:
  - Novel: Amrita Pritam, *Village No. 36*, translated by Shanti Dev, Delhi: Shilalekh Publishers, 2021, p. 75–80.
  - Poetry: Amrita Pritam, *Black Rose & Existence*, tr. Charles Brasch & Mahendra Kulshreshtha. Delhi: Shilalekh Publishers, 2019.
i)	'A Story of Fire'	p. 15–16
ii)	'Hand Reading'	p. 22–23
iii)	'Not Today'	p. 41–42
iv)	'Existence'	p. 54–55
v)	'Life'	p. 59–60
vi)	'Toast'	p. 85–87
- Translate and print:
  - Prose: Amrita Pritam, *Kainat se Aage*. Delhi: Shilalekh Publishers: 2013.
i)	'Paanch Sapne'	p. 20–22.
ii)	'Antar-dristhi'	p. 29–30.
iii)	'Vaama Shakti'	p. 38–39.
  - Novel: Amrita Pritam, *Urmi (Akk da Boota)*. *Ratna, Benu te Urmi: Tinn Novel*, Delhi: Shilalekh, 2017, rpt. 2020, p. 139–143.
- We thank Sahitya Akademi for permission to translate and publish an excerpt edited by Dr Vanita from Prof. S.S. Noor's essay, "Amrita Pritam di Kavita", *Amrita Pritam*, New Delhi: Sahitya Akademi, 2010, p. 15–54.
- This volume would not have been possible without the boundless generosity of Dr Amia Kunwar in sharing ideas, material and photographs. Our deep gratitude to her.

We are overwhelmed by the kindness shown by Dr Aman Kwatra, the grandson of Amrita Pritam and the copyright holder of the Amrita Pritam Trust, in granting permission to publish excerpts from Amrita Pritam's original writings and translations thereof, personal photographs and photos from *Nagmani*. We are deeply indebted to him for the trust reposed in us.

We also thank Routledge for the 'Writer in Context' series and for trusting us with this crucial volume on a doyen of literature, Amrita Pritam.

Our sincere apologies if we have omitted mention of any other fellow traveller on this journey.

Last but not the least, our special gratitude to our families for providing the strength and cosy comfort that allowed us a space to engage, absorb and fall in love with Amrita.

Figure 3 Amrita as a young woman

Figure 4 Amrita playing the sitar

INTRODUCTION
Daughter of Words

Hina Nandrajog and Prem Kumari Srivastava

Amrita Pritam, proclaimed as *akkharan di jaayi* (daughter of words), unlike other daughters in a feudal, patriarchal Punjab of erstwhile undivided India did not learn to stitch and sew – occupations seen as necessary for women in their roles as homemakers. She rather chose to stitch words together to create what she poetically calls a '*chaanan di phulkari*' – a tapestry of radiance – a metaphor for a borderless, equal and just world that she envisioned through her formidable literary oeuvre created over a period of seven decades of writing. Journeying from an intense desire as a motherless, lonely child for recognition and love from her father to supreme disregard of all criticism levied by contemporaries – kith and kin, writers and leaders alike – Amrita let nothing hinder the prolific pouring from her pen – her chosen tool – and carved a distinctive space for herself in world literature. She wrote primarily in Punjabi, although there is a substantial corpus published originally in Hindi, presumably for wider readership; and she enjoyed fame in both languages simultaneously. Noted Dogri writer, Padma Sachdev calls her 'an ornament of Punjabi literature; the sandalwood paste on its forehead, spreading fragrance ... one bank of the river where all five streams of Punjabi literature mingled' (Sachdev and Mudi 2005: 8).

Amrita's legendary persona as a writer and her striking, unusual personal life choices make her one of the most courageous and intriguing scholar-writers in the world. She lived and celebrated life on her own terms and her literature is a creative expression of her provocative iconoclasm. The stubbornly frozen gaze of her own generation, especially male writers and critics, viewed the trailblazing path that Amrita's radical self took on the road less travelled in an obverse light and designated her a rebel for interrogating status quo in gender relations and society. She questioned insidious structures of patriarchy, sought to redress social inequities and created new signposts in her life and her writings. Almost always swimming against the tide kept her in the cross hairs of society constantly and provoked her contemporaries and the media. The armour she built against this was hard-won and battle-worn; and she bore both fame and

DOI: 10.4324/9781003214656-1

1

notoriety with equal aplomb. This only deepened the aura around her and her present-day deification is in a large measure due to her distinctive progressive choices, both in her life and her writings. However, the hyperbolic status accorded to her is actually a matter of both service and disservice to her legacy. While it undoubtedly attracts present and future generations to revisit her prolific body of work and avant-garde sensibility, it draws attention away from the simplicity of her humanism which places her in the realm of the most distinguished writers and thinkers of the world. This volume on the writer provocateur, Amrita Pritam is a part of the 'Writer in Context' series which seeks to contextualise Indian writers in their own cultural and linguistic milieu, who yet demonstrate how they have made a significant contribution to Indian literature as well as the corpus of world literature by transcending narrow borders of language and region. The series highlights how the themes these Indian writers touch upon have universal resonance and are of immense value to readers and scholars all over the world. The impulse behind the present volume is not to build a romanticised, ivory-tower image of this much misunderstood yet admired-envied lady of letters who has dominated the Punjabi and Indian literary tradition, but to lay out an intertextual, literary and cultural site of exploration that is contextual, interventionist, critical and scholarly and most importantly, stimulating. Not only did her unconventional life choices roil the milieu in which she lived but her writings provocatively challenged stereotypes and dismantled conventions, both in choice of themes and modes of expression.

Proclaiming herself a citizen of a free world, Amrita's writings demonstrate two major impulses: freedom of expression and honest rendition of heartfelt, personal experiences. Both her life and writings advocate a transformation of societies and nations everywhere and attest to an idealistic, futuristic world populated by individuals who are pure at heart, cleansed of all unworthy thoughts and relate with others as equals. Called the 'Voice of Punjab', she embraces the entire world when she proclaims, 'wherever a glimpse of a free spirit exists / That will be my home' (Pritam, Singh 1982: 177). Her works, translated into numerous Indian and foreign languages, have taken her message of humanity like that of a dervish to the entire world.

Amrita wrote in myriad genres – 20 anthologies of poetry, 10 collections of short stories, 27 novels/novellas, 21 collections of prose, including travelogue, autobiography, letters and volumes on diverse themes – devotional, romantic, realistic and spiritual. Her literary journal, *Nagmani*, nurtured and shaped an entire community of creative writers in Punjabi. Extensive travels abroad, especially to Eastern European nations, brought her in contact with the wider world and she translated a great deal of foreign literature for a Punjabi audience. Having commanded considerable critical attention ever since she brought out her first collection of poetry in 1935, she won numerous national and international laurels – notable among which are the Sahitya Akademi award (1956), Bhartiya Jnanpith award (1981), Padma Vibhushan (2004) and the Sahitya Akademi Fellowship for Lifetime Achievement (2005). Her life and works have been adapted for multimedia platforms. She continues to charm successive generations of audiences and readers with her inspirational idealism.

Treading New Terrain

Amrita says in 'Kalam da Bhet' (The Secret of the Pen') 'Maan sucche ishq da hai, hunar da daava nahi' / 'I trust pure love, I lay no claims to talent.'

(Pritam 2019: 135)

Amrita Pritam redefined the literary canon in Punjabi and Indian literature. Progressing through various social and political movements, her uninhibited, provocative expression of the personal paved the way for greater articulation of authentic experience and ushered in modernism and experimentation in theme and style, form and content in Punjabi literature. Her natural talent for rhyming and her perusal of eclectic literature undertaken to assuage her loneliness was supported by the rich poetic tradition she inherited – the romanticism of the Middle Ages, *qissas*, *gurbani*, the idiom of Punjabi folk tradition and a study of poetics. Her diction breathed the lilt of spoken language and she sought to sculpt a new vocabulary to give utterance to her thought. Her relationship with everything, including words, was sensory; she says that she could not greet even the Gurus from a distance, she had to touch their sword or the falcon even in her dreams. (Pritam 1968: 3) Her poetry and other writings were woven with a wealth of imagery and a lyrical quality that drew inspiration both from the folk tradition and the love ballads. Popular characters in the romantic folk tales of Punjab pervade Amrita's poetic world 'not as mere literary allusions but as the embodiment of the Punjabis' aspirations and frustrations' (Dulai 1969: 69). An only child, born on 31 August 1919 to parents of a religious, ascetic bent of mind, Amrita Pritam nee Amrit Kaur was brought up in a restricted, religious environment in Gujaranwala, now in Pakistan. The death of her mother in 1930 despite Amrita's earnest prayers shattered her faith in God and had a profound influence on her personality and her writing. Her father recognised her gift for rhyming and taught her the basics of poetry to encourage her to compose devotional verse – which she did to please him; what she wrote her entire life was perhaps to seek validation from her father. (Pritam 1998: 11) On the other hand, her instinct impelled her to reject and rebel against prescribed dictates that forbade the articulation and fulfilment of the self; a frightening fate that had befallen her paternal aunt, Haako who had voluntarily buried herself in a solitary cell to escape an unwanted marriage. The germ of being a writer provocateur was sown when a pre-adolescent Amrita subverted her father's training and addressed her first poem to 'Rajan', a formless, unidentifiable, but real presence in her mind – a friend and confidante. The slap that she received from her father for denying authorship when he discovered her poem made her resolve to take full responsibility for all that she wrote henceforth – amply demonstrated over the next six decades of her writing.

The age in which Amrita started writing was the age of the romanticism of Mohan Singh that colours her early poetry as well. Their writings drew Punjabi poetry out of a mystic-romantic mould into modern forms and themes expressed in contemporary language. Marxism and the social consciousness of the Progressive Writers' Movement impacted Amrita's dreams of revolution against colonialism and capitalism and freedom from feudal, patriarchal shackles although she resisted being straitjacketed in any one category. From the traditional and devotional, her work evolved to the unconventional and iconoclastic – questioning stereotypes of gender, the iniquity of religion and the oppression of the state. The conventional, romantic trajectory in her first two anthologies of poetry, *Thandiyan Kirnan* (*Cool Rays* 1935) and *Amrit Lehran* (*Immortal Waves* 1936), turned to articulate the anguish of the common masses in subsequent collections such as *Jiunda Jeevan* (*An Exuberant Life* 1939) and *Lok Peed* (*Anguish of the Masses* 1944) and she addressed her poems to world leaders like Martin Luther King and Lenin. The birth pangs of a new nation-in-the-making jostling with values of an ancient civilisation began to find utterance, expressing both hope and anguish.

Palimpsestic Romantic Idealism

Writing the creative over the personal, Amrita recounts a dream about a garden of roses in her autobiography *Rasidi Ticket* (*The Revenue Stamp*) in which she equates love songs to red roses, songs of sorrow and pain to black and those for love of humanity to white (1998: 42), and one finds a blend of all these hues in her writings. Amrita's thematics string her entire oeuvre of poems, stories, novels, prose together with tropes of love, longing, sorrow – both personal and universal. The overarching frame that encompasses all her writings is the inscription of the personal into the creative and the transmutation of the personal into the universal; often becoming indistinguishable in the process. Her writing is not merely an abstraction sketched within the lines of a poem, story, or a novel but forged in the furnace of personal experience. Her childhood hunger for the attention of her solipsistic, scholarly father echoes in her work throughout and she felt she was like one of the books lying in the house. Her own experience with socially sanctioned/unsanctioned relationships made her interrogate patriarchy and the feeble, commodified position of women in it. She realises the restrictions imposed on women till their breath is stifled and they are reduced to being half-human, eternally doomed to serve men as daughters, sisters, wives, mothers. Her innate sense of the self refused to submit to a rationalisation of such a social arrangement; and her own rebellion against patriarchal shackles and the simple honesty with which she lived by her ideals is not only remarkable but extremely rare. The intensely private yet poignantly universal in her writings articulates the separation of the body and soul in a marriage in her poem 'Kumari' ('Virgin'):

When I entered your bridal chamber
I was not one but two persons.
One's marriage had been consummated and complete
The other had ever remained a chaste virgin.
                                                (Pritam, Singh 1982: 31)

In *Punjab di Aavaaz* (*The Voice of Punjab* 1952) Amrita says that woman has been on trial not only in the folk songs of Punjab but in the history of the world and mentions the three stages in a woman's life – daughter, mother and daughter-in-law: with other relationships flowing from it (qtd. in Kapoor 1982: 18–19). Her empathy for other voiceless and unheard beings gradually encompasses the universe to envision a world in which relationships are not transactional but bonded with purity of emotion because only such a world could provide a truly enabling environment for human beings to realise their true potential. Amrita feels that men and women have not yet met as two independent human beings (Pritam and Jha 1982: 188–189). For her, legitimacy of love is not achieved merely through social sanction but by the integrity of intention and complete commitment. Ostensibly, a large number of women in her stories and novels are socialised into patriarchy and endure the agony of separation and loss or die since such pure unions can rarely be found in life; and even if they exist, they are invariably doomed as society's walls are often impossible to breach. Yet, as Revti Sharan Sharma says, her heroines 'stand out for their pitiless honesty, subjecting themselves to the most hazardous experiments in unconventional and uncompromised emotional living' (Mahfil, 1968–1969: 119). Amrita's heroines reflect her own personality; she herself owns her kinship with Alka, the heroine of *Chakk No. 36* (*Village No. 36*) – a woman who willingly establishes sexual relations with a man without expecting anything in return from him, demonstrating the futuristic vision Amrita has of a woman's agency and her assertion over her body and her mind. Sharma finds Amrita's brand of feminism milder when compared to the stridency of Ismat Chughtai, Khadija Mastoor, Sarala Devi and Mannu Bhandari. 'Amrita genuinely feels in essence that the woman is her own captive and if she chooses to be a "full being", freedom and fulfillment will flow to her as naturally as water to fields below' (1969: 120). One could also place Amrita alongside two major rebel woman poet-writers, Adrienne Rich from America and Kamala Das from India, in building a case for a strong feminine tradition of the modern era.

Amrita's writings question not just the plague of patriarchy, but religious fanaticism and social inequality as well. Even as a child, she resisted, and ultimately prevailed upon, her grandmother to shun the discriminatory practice of keeping separate utensils for Muslims and Hindus. Witnessing, as a child, her father being browbeaten by religious fanatics into hiding pictorial slides created to preach Sikhism deepened this scepticism. She celebrates the traditional composite culture of Punjab in a folksong:

> One boy is called 'Fateh Mohammed'
> The second is 'Sardaru'
> 'Gama', 'Barkat', 'Saun', 'Chanan Singh'
> ...
> All of them go to the fair together
> To enjoy the giddha.
>
> (qtd. in Kapoor 1982: 18)

But this harmony is tenuous, and in 'Janoon' ('Frenzy') she expresses the threat it faces:

> When religion goes to people's heads
> Steel is sharpened
> Tongues grow cruel
> Poisoned by black snakes of hatred,
> ....
> And innocent children
> Delicate women
> Strong young men
> Are human beings no longer
> But animals for sacrifice.
> When religion goes to people's heads ...
>
> (Pritam, Singh 1982: 101)

The crescendo of religious fanaticism of 1947 compelled Amrita to interrogate the intersection of nationality, religion and gender. Forced to move across the border, first to Dehradun and then to Delhi with her husband and children, this was another major impulse for her writing – and her dirge to Partition, 'Ajj Aakhaan Waris Shah nu' ('To Waris Shah') was a universal lament for a lost world and resonated on both sides of the newly-drawn border. 'Ajj Aakhaan ...' oscillated sensitively to unite the personal and universal through evocative imagery and symbolism, and, in Khushwant Singh's words, made Amrita immortal. It travelled to Pakistan even before it was published and people are believed to have wept upon reading it and even carried it as an amulet. Her novel *Pinjar* (*The Skeleton* 1950) portrayed the shackles that chain women against the backdrop of Partition and evoked the significance of the autonomy of the individual. She stood for, and voiced, the idea of equality in all relations, leading to a vision of a universal humanism and harmonious global order. The journey of Pooro in *Pinjar* is envisioned later as being carried forward by Sheeri, the Muslim protagonist in the novel, *Unninja Din* (*49 Days*) in 1978. The Hindu protagonist, Sanjay echoes Amrita's thought when he says that just as danger lessens when two people walk together, the danger of the world will lessen if two religions walk together (Amrita, Devinder 1982: 316).

Even her personal anguish at her unrequited love for Sahir Ludhianvi, a fellow poet whom she met at Preet Nagar in a poetry festival and in whom she perceived the embodiment of the Rajan of her imagination, was not her agony alone. Her collection of poems, *Sunhede* (*Messages* 1956), was 'a letter she wrote to her lover all her life, a letter which has never reached him and is never complete. So it needs to be written continuously' (Dulai 1969: 68). This too was woven with the social and political angst of the marginalised, thus infusing it with deep resonance and winning her accolades as the first woman recipient of the Sahitya Akademi award in 1956. This empathy matured further in *Kaagaz te Canvas* (*Paper and Canvas* 1970) that won her the Jnanpith Award; an anthology she averred as her outlook and vision of life (Pritam, Jha 1982: 186) and which is imbued with a rare inner wisdom. Her comments on the historiography of her times, events and their socio-political register in poems such as 'Chup di Saazish' ('Conspiracy of Silence') and 'Mera Pata' ('My Address') became a representative manifesto of a courageous spirit that rebelled against any kind of oppression (Swarajbir, Mohanjit 2002: 188–189).

While contextualising Amrita's vast oeuvre, one finds her securely ensconced as a writer extraordinaire in the Punjabi literary tradition; while her uncompromising humanism extended her reach far beyond geographical boundaries. She had an unshakeable belief in the imperative to ensure agency to all human beings, irrespective of class, caste, creed, race, religion, gender. For her, the bounty of the earth is a shared heritage. In 'Still Life', transcending the local to global, she laments the common sorrow afflicting the world:

Jallianwala:
A silent wall scarred by bullets.
Siberia:
Broken cries buried beneath ice.
Concentration camps:
Smell of incinerated flesh.
Karogojawac:

An entire population in a single statue.
Hiroshima:
A torn ancient palimpsest.
Prague:
Trapped, breathless, in the censor's fist.
All, pale, lifeless.
This breath of disgust alone
My breath exhales.
The soil trembles.

(Pritam, Singh 1982: 107)

Progressive Humanism and a Writer's Role in Society

In an imaginary interview with noted Indian scholar, Rahul Sankrityayan, Amrita draws an analogy between the use of fire and words. Fire lit by some illumines paths and provides warmth to shivering bodies, while fire lit by others may burn households to ashes; similarly, the words of some show the path to people while words of others mislead them. And just as diamond cuts diamond, it is only words that can rip away the web of illusion spun by words (Pritam 1982: 11–15). It is her attempt to carve out a righteous path with words:

I write my song
So that none may have to write again
The songs of frustration.

(Pritam qtd. in Dulai 1969: 69)

Amrita's vision for a writer's role in society is to create fresh canons for a newer, more equitable world order. She believes that 'without values you cannot be an artist. The artist does not live in a void. When the old values die out or prove useless, the artist strikes new values' (Pritam, Jha 1982: 188). In an article about her own writing, she quotes an Australian aboriginal tale in which people crawled around in a dark world as the sky was very low. The birds raised the sky and the sun illuminated the world. She sees the soul of birds in writers, 'whatever little light one sees in the darkness of every society, every religion, and every state, it is because of those few who have made the effort to lift their sky' (Pritam, Mohanjit 1982: 261). Similarly, in her acceptance speech for the Bhartiya Jnanpith Award for *Kagaz te Canvas* in 1982, Amrita narrates a tale told by her grandmother about the gods sleeping in certain seasons, 'I think that all through my life all that I have written is only an attempt to wake up the sleeping gods' (Pritam, Mohanjit 2002: 254).

This commitment to society and art is what led her and her partner, Imroz, 'the one who broke the curse of loneliness of my heart' (Pritam 1998: 85), to birth and nurture a unique literary magazine in 1966;

'something like you've told me about *Mahfil*', she said to Carlo Coppola. (1969: 19) She explains the name 'Nagmani' as the precious stone supposed to be embedded in the foreheads of snakes with which they play on moonlit nights, symbolising one's intellect (1969: 18). She translated world authors for the magazine and invited fledgling, talented authors to write – even instituting a financial grant to encourage them. Poetic soirees, famed as 'Nagmani Shaam', were organised, often at her home, to enable writers to meet and learn from each other. The house that the two of them lived in became a kind of Mecca for generations of litterateurs and artists. That it was a service to society is evident from the fact that she and Imroz considered themselves to be 'labourers' rather than editors – writing, sketching, editing and everything else besides, to ensure delivery of the journal to its subscribers.

Speaking the Self

I don't know if my pen improves anything for anyone. I only know that my pen is my redemption. I tire of bobbing up and down in the waters of life, this bank gives me shelter. My written papers become books as they absorb the ink from my pen.

(Pritam 1968: 7)

Despite writing creatively and copiously, Amrita's compelling need for self-expression led her to write not just one autobiography but two, with the second one being revised repeatedly – *Kala Gulab* (*The Black Rose* 1968) and *Rasidi Ticket* (*The Revenue Stamp* 1976), in addition to *Aksharon ke Saaye* (*Shadows of Words* 2001). Unlike most autobiographies by women which tend towards the confessional mode – a mixture of assertion of a right and an entreaty to be heard – Amrita's autobiography, non-chronological and unapologetic, is a proclamation of a free spirit. That is what defines her; and any attempt to understand the persona of the poet or her vast repertoire of writings cannot be successful if the word 'free' is ever subtracted from her personality. It is precisely due to this reason that the prejudice of most of her contemporaries veered towards a highly scandalised disapproval of her; and it is precisely for this reason that she could be supremely unaffected by it.

Her self-reflexivity in her autobiographies lays bare the boldness with which she realised the autonomy of her being in the living of her life – her marriage, her relationship with Sahir Ludhianvi and later with Imroz – and it also illumines her creative process and its evolution from her early romanticism to later more nuanced work. Gayathri Prabhu says, 'When Amrita Pritam wove her autobiography around love, she also demonstrated the many ways to love' (*Scroll.in* 2019). It is:

9

not about explicitness in the mode of the 'confessional poets' (say, Sylvia Plath or Anne Sexton), for that would breach an intimacy that Amrita Pritam's words seek to cocoon and nourish, but the writing is candid and inviting in a way that turns the voyeur in the reader to an ally, a fellow-sojourner on the path of love.

(2019)

Although Khushwant Singh famously declared Amrita's life to be uneventful enough to be fitted onto the back of a revenue stamp, for Amrita the act of writing an autobiography was more in the nature of an attestation of her life – affixing a revenue stamp on the account of her life. It is important to remember that her scintillating and mesmerising personality may lead one to forget that a large part of what one knows about her is through her own account of her life – expansive enough to touch upon issues ranging from the tender burgeoning of romantic hope in the bosom of a young teenage girl to the profound, inner voyage into the soul of a sage who could yet be as playful or pettish as a petite child at the age of eighty and more. A Greek poet that Amrita admired, Nikos Kazantzakis, said that one should create one's idealised image of oneself as a free being and unceasingly strive to resemble that image. This is the strand that strings all the motifs in Amrita's writings together – to be an authentic being for one's own self and for others.

Towards Transcendental Mysticism

'Poems ... are after all, not some material things, they can be seen melting into colours, soaring in the sky like divine birds, changing colours every moment ...' (Pritam, Mohanjit 2002: 263).

The evolution of Amrita's poetic genius is a journey from the self to transcendental mysticism. This stage also segued in with the inner contentment that she found with her artist-partner, Imroz, a contentment that no marriage ritual could pledge. It was only after this that Amrita Pritam's outward search ended as she retreated from the material world to wander amidst the inner recesses of the mind; her life henceforth became an odyssey into the inner self, again giving direction to her writing in the latter phase of her life. Her poetry and prose delved into different planes of consciousness and her densely woven world of imagination and dreams now began to fall into place like a jigsaw puzzle to complete the circle of life. The extensive reading of literature and scriptures became signposts for her journey within the soul and beyond the universe. Dreams and journeys into the inner consciousness become the primary focus in books such as *Darveshan di Mehndi* (*The Dervishes' Ecstasy*) (1996) and *Utth ni Sahiba Suttiye* (*Wake up Slumbering Sahiba*) (1998), while in *Main Tainu Pher Milaangi* (*I Shall Meet You Yet Again*)

(2004) her consciousness transcended the entire universe even while plumbing the depths of an individual soul. Her ardent self, however, remained undimmed and was expressed evocatively in her impassioned promise to Imroz, 'I shall meet you again' – as a line on his canvas or as a ray of sunshine. The two are forever united also in the mingling of word and image as all of Amrita's writings are adorned with Imroz's sketches and paintings for posterity.

Amrita's swan song was a promise not only to Imroz but also to her galaxy of readers and admirers – like the motif of the phoenix in her writings, she has been resurrected time and again in various renderings of her rich life and literature through diverse media. Her bold and independent feminine sensibility nurtured by an absolute faith in romantic love woven with the mellow glow of mysticism is an unforgettable experience for anyone traversing through her writings.

Mapping the Volume

To contextualise this writer provocateur within the mutative and evolving socio-politico-literary milieu of the early decades of her writing when the progressive trope was favoured, or within the charged debates around nationalism and democratic idealism of the evolving, independent Indian nation state through the 1950s to the 1970s, or within the later liberalised and globalised climate of 1980s and the 1990s and finally within the debates of postcolonialism, postmodernism and radical feminism of the end of the century and till 2005 was a difficult task. Serious and sustained engagement is required with Amrita's interventionist dialogues and innovative sites of exploration of the literary and cultural registers of Punjab, India and the world. Seeking to fulfil this purpose, this volume is arranged thematically into the above-mentioned debates and the diverse genres of Amrita's writings. Though by no means representative of all her dimensions, some nuggets of her original creative writing provide the readers a flavour of Amrita's rich palette and exhibit her indomitable rebellious spirit to vouch for the purity of the soul in the face of societal pressure. Among the poems presented are 'A Call to Waris Shah', the one that immortalised her, 'A Story of Fire' which stands out for the intensity of ardour that Amrita felt for Sahir, while her swan song, 'I Will Meet You Yet Again' is for Imroz – a journey traversed from the heat of passion to the contentment of the transcendental. *The Skeleton* stands tall in her vast oeuvre of literary fiction as one of the most authentic sagas of feminine trauma during the cataclysmic Partition of 1947, while *Village No. 36* presents a female protagonist who is admittedly moulded upon Amrita herself. She discusses issues related to transactional relationships, marriage, dowry, illegitimate children, honour killing; the last one being presented through an extract from the novella, *Urmi* where a woman is killed by her parents and in-laws for daring to love outside marriage. A sample of her short story is presented through 'The Shah's Harlot' which is unusual in its treatment of two women – a wife and a mistress who are by turn victim and victimiser, while glimpses of her spirituality, seeded perhaps by her parents, are presented through three short samples of her later writings. An excerpt is taken from her autobiography, *The Revenue Stamp* – a woven tapestry of the self that envelops her readers in a willing suspension of disbelief to devour it as *itihas* or 'so it happened'.

The various essays in this volume analyse diverse elements of her multiple genres. Amrita's autobiographical writings are examined to see how the genre of life-writing was used by her to register a constantly changing self and hold disjunctive life experiences together, and to elaborate the relation between Amrita's biographical and poetic self. The focus in her writings on gender, nation and state within the rubric of the traumatic Partition of 1947 is attempted through survivor accounts, fiction and cinema that function as testimony to explore concepts of historical and structural trauma in Amrita's magnum opus, *Pinjar* (1950) and its film adaptation (2003). A study of three of her poems shows how Amrita subverts the taboos imposed by local and nationalistic patriarchies; and how they are reinterpreted in Amrita's gendered, syncretic voice, thus empowering several voiceless women. Also explored is the (re)production of upper caste/middle class women's sexuality at the interstices between patriarchal, virilocal and patrilineal structures on one hand and legislative adjudicatory framework of the Hindu Code Bill on the other through a reading of three of her novels. Women's negotiation with the structural inequities of marriage is explored through the universe inhabited by her extraordinary heroines seeking to redress social biases, drawing from Amrita's own words about her heirs who would take forward her dream of an equitable world and to proclaim women's inalienable right to cultivate an autonomous identity. Her social commitment to widening the horizon of Punjabi literary landscape is borne out by her eclectic creativity as an editor, or a tireless 'labourer' along with Imroz for *Nagmani*.

The essays go on to critically interrogate the evolution of her poetic sensibility and showcase her enduring legacy. Her mysticism tempered by her materiality is explored as well. The language discourse in her writings is examined by taking her literary texts as objects of study, and also through a critical study of the unique harmony of intellect and instinct in her language that focusses on meaning rather than words, with an awareness that the existential experience of women cannot be expressed in a male-centred language.

Trained early in expounding religious verse to congregations in gurdwaras as a child, then addressing the public on the radio in Lahore and Delhi, Amrita romanced the media, and the media in turn romanced her.

Her numerous interviews, adaptations on her love and life on stage and screen possess an irresistible allure. Her continuous and continuing glamour for multimedia – radio, television, theatre and celluloid – is foregrounded through Amrita's candid interface with popular media of successive eras as it evolved and transformed from the 1950s to the present day. The volume concludes by turning its gaze on the enduring fascination for this peerless writer whom 'age does not wither, nor custom stale her infinite variety'. She has inspired a galaxy of admirer-writers, scholar-critics and awe-struck young authors who bear the mantle of her legacy of a liberal and liberated spirit and are inspired to write their 'own truths'. Amrita transcends any appellation used to define her and all her pen portraits are but incomplete shards of a holistic portrait of her.

Conclusion

(D)dare[d] to live the life she imagine[d]
(Tharu et al. 1993: 161)

Amrita's writings testify to her living by her words and bear the imprint of her revolutionary streak. The mantle of her early outward conformity gradually thinned and dissolved, revealing the radiance of her rebellious self-assurance that transformed a clinging ivy to a girl with a 'steel spine'. She lived her life with a belief in the sovereignty of the self; rewrote conventions of prevalent poetics, aesthetics, themes considered legitimate and universalised the intensely personal (and vice versa). Like the motif of a phoenix that she narrated, she has soared high above anyone's reach, exactly as in her dreams. Her appeal has endured and deepened, and she is acknowledged today not just as a Punjabi writer, or a woman writer, but an eminent Indian writer who has achieved rare world recognition and respect. She transcends all borders and continues to remain relevant in establishing the autonomy of one's identity. All her writings are the living of her dream of a borderless, casteless, religionless, race-less, gender-less world.

The legacy that Amrita bequeaths is unique and empowering. The feminist and humanistic concerns that she foregrounds in her vast body of work have inspired later poets and novelists for generations to come. This is what she envisaged herself in 'Vaseeyatnama' ('Will') published in the July 1984 issue of *Nagmani*; Amia Kunwar recounts that there was no mention of a traditional will of any property or land; in fact it was a will written about the dreams and thoughts of a writer:

I desire … now whenever it's time to say goodbye I can do so easily. I just want that those who were in no way connected to me while

I was alive, should not be connected to me when I am dead.... the pen that remained with me throughout my long journey, I desire – it remains with me till my flesh turns to dust.

(Pritam 1984)

Amrita's pen has spoken in a true and clear voice to be heard by, and to provoke to action, not only her contemporaries but later generations too. As Russian poet and translator of Amrita's poetry, Rimma Fyodorovna Kazakova, said, 'thousands of arms are eager to embrace her in their warm embrace' (Kazakova, 1982: 390), this volume is another reverent embrace in the enduring legacy of Amrita Pritam, the daughter of words.

References

Coppola, Carlo and Amrita Pritam. 1969. "Amrita Pritam", *Mahfil*, Vol. 5, No. 3 Amrita Pritam Number (1968–1969): 5–26.

Devinder. 1982. "Hunar da Daava Nahi", in Ajit Singh Kakkar (ed.), *Punjabi Duniya*, pp. 314–318. Patiala: Directorate Bhasha Vibhag.

Dulai, Surjit Singh. 1969. "Pebble Playthings to the Serpent's Jewel", *Mahfil*, Vol. 5, No. 3, Amrita Pritam Number (1968–1969): 53–73.

Jha, Rama and Amrita Pritam. 1969. "An Interview with Amrita Pritam", *Indian Literature*, Vol. 25, No. 5 (September–October), 1982: 183–195.

Kapoor, Navratan. 1982. "Punjabi Lok Sahit nu Shrimati Amrita Pritam di Den", in Ajit Singh Kakkar (ed.), *Punjabi Duniya*, pp. 14–28. Patiala: Directorate Bhasha Vibhag.

Kazakova, Rimma Fyodorovna. 1982. "Main Kaun Haan", in Ajit Singh Kakkar (ed.), *Punjabi Duniya*, pp. 380–384. Patiala: Directorate Bhasha Vibhag.

Prabhu, Gayathri. 2019. "When Amrita Wove Her Autobiography Around Love, She Also Demonstrated the Many Ways to Love", Memoirs, *Scroll.in* (13 October 2019). https://scroll.in/article/940264/when-amrita-pritam-wove-her-autobiography-around-love-she-also-demonstrated-the-many-ways-to-love (accessed on 13.12.2021).

Pritam, Amrita. 1968. *Kala Gulab*. Delhi: Navyug Publishers.

———. 1976, rpt. 1998. *Rasidi Ticket*. Delhi: Shilalekh Publishers.

———. 1982. *Amrita Pritam: Selected Poems*. Trans. Khushwant Singh. Delhi: Bhartiya Jnanpith Publication.

———. Ed. 1982. "Interview with Rahul Sankrityayan", *Akshar Bolte Hain*, Delhi: Saraswati Vihar, pp. 11–15.

———. 2019 (2006). *Kagaz te Canvas ton Pahilan*. Delhi: Shilalekh.

———. 2002. "Sookham Kanan di Ibarat", in Mohanjit (ed.), *Goode Akkharan vali Varanmala: Writings on Amrita Pritam*, pp. 254–264. Delhi: Punjabi Academy.

Sachdev, Padma and Amar Mudi. 2005. "Amrita Pritam: The Flame on the Smoke Ball", *Indian Literature*, November–December 2005, Vol. 49, No. 6 (230): 8–12.

Sharma, Revti Saran. 1968–1969. "The Search for Feminine Integrity", *Mahfil*, Vol. 5, No. 3, Amrita Pritam Number (1968–1969): 119–131.

Swarajbir. 2002. "Itihaas, Kavita atey Kavi", in Mohanjit (ed.), *Goode Akkharan vali Varanmala: Writings on Amrita Pritam*, pp. 179–196. Delhi: Punjabi Academy.

Tharu, Susie and K. Lalitha, eds. 1993. *Women Writing in India: 600 BC to the Present*. Vol 1&2. New Delhi: OUP.

Family Album

Figure 5 Raj Bibi, Amrita's mother

Figure 6 Kartar Singh 'Hitkari', Amrita's father

Figure 7 Amrita as a child

Figure 8 Amrita with husband Pritam Singh Kwatra, and son and daughter, Navraj and Kandala

Figure 9 Amrita and Imroz

Figure 10 Amrita with grandchildren, Shilpi and Aman

Part I

THUS SHE WROTE ...
Amrita Pritam's Creative Oeuvre

I (a)

AMRITA'S POETIC SELF

1

SELECT POEMS

'A Call to Waris Shah'

Waris Shah I call out to you today to rise from your grave
Rise and open a new page of the immortal book of love
A daughter of Punjab had wept and you wrote many a dirge
A million daughters weep today and look at you for solace
Rise o beloved of the aggrieved, just look at your Punjab
Today corpses haunt the woods, Chenab overflows with blood
Someone has blended poison in the five rivers of Punjab
This water now runs through the verdant fields and glades
This fertile land has sprouted poisonous weeds far and near
Seeds of hatred have grown high, bloodshed is everywhere
Poisoned breeze in forest turned bamboo flutes into snakes
Their venom has turned the bright and rosy Punjab all blue
Throats have forgotten how to sing, the yarn is now broken
Friends are lost and the spinning wheel has gone silent
Boats released from the harbour toss in the rough waters
The peepul has broken its branches on which swings hung
The flute that played notes of love is now forever lost
Brothers of Ranjha have lost the hero's devotion, his charm
Blood rains on the earth, even the graves are oozing red
The princesses of love are now weeping midst the tombs
Today all have turned into Qaidon, thieves of love and beauty
O where on earth do we go to look for a Waris Shah once more
('Ajj Aakhaan Waris Shah nu', Pritam, Dutt Scroll.in)

A Story of Fire

This is a story of fire
You told me that story;
This is the cigarette of life
The one you lit.

DOI: 10.4324/9781003214656-4

The spark was of your giving,
My heart has been smoking ever since;
Time with pen in hand
Is smiling and counting.

The cigarette took fourteen minutes
To smoke;
To write this
Took me fourteen years.

My body was an unlit cigarette.
It was your breath that gave it life.
Earth is witness
To its constant burning.

The cigarette had burned out,
You inhaled a little
Of the scent of my love,
The rest has blown away on the wind.

Here is the butt.
Throw it away
That my love's fire
May not burn your fingers.

Don't think of what it burned.
Mind the spark in the butt.
Take care of your hand –
Light another cigarette.

('Agg di Baat', Pritam 2019: 15–16)

Hand Reading

The line of faithfulness
No one knows how to read it
I know there is a line of faithfulness
On my hand
The line of faithfulness

I don't know how to define it
How to tell
What its limits are
How far thought should be free to stray
And at what point danger lies.

24

How much nearness of other's lip
How much intimacy of talk
How much warmth of hands
Goes with the notion of faithfulness?
The line of faithfulness

How can one deepen it
And strengthen it
When so many promises
Cross one's lips –
As if words could measure it!

I know there is a line of faithfulness
On my hand
It may be invisible
But I can see it
It is the long one, deep one
On my small hand

And there are five fingers
Five senses
Five gods
To witness
The line of faithfulness.

('Wafa di Lakeer', Pritam 2019: 22–23)

Not Today

I always do the right thing
But not today,
I always do what people ask
But not today –

No!
In Nilchander valley
Where nothing grows old
Nothing changes
Flawless
Starless
Stormless
The blood in my hot veins is rebellious
I want to see a storm
Passionate as my blood
Giant hills

Demonic stones
I want to see the clouds
Breaking their heads
And I want to see deep gulfs
Like the gulfs of sin
I want to see the clouds
Fall into those gulfs
Their limbs shattered
I don't like pure blue sky.
I always do the right thing
But not today

I know society has a loud voice
But my purse is full
I can buy the voice;
I know religion will be outraged
But I shall bow my head for a while
And it will be appeased.

I know something will cry in my soul
But psychology will find me an explanation
And keep my soul quiet

I always do the right thing
But not today.

('Ik Gunahgaar', Pritam 2019: 41–42)

Existence

I'd heard
That the blue robe of the sky,
Stitched by Adam so long ago,
Belonged,
By hereditary right,
To me.
One night
I plucked the stars off –
Ripped out all its stitching –
And tearing a piece from it
Tried to wear it on my body.

I swear by this naked, shaken flesh
That one of Ghalib's ghazals
Dangled in the mind that day.

And, from a corner, a spider in its web
Began humming a new song.

Human limbs, rubbed, strike sparks.
I see face after grey face
In the light of burning wood.
I've swept out the ashes of dead fire:
I'd to sweep it out.

Only last night
I'd filled up the moon-pitcher,
And now I notice a crack in it.
I've wiped my lips clean
Of the rubai of Omar Khayyam
That played on it.

I stand between Newton and Kalidas
I glance for a moment to the right
I glance for a moment to the left
And the question arises:
I've to walk these distances.

I stand between Newton and Kalidas.
These distances are yet to walk.
The question is mine
But the answer is also mine:
I've to walk, not the distances,
But their meanings.

('Hond-Vaad', Pritam 2019: 54–55)

Life

Six steps full and one step half
A room in a prison
Sufficient
For a person to move about
And to take rest

Stale God-bread
Tasteless patience-curry
You can eat these to your bellyful
Every morning and evening

A pool of stagnant water –
Water of knowledge

You can wash your face with it
And drink it if you like
(of course after wiping
its surface of the mosquitoes)

(A wound in the soul
is a common disease)
If you're ashamed too much
Of its nakedness
You may tear off a piece
From your dreams
And cover the wound with it
No one would dare to talk
The matters of the prison
But for the cancer of hope
Revolts rise like waves of heat
And heat subsides in due course
Yet they rise again and again.

('Zindagi', Pritam 2019: 59–60)

Toast

Last night
I filled my goblet
With the wine of thoughts
– thoughts deep red
Friends drank the wine
And exchanged toasts
With words
That do not grow
 In the bosom
Where are the trees
On which they grow

And how they appear
On the flowerpots of the lips –
I had no time to think
Or perhaps I dared not think
It was a festival of words
An anniversary of illusions

And there were we:
I, the night,
The wine of thoughts

And friends –
Friends, some of whom
Had come on invitation
Others without it
But there was one
Who had not come
Despite reminded calls
... ...
The day had just broken
A ray of the sun
Has pierced my bosom
And entered deep into it
Just now I saw a dense forest
Thick with trees of pretense and falsity
I also saw the autumn visiting on them –

The autumn that visits
Not the words
But their meanings
The words spoken by friends
Are still fresh
Like flowers in spring
I witness
Only their meanings falling from them

I am alone in this forest
Utterly alone –
And there is the silence
A ray of the sun
And the empty goblet

Someone has just arrived.
There is the silence
Which includes
The sound of his footsteps
– a piece of silence
 broken from the silence whole
– a piece of ray
 broken from the ray complete

The one who has just arrived
Is he
Who had stayed away
Despite reminded calls

I am alone no more.
My self is with me
I've filled the goblet once again
Filled it with the wine of looks
And we're both drinking

He's offering toasts
With words
That grow only in the bosom
It is a festival of meanings
And there are we:
I, he by my side,
And the goblet
Filled with the wine of looks

('Toast', Pritam 2019: 85–87)

'I Will Meet You Yet Again'

I will meet you yet again
How and where
I know not
Perhaps I will become a
Figment of your imagination
And maybe spreading myself
In a mysterious line
On your canvas
I will keep gazing at you.
Perhaps I will become a ray
Of sunshine to be
Embraced by your colours
I will paint myself on your canvas
I know not how and where –
But I will meet you for sure.
Maybe I will turn into a spring
And rub foaming
Drops of water on your body
And rest my coolness on
Your burning chest
I know nothing
But that this life
Will walk along with me.
When the body perishes
All perishes
But the threads of memory

Are woven of enduring atoms
I will pick these particles
Weave the threads
And I will meet you yet again.

('Main Tainu Pher Milangi', Pritam, Dutt *Scroll.in*)

Sources

2016. "I Will Meet You Yet Again", tr. Nirupama Dutt. https://scroll.in/article /815278/the-story-of-amrita-pritams-final-love-poem (accessed on 12 December 2021).

2017. "A Call to Waris Shah", tr. Nirupama Dutt. https://scroll.in/article/847004 /when-amrita-pritam-called-out-to-waris-shah-in-a-heartrending-ode-while -fleeing-the-partition-riots (accessed on 16 May 2022).

2019. Amrita Pritam, *Black Rose & Existence*, tr. Charles Brasch & Mahendra Kulshreshtha. Delhi: Shilalekh Publishers.

I (b)

AMRITA – THE STORYTELLER

2

THE SKELETON

That morning Pooro planned her escape. To avoid suspicion, she ate all the sweet rice and curry Rashid brought for her. At night she stole the key of the door from beneath his pillow. Later, when he was fast asleep, she quietly unlocked the door and stepped out of her prison.

The pitch black of the night terrified her; she almost turned back. She was not sure if she would be able to find her way to Chatto. She might fall into the hands of some rustic worse than Rashida! Then the faces of her mother, brothers and sisters appeared before her eyes. She took the path she believed led to her home. The dim light of the coming dawn made the landscape somewhat clearer. She found herself on the right path and saw the outlines of her village.

Now the die was cast. She used all her strength and began to run. She came to the village and reached the land that led to her home. The sky had not turned grey when she found herself before her father's threshold.

Pooro rattled the chain. The door opened from the other side and she fell on the courtyard. She had used up all her strength; as soon as she reached the winning post, she had collapsed. She lay on the mud floor moaning like a wounded animal. She found her parents standing above her with oil lamps in their hands; she saw tears streaming from her mother's eyes. She felt her mother take her in her arms and clasp her to her bosom, as a cry of anguish broke from her heart.

'The neighbors will hear. There will be a crowd,' warned her father. Pooro's mother stuffed her mouth with the hem of her shirt.

'Daughter this fate was ordained for you; we are helpless'. Pooro heard her father's voice. She clung to her mother. 'The *Shaikhs* will descend on us and destroy everything we have'.

'Take me to Thailand with you!' cried Pooro.

'Who will marry you now? You have lost your religion and your birthright. If we dare to help you, we will be wiped out without a trace of blood left behind to tell of our fate'.

'Then destroy me with your own hands'.

DOI: 10.4324/9781003214656-6

'Daughter, it would have been better if you had died at birth! If the *Shaikhs* find you here, they will kill your father and your brothers. They will kill all of us,' said the mother, hardening her heart.

Pooro remembered Rashida's words: 'You have no place in that home now'. But what about her fiancé, Ram Chand? What was the difference between being engaged and being married? Why had he not bothered to come to her help? There was one hope for her: escape in death.

Pooro got up and went out of the door. Neither her mother nor her father tried to stop her. When she had come this way earlier, she had believed she was returning to life; she had wanted to live again, to be with her mother and father. She had come full of hope. Now she had no hope, nor any fear. What more could anyone take from her than life? The thought dried up all her tears.

Rashida came running breathlessly towards her. Pooro stopped in her footsteps. Even death had slammed the door in her face. Rashida grabbed her by the arm. She followed him without a word.

The third day the *Maulvi* came with another two or three men. They performed Pooro's marriage ceremony with Rashida. A few days later, Rashida told her that her parents had left for Thailand.

Rashida's parents were dead. He had no sisters; only brothers and uncles. He decided to leave his village for another, called Sakkar, a few miles away, where a distant cousin, Rahima, had some land. He could exchange some of his land with Rahima's and make his home there. He told Pooro of his plans. There was no reaction from her – after her parents had turned her away from their door, leaving the ancestral village did not seem so momentous. All said and done, what difference did it make? All villages were alike.

Rashida packed his odds and ends in a few steel trunks and set out for Sakkar. Pooro followed him as the blind follows a guide. They found a small house some distance from Rahima's. The first relations of Rashida's that Pooro met were the women of Rahima's household. They did not pester her with many questions; they only wanted to find out if she needed anything for her new home and whether they could be of any help. Nevertheless, Pooro felt like a stray calf in a strange herd of cows.

There were more changes in store for her. Till then Rashida had called her by her proper Hindu name. One day he brought a stranger with him and asked his wife to stretch out her arm. The man tattooed on it the new name she had been given when she was married to Rashida. From that day 'Hamida' was not only inscribed on her skin in dark green letters but everyone began to call her by that name.

In her dreams, when she met her old friends and played in her parents' home, everyone still called her Pooro. At other times she was Hamida. It was a double life: Hamida by day, Pooro by night. In reality, she was neither one nor the other; she was just a skeleton, without a shape or a name.

Six months later a tiny life began to stir inside her frame.

Source

Excerpt from Amrita Pritam, *Pinjar*, 1950, translated as *The Skeleton* by Khushwant Singh, Delhi: Dynamic Publishers, 2021, p. 17–20.

3

VILLAGE NO. 36

Kumar clambered to his feet and strode out, just in time to stop Uncle Chetu from unloading the baggage. Would he be good enough to carry it across to the house and would he get Haria to cook something for him to eat, he asked him.

Coming back inside, he noticed a huge big painting on the right wall. The nucleus of an interminable set of black lines suggested the form of a man; and that in the red tangle of lines, a woman. Towards the back of the man was the sun with a good part of it eclipsed; the same sun was a ball of fire behind the woman – radiating an aura of light. The man's eyes seemed to be viewing the world – full of wonder, the woman's seemed wrapt up in the man's shadow falling on them. Dumbfounded, Kumar kept admiring the handiwork for a good few minutes, then he looked askance at Alka.

'I know I don't have the maturity or talent for anything better…'

Kumar was not yet thinking of Alka's inherent talent, he was concentrating on the conception of the entire idea. Behind the spot where the man stood, there was very little space – to convey as it were, that he had not walked too far to reach where he was; the distance measured by the woman's steps seemed on the other hand, infinitely longer. The varying depths of the red and maroon colours marking her journey suggested an anxiety-ridden search for something; the man's, on the other hand, was suggestive of a brooding thought marked by as many shades of depths to the shadows surrounding him.

Placing an arm around her shoulders and touching her forehead with his lips, Kumar stated intensely, 'I want to bow in deep reverence to that woman.' Alka put her head on his shoulder and shut her eyes, her ears too perhaps. After what she had heard, she wanted to hear nothing more.

'Do you know why I named this place "Village No. 36"?'

'Did you name it?'

"You don't have numbers to names of villages in the hills. Nowhere else, with perhaps the rare exception of my native district, Baar. The village I was born in was called 'No. 36'. When both my parents died within a year, my

38   DOI: 10.4324/9781003214656-7

Uncle grabbed all he could lay his hands on. I was then simply an art student in Bombay."

'Did you not clamour for your claims when you were through?'

'I did, once. Settling disputes over land, I discovered, was beyond me. Anyway I couldn't have lived there always ... used to high life in cities though I was. After many years when I'd earned enough, I bought this land.'

'And you thought you'd bought back "Village No. 36"?'

"Exactly! I had, in fact, completely forgotten all about it until this moment. I was standing here wafted back on the wings of memory to my old village, back to my old hut. I am drawing no parallels, yet my mother had spread a hand-embroidered sheet on a cot the same way you have on that platform; she had painted a portrait of Goddess Lakshmi with reddle. This study of yours brings a nostalgic feeling. Her Lakshmi seems to have walked straight out of the village-hut-wall into this!"

It was rather unlike Kumar to be talking of such sentimental things – saturated with nostalgia. Alka grew nervous lest, lost in ruminations of fond old days with old folks, he should relapse totally into his former self and fetter his feelings. So she caught hold of his hand and said, 'Come now, eat something.'

'Do you live here? I mean do you sometimes go to your apartment?'

'Here only. I have now given up the other place.'

'Aren't you going to take me round to the other huts?'

'Have your dinner first. Later I will.'

'What about electricity?'

'It didn't quite fit in with the atmosphere of the huts.'

'With what difficulty I had got it for my studio! Gosh! It took me eternity before I did.'

'It was essential there.'

'But don't you have that creepy-crawly feeling – at night especially?'

'I did, twice so far. But not because of the area around. I had such terrify-ing dreams both the times that, that...'

'That... what?'

'That I have just told you about... about your calling out to me. The other dreams I had had seven or eight nights earlier.'

'Seven or eight nights, did you say?'

"Yes. I was in a tearing hurry to get somewhere, I don't know where to exactly. It was pitch dark. In the dark density of the night I was racing along the roads, I distinctly remember, of some big city. In the darkness I tapped at a window. I knocked at a door and then I woke up. I couldn't of course make head or tail of what all the dream was about. Where I was going, I knew not; why I was knocking at a door, I knew not either; why that door would not open I could not for the life of me understand. This much I know: I lay shivering from fear for quite some time."

A shiver went through the arm Kumar had thrown around Alka's shoulders. He involuntarily exclaimed, 'You devil!'

Alka stared stonily into Kumar's face – and staring still, she said, 'I thought by now you would have forgotten to call me "devil".'

Perhaps he was too rapt in winding his own experience to hear her speak. He took her by the hand and sat her down on the platform and for a fleeting moment thought he might as well tell her of that night in Delhi when Kanta had sat in his room and Alka's shadow had flickered across the window and he had heard her steps outside the door. But he held his lips tight: afraid of the story tumbling out, should he open them. Rather than tell her anything, he held back, 'Had you worn bangles, in your dream, I mean?'

Alka did not quite understand his question. Holding out both her arms instead, she said, 'I had got these new bangles on that very day. Or, just a moment, was it the day before?'

It was difficult keeping that groovy bit to himself, yet Kumar wanted it that way. Not being able to keep his lips sealed, he pressed them hard on Alka's so as to shut it up tightly inside.

He had had the conviction when in Delhi, that he had overcome his hunger for a woman's body. He had subjected himself to the test. Even when Kanta lay there in his bed, he had not wanted her. But Alka's breath fanned the fires of his desires again, he felt each part of his body aflame. He shut the door, fed the fire on the hearth with another dry log lying by, tore her clothes off and, when he held her naked form to himself, felt that the whole hut was ablaze and that his entire being was being cleansed by the flames.

What he did not want to tell her, he sensed it being poured out sequentially from each pore of her body.

And when they had both eaten in his room, and he got Haria to light a lantern, his curiosity could not be contained any longer. 'Let us go and see the other two huts.'

The three huts were not, as might be expected, all in a row. One faced the beds of flowers; the second overlooked the valley; and the third commanded a full view of the fields of corn. A common courtyard held the backs of the three together. Each of them had a spacious verandah in front which was linked up with the others by the continuity of the slate roof. So it was easy enough for Kumar to get into the second hut by the light of the lantern in hand.

As in the first, the window was of pleated leaves in this hut too. For operating the wooden latch with ease, was attached a tasselled string of cowrie shells. Likewise, there was the mud-plastered little platform to sit on. The only unique feature was in the adjacent wall studded with innumerable little alcoves of varying depths, each with an earthen lamp in it.

'It we lit all these ...' Kumar said so excitedly that his voice did not sound his own. That was perhaps why Alka desisted from attempting to complete his conjecture.

Kumar held the lantern up to the other wall. Rippling streams of water seemed to be flowing from it. With alternating use of indigo and chalk, Alka had caught that scene from nature with a vividness all its own. As he looked minutely into every touch, he observed a very fine line in the water.

'You can't draw a line in water they say.'

'Would you say so as well?'

'I couldn't – since I've put my foot on the line!'

Alka smiled at the smart way he conveniently went off on a tangent by trying to be witty.

'I couldn't say why you drew it, but I could give my own interpretation of it.'

'And that is?'

'I have drawn a line in my own mind where from one end flows hot water and cold from the other.'

'From one side, love; from the other, hate!'

'Alka!'

'Yes?'

'I wanted to say as much, but couldn't bring myself to. You have articulated my words literally. I don't know what there is to my nature: I love you, but I hate you too.'

'I know it.'

'I stand precariously on this line. I can never say when I will slip off; nor on to which side...'

Alka stood silent.

Kumar lowered the hand with the lantern and stepping out, went towards the third hut.

'That is still incomplete,' she informed him.

When he turned to go, he offered to share his room, should she feel afraid being there all by herself.

'Thanks. I prefer to sleep in my own hut,' she politely refused while entering. She fed the lamp with more oil, nicked the wick and got the flame going steady.

Back in his room, Kumar ruminated. There was no other woman in the whole world who could so tie him down. Alka alone held both his hands and the reins of his thoughts firmly in her grip.

He loved her, yet was angered by her power of possession. He admired her for the truth analysed and expressed in her painting. The waters of his life were indeed divided by a line; he was indeed precariously balanced – both feet together – on this line; he was bound to fall sooner or later, one way or the other, but he still could not tell whether he would for ever and ever be on the side of Love or Hate.

Source

Excerpt from Amrita Pritam, *Chakk No. 36*, 1964, translated as *Village No. 36* by Shanti Dev, Delhi: Shilalekh Publishers, 2021, p. 75-80.

4

URMI

Listen!

Here I stand, at the crossroads that radiate in four directions.

One road goes towards a blind well in which lies the corpse of Urmi ...

One road goes towards a river in which floats the corpse of Urmi ...

One road goes towards a pit in the ground where lies buried the corpse of Urmi ...

One road goes towards the pyre on which burns the corpse of Urmi ...

And I – as if I am walking on all the four roads ...

A noxious stink rises from all four sides, but the hustle and bustle of the world goes on as if no one can smell that odour ....

I, after all other options were closed, had gone to knock at the portals of justice of the country; I'd heard that it can detect even the slightest hint of odour but I found that it quickly covered its nose with a bag of money and mocked me, asking, 'Where? There is no stink anywhere....'

Urmi had been sweetly fragrant, but someone has turned her into a stink....

The two villages were adjoining – one where Urmi's parents lived, and the other in which her in-laws dwelled. It was as if both villages had been afflicted by a stroke; their lips could utter not a word ...

No, this is not a stroke, this is an epileptic fit, because both villages are frothing at the mouth ...

They say that one in the throes of an epileptic fit should be given a kind of snuff to bring one back to consciousness. This snuff is prepared by soaking rice in the milk of the toxic *akk* plant and grinding it. The truth is also as bitter as the *akk*. Urmi's words were like the grains of white rice, if I soak them in the *akk* of truth and ram the snuff into the nostrils of both these villages, then their fit will definitely come to an end ...

It is true – that one village coerced Urmi into a marriage and shoved her into the other village. And now one village held one of her arms, the other village held the other arm, and they beat her to a pulp and killed her ...

Neither village has any concern for Urmi. That is all right, no patient of epilepsy should have any worry ...

DOI: 10.4324/9781003214656-8

43

No trace of Urmi remains; it is as if she never existed. When I mention her, her kith and kin stare at me as if I am talking of genies and ghosts. And as if only I had ever laid eyes on Urmi – no one else seemed to have ever seen her …

Statements of all the witnesses have been recorded. Only one witness remains – the page of the village school register where at the time of her admission, it had been written, 'Urmi, age six years, father's name, Hari Chand'. As if what happened, and what followed, is still alive and present before one's eyes. One day I ask, 'Pita ji, Raja Hari Chand was the twenty-eighth king of the Sun Dynasty, wasn't he?'

'Yes,' Pita ji says, and begins to tighten the cords of the rope bed….

'Your name was kept on Raja Hari Chand's name, wasn't it?' I say again. Pita ji does not answer….

My tongue seems to have got twisted into a knot, but I still say, 'Raja Hari Chand was a truthful man. Even if you never speak the truth again, please answer me honestly once – Where is Urmi?'

Pita ji yanks the cord of the bed so hard that the rope snaps …

Ma sits huddled like a bundle on a cane stool. The village hakim massages her spine with an unguent every day and says that she should never be allowed to sleep on a sagging cot – that is why Pita ji tightens the cords of her cot every day …

A bundle is all what I can call her; had she been a mother wouldn't she have wept and wailed loudly …

I think that if Urmi had not been a beautiful, vibrant girl and had instead been the coarse rope of a cot, this knot would not have formed in her life …

Then the niche in the room glances at me, and I towards it. Its breast has been gouged out just as my breast has been wrung. There – in the niche – used to be a picture … of Urmi and me. Once Pita ji had held us both by the finger and taken us to a fair. Urmi had been about seven then, and I about five. And he had had a photograph taken of both of us – brother and sister, and today that picture is not there …

The niche and I ask in unison – 'Pita ji! Where did that photograph go?'

'What do you need the photograph for?' Pita ji jerks the cord so angrily that I think it will snap again …

I say – 'There was only one memento of hers!'

Pita ji says in a goaded voice, 'What the hell will you do with a memento now?'

I say doggedly, 'If you didn't want it, you didn't need to keep it; you could have given it to me and I would have put it in my room in the city.'

'Damn the curst room in the city…!' Pita ji's entire body is coiled like the coarse cord. And perhaps the splinters from his own body pierce his palms; he rubs his hands together and glares at me …

I know that when I had taken a room in the city to study in the college there, Urmi had also pleaded with her parents and in-laws to allow her to study further in the city. Her husband had gone to Kenya for a few years to earn money and she had nothing to do at home. She had come to the city and taken admission in the college; and both of us had lived in the rented room together.

From the mention of a memento, it occurs to me that had Urmi been alive, or had she lived just three or four months longer, then her child would have been her souvenir ...

Pita ji spreads a *khes* on the cot, picks up the hunched heap of Ma from the stool and places it on the cot. Then he washes his hands and serves food in three plates ...

Earlier four bronze plates had always been placed side by side on the shelf in the kitchen. Ma used to keep scrubbing and scouring to keep them gleaming. These engraved plates had been of a brand-new design, bought as a set at a fair once. And as she used to place the shining plates on the kitchen shelf, Ma would always say, 'This is my Urmi's plate, this is for Urmi's brother, this is mine, and this is your father's ...'

That day when Pita ji takes down three plates from the shelf, 'This is Urmi's plate ...' bursts from my lips before I can stop myself.

Pita ji scowls, I don't know whether at me or the plate ...

I concentrate my attention on my plate, break off a piece of the roti, dip it in the bowl of dal and put it in my mouth. The dal has a burnt taste. But all three of us start eating our roti with the burnt dal without uttering a word.

I don't know what kind of a crossroad this is; it travels with me wherever I go. It wraps itself around my feet. And everywhere the same four roads radiate from it – one that goes towards a blind well in which lies the corpse of Urmi, the second that goes towards a river in which floats the corpse of Urmi, the third that goes towards a pit in the ground where lies buried the corpse of Urmi and the fourth that goes towards the pyre on which burns the corpse of Urmi ...

I return to the city from the village and this crossroad also comes with me ...

There used to be another road – on which Urmi used to walk ... no, perhaps there was no road and Urmi had carved it out herself by plucking out the thorns ... and she had barely walked ten steps or so when the road had disappeared under the blood oozing from her feet ...

Urmi's bed is still placed against the facing wall in my room as before. A small table still lies between the two beds as before. The same electric lamp sits on the table with the scarlet red flower that Urmi had painted on the shade ...

While painting the flower she had said, '*Veer*, don't touch it just yet. The paint is still wet; let it dry...'

This was last year, but the paint is still not dry ... I touch the flower with my finger and the colour sticks to my fingertip ...

Perhaps a few tears from my eyes have fallen on it ...

By now even the place where Urmi's blood had been spilled, must have dried ...

I think, it is almost two months since ...

Perhaps she had been hacked to pieces with an axe. The hands holding the axe must have been coated with her blood ... and then that blood would have dried on those hands ... he would have washed his hands, but at least some of it would have seeped through his pores and stained his palms ... it will forever be inked into his palms ... it will dry there ... but at times, perhaps some tears would well up in his eyes – may be in the middle of some night – and the blood dried in the palms would again become damp ...

Perhaps only colour becomes wet, not blood ...

Opening the closed door, he slides in – ghost-like ... he, whom Urmi fell in love with ...

The hair on his head is matted and a shawl is wrapped around him; he stands in my room like a dense darkness ...

The darkness doesn't lighten, only the silence snaps. He asks, 'When did you return from the village?'

'Only today.'

'Found out anything?'

I shake my head.

He, like a bundle of darkness, first stares at Urmi's empty bed, then sits down on it ...

A voice rises from Urmi's bed, 'People say that ardour and odour cannot be hidden at any cost... this is half true and half lie ... ardour couldn't be hidden, but the odour could be....'

Source

Excerpt from *Urmi* (*Akk da Boota*, 1974), *Ratna, Benu te Urmi*, Delhi: Shilalekh Publishers, 2017, rpt. 2020, p. 139–143. (Translated by Hina Nandrajog.)

5

'THE SHAH'S HARLOT'

No one called her Neelam, she was the Shah's harlot to everyone. Neelam blossomed into youth in a courtesan tenement in Lahore's Hira Mandi. A sardar from a princely state performed the ritual of removing her nose ring to deflower her for a precious sum of five thousand rupees.

Then one day, she left the cheap tenement in Hira Mandi and moved to Falleti's, the most expensive hotel in town. Although she had not moved away from Lahore, the whole town seemed to have forgotten her original name overnight and started referring to her as the Shah's harlot. She was known for her sonorous voice. No girl could render Mirza as well as her. Although people had forgotten her name, no one had forgotten her voice. Every home with a gramophone was sure to have her records. At any get-together there were always requests for her records to be played over and again.

Her relationship with the Shah was no secret and his family knew of it. Not only did they know of it, they had also accepted it. Though when the Shah's son, who was to be married now, was still a baby, the Shahni had threatened to take poison and kill herself. But the Shah, clasping a necklace of the purest of pearls to his wife's neck, told her:

'Shahni! She is lucky for your household. I know a gem when I see it. Haven't you heard of the qualities of the neelam gem? The sapphire can make or mar someone. This Neelam has made me. Ever since I took her, even the mud that I touch turns to gold'.

'But she will ruin the home one day. We will be left with nothing'. The Shahni, swallowing the pain that rose in her heart, tried to counter his argument.

But the adamant Shah said, 'On the other hand I am scared. One can never tell with these harlots. If someone else lures her away, our fate may be marred forever'.

The Shahni could say nothing more and left everything to time. But time did not move on for many years to come. True enough more wealth came into Shah's hands in comparison to what he spent on Neelam. Earlier, he had a small shop in the city but now his was the largest showroom with

DOI: 10.4324/9781003214656-9

cast-iron railings. He owned not just his house, but the entire colony that was rented out to well-off tenants. And the Shahni did not let go of the keys to the lockers of her home.

Long ago while locking the box with the gold coins, the Shahni had told her husband, 'Keep her in the hotel if you will or build a Taj Mahal for her, but she must never enter my home. I do not wish to see her'. True to her word, the Shahni had not seen the harlot till date. When she had said this, her elder boy was still in school. Now he was to be married but she had not even allowed Neelam's records to enter her home nor could anyone talk of her. But her sons had heard her records all over the bazaar and had also heard innumerable people referring to her as 'the Shah's harlot'.

The elder son's marriage had been fixed. Tailors and embroiderers had been sitting in the house for the past four months. One was embellishing a suit with gold, another with silver, yet another was bespangling dresses and edging dupattas with golden trimmings. The Shahni was flush with money – she would take out a pouch full of rupees, spend it and return to the locker to fill it again.

The Shah's friends insisted that they wanted to hear the harlot sing at the boy's wedding. They put the proposal forward with tact. 'Shahji, many singing and dancing girls are available but you must make sure that your melody queen comes, even if she sings just a verse of Mirza'.

Falleti's was not just any other hotel. Only the Britishers used to stay there. It had not only single and double rooms but also suites of three big rooms. Neelam lived in one such suite. The Shah thought he would humour his friends by organising an evening of music in her suite.

'That would be like going to a house of entertainment,' a friend objected and everyone joined him saying, 'No Shahji, only you have the right to go there. We have never said anything for so many years. She is all yours. But we want to celebrate our nephew's wedding so in the true feudal tradition; you must call her home, the home of our sister-in-law ...'

The proposal appealed to the Shah. It was wise not to take his friends to Neelam's abode although he had learnt that a few aristocrats were visiting her in his absence. He also wanted Neelam to see the grandeur of his home. But afraid of the Shahni, he did not concede to the request of his friends.

Two of his friends found a way out and approached the Shahni, 'Bhabhi, won't you arrange an evening of music for the boy's wedding? We don't want to miss out on any ceremony. The Shah wants to arrange a get-together at Neelam's place. It is all right but thousands of rupees will be wasted on it. After all, you have to take care of the finances. He has already spent enough on the harlot. Be wise and call her to sing here one evening. We will enjoy the music and a lot of money will be saved'.

First the Shahni resisted. 'I do not wish to see the harlot'. However, the friends persisted. 'This is your empire. She will come as a servant obeying your orders. It will be her humiliation, not yours. She will be just another entertainer'.

The Shahni finally saw the merit of their case but she laid down the rules. 'Liquor will not be served. Everyone will sit as they would in a decent home. You men can join us. She will just come, sing and leave. I will give her the four patasas that I will be giving the other girls who come to sing the ghodhis'.

'That is exactly what we want'. The Shah's friends flattered her. 'You have saved this home with your wisdom otherwise God knows what may have happened'.

And the harlot came. The Shahni had sent her personal carriage to fetch her. The home was full of relatives and friends. White sheets had been spread out in the big room with big round cushions and a dholaki was placed in the middle. The women of the home started singing the ghodhis, the wedding songs for the groom.

As the carriage stopped outside the house, many eager women ran towards the windows and the staircase to catch a glimpse of the woman they had all heard about but never seen.

'It is an ill omen to leave the song unfinished,' the Shahni scolded. But she found her own voice weak as though her heart was sinking. She slowly walked to the front door. She rearranged the borders of her pink sari as though she was seeking courage from the auspicious pink colour to face the other woman.

There was Neelam! She was resplendent in a shimmering green garara trimmed with gold and a bright red shirt. A green silk dupatta was draped on her head and trailed to her feet. She seemed to be twinkling and the Shahni felt that the shimmering green colour of her attire had spread itself out in the doorway.

Then her green glass bangles tinkled and the Shahni saw a fair hand rise in a salaam. A musical voice spoke out, 'Many congratulations, Shahni. Many congratulations to you'.

She was a dainty little thing. The Shahni pointed towards the round cushion and asked her to sit down and doing so she felt that her fleshy arm looked very unsightly. In one corner of the room, the Shah sat with his friends. The delicate woman glanced at them and gave her stylish salaam and then sat by the cushion. Her glass bangles tinkled again. The Shahni looked at those arms once again, bedecked with green glass bangles. Then spontaneously she moved her gaze to her own gold bracelets.

The whole room was bedazzled. All eyes were looking in one direction, including the Shahni's, but she was annoyed at the other admiring stares. She wanted to scold everyone and ask the women to continue with the wedding songs. But she could not find her voice. The others too seemed to have lost their voices. She looked at the dholaki in the middle of the room and wanted to go and beat it hard to break the stunned silence.

49

She who had caused the silence broke it too. She said, 'First of all I will sing a ghodi. Is that all right Shahni?' And looking at the Shahni, she started to sing:

> *Nikki-nikki bundi nikeya meen ve ware*
> *Teri maan ve suhagan tere shagan kare*
> (Tiny droplets, my young one, come down in rain
> As your lucky mother performs the sacred ritual)

Hearing the song, the Shahni felt a little at ease because she was the mother and was being sung about. Her husband was only her's and only she had the right to perform the rituals. Smiling, the Shahni sat right in front of the woman who was singing about the rites and rituals of her son's marriage.

The ghodi ended and conversation resumed in the room. The women wanted a dholaki song and the men wanted to hear the verses of Mirza. The singer paid no heed to the request from the menfolk and put her knee on the dholaki. The Shahni was pleased with the fact that instead of pandering to the men, the harlot was fulfilling the requests of the women.

Some women did not know of Neelam. They were asking one another about her. The Shahni heard whispers, 'She is the one, the Shah's harlot'. Even though they had whispered softly, the words were piercing through the Shahni's ears – the Shah's harlot, the Shah's harlot – and her face went pale again.

> The beat of the dholaki got louder as did the singer's voice:
> *Soohe ve cheere waalea main kehani aan...*
> (I call out to you, the red-turbaned one ...)

The Shahni's heart sank. God forbid! The red-turbaned one was her son and today he was to mount a horse to bring home a bride. There was no end to the requests. One song would finish and another would start. The singer would oblige the women in one song and the men in the other. Every now and then she would say, 'Let someone else sing now, give me a breather'. But who had the courage to sing in front of her. Singing came naturally to her and her voice was so melodious. She was just saying this for effect because when one song ended, she would start the next one.

It was all right as far as the wedding songs went but once she started singing the verses of Mirza in her sonorous voice, even the breeze stopped blowing to listen to her. The men in the room froze. The Shahni started feeling uneasy. She glanced at the Shah. He was a statue like the others but the Shahni felt he had turned to stone.

The Shahni panicked. She felt that if she lost this moment, she would be reduced to a clay statue forever. She had to do something, something to prove her existence. It was late in the evening, and the function was coming to a close. The Shahni had said that she would distribute only patasas but once the singing ended, tea and delicious savouries were served. The Shahni took a rolled hundred-rupee note in her hand touched it to her son's head and then gave it to the one who was known as the Shah's harlot.

'Let it be, Shahni. I already live off your morsels,' she said and laughed. Her laughter twinkled as did her silence. The Shahni's face went white. She felt that the Shah's harlot, by referring to her liaison with her husband openly, had belittled her. However, she took quick control of the situation. Pressing the note firmly in the other woman's hand she said, 'You will take from the Shah always but when will you get the chance to take something from me? Come on, take it today'.

The Shah's harlot accepting the note seemed most humbled. The auspicious pink colour of the Shahni's sari had spread itself all over the room.

Source

Amrita Pritam, "Shah di Kanjari", translated by Nirupama Dutt. https://scroll.in /article/875515/on-baisakhi-two-classic-short-stories-that-capture-the-spirit-of -punjab (accessed on 17 December 2021).

I (c)

AMRITA – TRANSCENDING THE SELF

6

SPIRITUAL WRITINGS

'Five Dreams'

The night of 30 January was still young, when I see – a mountainous terrain, where in some building there are a great many paintings. When I and Imroz emerge outside after seeing those paintings, I am enchanted by the vistas of nature's bounty. Big crimson and white flowers are blooming. It's raining and all the flowers, drenched, go on looking upwards at the sky. I say, nothing could surpass this beauty, and step forward to partake in the torrent. My heart is drenched in it too …

Then it was the morning of 8 February, I see Sai standing by my side. I quickly spread a sheet for him to sit, but who knows where he goes off to. I am left searching for him; he was right here, where could he have gone?

Then the night of 18 March is edging towards its end; I see that the picture of Sai is missing from its place near my pillow… and Sai himself is sitting there. And the place where I would offer flowers in front of the picture is now illumined with numerous diyas….

On the night of 20 March, I see a peacock spread its plume in a dance. Each feather has a painting on it. One painting is of Baba Devaraha Hans, another of Rajneesh, and of Sai….

Two days later on 22 March around midnight, I find my right palm clenched into a fist. When I open the fist, I see several paintings on my palm. I can see pictures of sages on my fingertips too … I stare, stupefied and then I hear several chants from my palm….

And I see Shri Yantra etched on my entire palm … All that I saw was so precious that I was wrapped in its trance…. I wrote a poem after about a year, which captures the essence of these dreams.

> Sometimes even when Death –
> writes a book
> it approaches Life –
> to script a preface.
>
> As she crossed the Bodhi tree
> Wondering when Buddha would open his eyes

DOI: 10.4324/9781003214656-11

Trembling like a leaf
When she placed forth the parchment of the winds
Buddha had spoken the tale of compassion ...

When she heard Krishna's flute
Hidden behind a tree
and watched the *gopis' raas-leela*,
herself trembling like an anklet bell.
Then traversing weapons and corpses
She caught the reins of a chariot
And when she placed forth the parchment of the winds
Krishna had laughed and recited Gita ...

Once she stepped into the Vai river
And pressed Nanak's feet for three days
Then sitting on the river's bank
When she placed forth the parchment of the winds
Then Nanak's rapture had chanted *Japji* ...

There are several black books of death
And many prefaces
like the light of sun and moon
Which belong to us –
Treasure belonging to us earthly mortals ...

And then there was a Sai Rajju
Who told us of treasures
And the treasure's serpents –
leaping away from hands
wiped off the dust of ages from the pearls
And gave away wealth with both hands
Death laughed –
No one reads my books, nor understands
People just fling them away
And reading prefaces
And casting them in iron
They become the serpents of treasures,

She then began to say –
Who knows how he came in the world,
But – I became his co-writer
And have come to greet him today....

24 February 1995
(Pritam 2013: 20–22)

'In-Sight'

My eyes remained teary on the night of 9 November. Saw – just ahead, a little to the left side, the eyes of some birds, which kept gazing at me relentlessly. The birds can't be seen, but I can sense that the watching eyes belong to birds. Suddenly a hand comes towards me, towards my mouth, I can't see the person, but can make out that it's a man's hand, trying to feed me the eye of one of the birds....

Will I have to eat the eye? – This sensation made me shudder, so tears filled my eyes and kept staring in the distance, and the eyes of the birds continued to stare back the same way.

I was shaken up by this experience of the night when Sai Kaka came visiting. Kaka heard the tale and began to laugh. 'The eye is the means to see, what is important is vision, the perspective; Sai has offered insight. This is what the birds had agreed to, that first we'll give a mantra, then go dig for things in the ground. That eye is the mantra given by the birds....'

Four days passed by. Suddenly, I saw that I stood in a vault-like space below the ground. It's a big place and big brass pots were kept there. The whole vault was full of brass pots. But the pots look as if they have lain in the ground for ages. I stood in the vault for a very long time. Didn't pick anything, just watched....

Morning came. I couldn't fathom why such a vault had been shown to me. Sai Kaka comes to my aid in all moments of difficulty; he told me, 'Once the birds had forbidden you to dig the vessels out of the ground, and now they themselves showed them to you. This means that you come from the tradition of those yogis to whom these things belong. Now all of it will be discovered through your medium. That's why it has all been revealed to you'.

I remembered that the birds too had said, 'Let it all remain as it is for now. But this will all come to pass through your hands only'.

Kaka began to say, 'Every hermitage has its own tradition. When any yogi leaves his corporeal body, his vessels are put in the ground for safekeeping. Thus does the ground around a hermitage becomes a treasure – of the belongings of the yogis, of spiritual power.... You are going to receive an important spiritual revelation'.

(Pritam 2013: 29–30)

'Feminine Principle'

The room was dark, but I wasn't asleep. I was in bed. A woman came from the left, carrying a baby in her arms. I was struck by the beauty of the child. The woman knelt and placed the baby close to me, on my left side. That kneeling woman's head was covered with an *odhni* which veiled her face, so I couldn't identify her. I kept looking at the baby, it too stared back at me with big, calm, steady eyes – I realised on my own that it was a fairy girl child … I was looking at her, staring at her … when the whole vision dissolved.…

Couldn't quite understand what exactly had happened and some five days elapsed like this. Then it was the morning of December 27 when Sai Kaka came. He had returned from Vrindavan and was headed to Pune in three days for a couple of months. So he had come to meet me. When I asked him about his experience in Vrindavan, he laughed and said, 'You were there too … I was sitting at the tomb of Haridas ji, when I was graced by Lalita ji's presence. It is said that Haridas ji was a reincarnation of Lalita ji herself – she emerged from the tomb – first in a blueish apparition, then appearing as herself she asked, "Have you come alone? Where are your *sakhis*?" I was about to say, "I've come alone", when Shirdi Sai also arrived, as did Imroz, and so did you. I laughed and said, "Here, my *sakhis* have arrived.…"'

Sai Kaka is a revered darvesh who travels the whole world quietly, so I laughed and said, 'You call me mother, right? And in Vrindavan you referred to me as *sakhi*. So now I am friend and mother.…'

We discussed several such things when I narrated the experience I had had five days ago to him. I said, 'I couldn't understand anything, Kaka. What happened exactly? Who was that woman? Why did she leave the child with me on my bed?'

Sai Kaka has seen my bedroom. When I am unwell, he sits in that very room. Though when he visits, he prefers to sit in the library. He said, 'That woman was "Vaama Shakti" / "Feminine Principle". That is why she didn't come from the right side. Although there's a wall to the left of your bed, and there is no way to enter. The bed can be accessed only from the right…'

All I know of Vaama Shakti is that Shiva's sculpture as *ardha-narishvara* has two aspects: the man is on the right, the woman on the left – and the left side is called Vaama. I didn't know more than this so Sai Kaka began to elucidate the strengths of the feminine principle. 'Vaama is the power of the outer self, of *maya*, of *maya*'s entrapment, *maya*'s walls, which is why she came through the wall. When the same power becomes inner power, she becomes *kundalini*, the mark of self-knowledge. That child is the sacrament of that Vaama Shakti which she offered to you. This is a marvellous development'.

Kaka left around four, but it was as if Rajneesh came near, saying, 'Dharma doesn't ask if God is or isn't. Dharma asks how one can be God'.

27 December 1994.
(Pritam 2013: 38–39)

Source

Excerpts from Amrita Pritam, "Paanch Sapne", "Antar-drishti", and "Vaama Shakti", *Kainat se Aage*. Delhi: Shilalekh Publishers: 2013. (Translated by Anupama Jaidev Karir.)

I (d)

AMRITA – WRITING THE SELF

7

THE REVENUE STAMP

I was ten then. Forty years later, now when I think of that prank of mine, it seems that whatever I have wanted with all my heart, I have found. Around me, forts have been raised and demolished but the reality of the One, has in one form or the other, always been with me. At one time in the features and form of a man's face; at another in what has taken shape from my pen and at yet another some sort of divinity has arisen from the leaves of a book or has stepped out from a canvas to be with me. Like a genie from a streak of smoke it emerges – sometimes from the anguish that goes into the making of a song, from the budding leaf of a twig, even from the moon as it shines on the waves of the sea. At times, when I am engulfed in my loneliness, I have found it gushing forth – coursing in the veins and speeding up the flow of blood in my body. And with all this, the pallor that should otherwise come with weariness of a kind takes on a fresh colour.

It pervades all my thoughts and dreams to such a degree that even fleeting goodness seems to be a manifestation of that One. And it is so beautiful that I cry....

Abstractions have no meaning for me. Each entity must take on some sort of shape or form ... that I can touch, that in fact, can thrill me with a touch.

In the years, of my nonage, whenever I dreamt of the Gurus – Har Gobind or more often of Gobind Singh – I always ran my fingertips over the portrait; the horse he rode on, the sword he carried, the falcon he held in his hand, anything. I would never pay homage from a distance. If in a slightly different way, flowers or leafy boughs too I hold to myself as in embrace. My entire being is filled with such a sense of belonging as to make my very breath heavy.

Many, many years ago, the One sat by my side. He had a soiled handkerchief. I took it away giving him a clean one. His, I kept for years. My forehead burned with a yearning whenever I touched it.

There are certain seeds that once fertilised in the soil, can survive without leaf and branch, no matter how furious the tempest, how searing the hot wind of drought. They just cannot be uprooted. In the same way is the longing for the One, and respect for the Word. Such seeds indeed sprouted

DOI: 10.4324/9781003214656-13

in my womb in the prime of my life, but faith was shattered – utterly. I feel both these trees should have been uprooted. Sometimes deep down I have a feeling that they no longer exist. But from the dry dusts of the mind, they sprout forth again and become sturdy branches; branches strong enough to blossom and bear fruit. And with the branch of my life, I receive their fragrance.

One seed I sowed myself; for the other, Father was responsible. Should a page from a book be found on the floor, he would pick it up with solemn respect. Should my foot by chance fall on it, he would be angry. Thus has been deeply engrained in my mind, respect for the written word – and with that for all those who wield the pen. That was how I came to look up to Bhai Sahib Kahan Singh, Father's friend. The very threshold of our house seemed benigned when he entered. A portrait of Father's Guru, Dayalji, that rare scholar of Sanskrit, hung at the head of Father's bed. Even to sit with feet stretched out in the direction of that portrait was forbidden.

So when I grew up, I had the utmost respect for my contemporaries. But my sad experience with them leaves me wondering why this respect for the word and the pen has not vanished long ago.

Sometimes I wonder whether my contemporaries are the only ones with whom I have dealt.

* * *

In the totality of myself as a writer, the woman in me has had only a secondary role to play. So often have I nudged myself into an awareness of the woman in me. The writer's role is obvious. But the existence of that other being have I increasingly discovered through my creative works.

When she came to life, three distinct incidents come to mind. Paradoxically again, there was no possibility of finding a place for her as she exists in the world of creativity. This fact I can realise and assess since the distance of years alone can make possible such a vision.

The first time was when I was twenty-five years of age. I had no child until then. Very often I dreamt of one: a fair face with finely chiselled features looking into my eyes. I began to recognise it after its repeated appearances. I used to dream of it speaking to me – so I began to recognise the voice as well. In one of these dreams I was watering plants. From one of the pots, instead of a flower, the face would suddenly spring up. Aghast, I would ask: 'Where were you?' 'Right here!' He would break out into laughter with the reply. And I would hurriedly lift the little one from the pot.

But when I would wake up, I would find myself all alone – a woman in name, who, if she could not become a mother, could find no meaning at all in existence....

The second time was when Sahir had turned up with a fever. He had racking pain all over and was finding it particularly difficult to breathe. I rubbed Vicks on his throat and chest – in fact I went on and on, as if I could spend the rest of my life doing it. The mere contact had magnetically rendered me into a mere woman, with no need at all for paper or pen.

The third time the woman in me came to the forefront was when Imroz sat once, working in his studio. On completion of the canvas, he dipped the brush into the red paint and with the tip of it, dabbed a mark on my forehead.

This secondary role as a woman, however, rakes up no quarrels with my main being as a writer. Rather, the woman in me has in a disciplined manner learnt to accept that secondary role. Only three times over the years did she wish to assert herself and the writer move aside to make way for her.

* * *

A damsel of twenty years or so, stood by my side. She was the very picture of perfection. But she was ebony-black, carved out of black marble....

'Who is she now?' someone asked of me.

'My daughter.'

'Come now! You're pulling a fast one on me, aren't you? I've seen both your children. So fair ... so charming they are ... but this one....'

'The fair ones are small.... She is the eldest.... Do you know something about the manifestations of my art? The Goddess Parvati was churned from my wrath. And do you know that her son Ganesh was in turn kneaded from the dough of her own body?'

I passed through a desolate region with neither face nor form in sight. A voice came to my ears. It was a song. 'You've been the undoing of me, Sahiban, you've hung my arrows on a silver'.

'And who are you?' I looked around on all sides and asked.

'I am the valiant Mirza. Sahiban, my beloved, went and hid my arrows.... That was not fair... the way she had me shot dead....'

I again looked all around. Seeing no one, I said: 'Stories have a way of changing sides.... Today a certain Mirza has gone and hidden my arrows ... is it fair ... the way he has had a courageous woman like me shot dead...?'

The clouds thunder and roar. The sky shakes with wind and rain. A jagged streak of lightning flashes through the sky and falls on my right hand.

The shock of it goes right through my body. When I regain balance, I look at my hand and shake it. It is a relief to find only a slight scratch, from which oozes a drop of blood.

Another peal of thunder, and on the same hand, strikes lightning again. Recovering from it, I examine the hand. A slight scratch....

Thunder and lightning a third time. Now I cannot move my hand – one finger is bent. Holding the parallel finger of my other hand as a supporting splint, I press it hard again and again. It straightens out – as before. And as a last test, I take up my pen. I can still write, as well as ever. My mental state at the time is like Baudelaire's in his *Ode to Beauty*.

63

On the eve of Republic Day the same year I was deputed to go to Nepal. I was still a mental wreck when I wrote the following two letters to Imroz:

Yesterday Nepal honoured the same pen with which I had written my love songs for you. All the flowers showered upon me are therefore my offerings to you. How did some light kindle this inky night of separation? Thoughts of you will ever remain lit in this poem of mine. Talk of this light – and much more besides, went on until as late as late could be. A Persian poet's lines come to mind:

> Under the desert sun they run.
> The shimmering sands as though water,
> But the tortuous illusion soon passes.
> 'How can sandshine,' wise men opine –
> 'Blinding sand's continuity
> Confine them?' But the thirst of those
> Must, say I, first be seen – how it goes.

I might have illusions about my wisdom, but not of my thirst....

27 January 1960

> Wayfarer! Why did you the first time meet me at an
> evening hour!
> I am approaching the turning point of my life.
> If you had to meet at all why did you not meet me at
> high noon
> When you would have felt its heat.

The Hindi poet, Shiv Mangal Singh Suman, read this poem.

Each feels his own pain. But sometimes such pains bear striking similarities. These longings of mine have been bruised against that stern citadel of yours in the same city of my earlier hopes. The first waiting too lasted a good fourteen years (like Lord Rama's period of exile); the remaining years too might well get added to those gone by....

1 February 1960

Meeting with Centuries

According to the Hindu religion, each man must pass through four stages – four *varnas* and four *ashrams* in the course of his life span. I do not presume to know much about this. All I know is that in the course of my life's journey I can discern four milestones.

During the first phase, like a *Bodhisattva*, I sat looking upon everything with an eye of wonder: the minutes were somehow magnified, though for no reason that I can explain.

By the second, I had developed an overwhelming consciousness – it was the vigour of youth in revolt against the bastions of social tradition. The hatred and wrath rising up in me was like the precious stone in a toad's head.

The third one was the courage to forget and demolish the present and to build a new future, the courage to shuffle dreams like cards before they are dealt out ... the courage to take the losses in a game and to shuffle the cards again and deal them out afresh in the hope that luck would change.

The fourth is this sense of isolation.

Three or four years back when Ho Chi Minh, the President of Vietnam, came to Delhi, he kissed my forehead and said: 'We are both fighting the wrong values, are we not...? You with your pen; I with my sword'.

Source

Excerpt from Amrita Pritam, *Rasidi Ticket* 1976, translated as *The Revenue Stamp* by Krishna Gorowara, Delhi: Tarang Paperbacks, 1994, rpt. 1996, pages 7-8, 26-27, 37-40. https://apnaorg.com/books/english/raseedi-ticket/book.php?fldr =book (accessed on 24 May 2022).

Part II

DECONSTRUCTING THE SELF

8

LOVE AND DISSENT

The Making of a Self in Amrita Pritam's Autobiographical Writings

Arti Minocha

There was a pain
I inhaled it
Silently
Like a cigarette
There are a few songs
I've flicked off
Like ashes
From the cigarette

Mahfil (1968–1969: 3)

The intensity, irreverence and performance of pain in Amrita Pritam's creative oeuvre that the above lines indicate came to be identified as the hallmark of her writing and earned her much criticism in her lifetime before she achieved state and public recognition. For a writer who wrote about her censure and vilification at the hands of her social, political and literary milieu that she described as a 'deep, black corrosive poison' (Amrita 1994: 113), the autobiographical impulse in her three life narratives may partly be located in an audacious defiance of cultural prescriptions – 'Our offences are not heinous' (Amrita 1994: 117). Yet simultaneously, in an act of self-diminution, she titles her autobiography *Rasidi Ticket* (*The Revenue Stamp*); a revenue stamp that she says can never overreach its insignificant form and stature. These contradictory impulses of dissident assertion and quiet interiority run through her autobiographical writings that in their final shape came to be densely textured with philosophy, contemplation and creativity.

Although written in different modes, *Kala Gulab* (*Black Rose*, 1968), *Rasidi Ticket* (*The Revenue Stamp*, 1976, revised edition 1991) and *Aksharon ke Saaye* (*Shadow of Words*, 2001) together form Amrita's autobiographical writings. The modes of her autobiographical practice in these three works traverse a whole range from *atmakatha* (autobiography), to *nazm* (lyric), *kahani* (short story) and *antaryatra* (interior journey, the

DOI: 10.4324/9781003214656-15

subtitle of *Aksharon ke Saaye*), thus making the genre of autobiography more commodious. This essay discusses Amrita's three autobiographical writings to see how the genre of autobiography/life-writing was used by the author to register a constantly changing self and to hold disjunctive life experiences together through the central *topos* of love and dissent.

Contemporary and later critical responses to her life-writings ranged from dissatisfaction with the lack of chronology and temporality in *Rasidi Ticket*, to the charge of it being a series of dreams and nightmares that did not reveal the 'truth' about her life, and that it defied expectations from an autobiography. The attempt in this essay is to see these 'broken' literary pieces as Amrita's attempt to assemble and narrativise a gendered self, torn apart by love and longing, romance and rebellion, in the cultural matrix that she inhabited.

Autobiography/life-writing/life stories, a genre variously named and defined, was used especially by women in India in the second half of the 20th century, a period of nation-in-the-making, to dramatise identity-formation and negotiate the 'shifting landscape of privacy and publicity' (Bruno 2018: 17). Ajeet Cour's *Pebbles in a Tin Drum* (1998), Kamala Das's *My Story* (1976), Nayantara Sahgal's *Prison and Chocolate Cake* (1954), Dhanvanthi Rama Rau's *An Inheritance* (1977), the self-narratives of Nazr Sajjad Hyder (1942–1963), Maharani of Kapurthala's *Maharani: The Story of an Indian Princess* (1953) and Ismat Chughtai's *Kaghazi Hai Pairahan* (1988) are some eminent examples of autobiographies in which women have reframed terms of their subjectivities and inhered the self into specific historical moments in postcolonial India.

Life-writing in its late-19th and 20th-century form in India is considered to be a genre of modernity that became possible with the emergence of the new individuated subject at the end of the 19th century but the form as it was known in the west was also mediated through local intellectual traditions and literary practices.[1] Generally interpreted through the oppositional tropes of 'fact' and 'fiction', critical assessments tend to instrumentally connect autobiography to 'context' or history as revealing personal and historical 'truths' through an assumed transmissible and transparent voice. Such assumptions of history as a site of the 'authentic' end up fixing history as immutable truth rather than analyse the subject herself being implicated in the formation and articulation of this history. Some life narratives, such as that of Amrita, are liable to be read as interiorised narratives that presume a core of 'unconquered autonomy' (Kaviraj 2015: 137), a unified self in rebellion against social conventions and orthodoxies that lie outside the self. Such readings may run the risk of fetishing rebellion itself as well as assuming an apriori, self-expressive 'I' that possesses a wholesome psychic interiority.

There is no essential, original, coherent autobiographical self before the moment of self-narrating. Nor is the autobiographical

self-expressive in the sense that it is the manifestation of an interiority that is somehow ontologically whole, seamless, and 'true'.
For the self is not a documentary repository of all experiential history running uninterruptedly from infancy to the contemporary
moment, capacious, current, and accessible. The very sense of self
as identity derives paradoxically from the loss to consciousness of
fragments of experiential history.

(Smith 1998: 108)

The act of reading life narratives, thus, poses methodological challenges
about questions of authenticity, truth-telling, memory, history, subjectivity,
agency and authorship. In this essay, the autobiographical act is seen as an
attempt to bring together the contradictions of a material life and 'fiction-
alise subjectivity' (Rhodes 2005: 3) and to imagine a stable self in a legible
space, thus claiming a political as well as textual agency.

The first part of the essay briefly examines some theoretical and conceptual shifts mentioned above that have occurred in our understanding
of the genre of life-writing and autobiography, and how they bear upon
South Asian life-writing and women's life-writing. The second part of the
essay traces possible connections of Amrita's autobiographical writings
with women's enunciations in late-19th and early-20th century Punjab
and the development of gendered modernist aesthetics in the period.
The third part of the essay looks at Amrita's *Rasidi Ticket*, *Kala Gulab*
and *Aksharon ke Saaye*, and the author's own comments on the use of
the autobiographical genre in her work to see how she weaves together
the dialectics of reality and fiction, convention and dissent, dreams and
failures.

Conceptual Shifts in Understanding Autobiography

Conventionally, autobiography has been understood as Lejeune says, 'a ret-
rospective narrative in prose that a real person makes of his own existence
when he emphasises his individual life, especially the story of his personality' (qtd. in Stanton 1998: 136). Central to this idea of autobiography is the
'individualistic paradigm of centrally located isolate autobiographical self'
(Gusdorf 1980: 29). It is because of the cultural specificity of the require-
ments of atomistic individuality, interiority and introspection in these definitions that Pascal asserts, 'Autobiography is essentially European' (1960:
22). This western template of autobiography was subsequently rejected on
several grounds, not only in the Anglo-American academia and literary
world, but also in other locations such as South Asia. Alternative generic
categories such as life-writing, life narrative and life story sought to counter
the 'politics of exclusion' (Smith and Watson 2010: 3) and western cultural
assumptions inherent in the term 'autobiography'.

Another important conceptual shift in the understanding of autobiography/life-writing came with poststructuralist interventions. These theories reconceptualised the fixed and knowable 'individual' as a decentred and dynamic subject constituted through dominant discourses of morality as well as through linguistic constructions. This poststructuralist questioning of a neat dichotomy between the interiority of the individual and the normative structures of the society located outside the self especially has implications for the study of women's life-writings. We can therefore read the trope of dissent in Amrita's writing, not simply as individual contestations with oppressive structures outside but as those that constitute her very self. The autobiographical act can be interpreted as a self-fashioning to negotiate the very 'invasion of an epistemological space' (Cohn qtd. in O'Hanlon 1988: 217) by the languages and laws of a universal Father:

> Half a century later I feel that both riches and renunciation have taken twin birth in me as well. This I have inherited, like my features, I think, from Father. Perhaps I see things with the same eyes that he did. Only, I keep wondering if I have accepted myself for what I am. That is why perhaps I have written all my life – so that whatever I could not accept in me, I would in time not reject altogether ... My only desire was to please Father. It is the same now.
>
> (Pritam 1994: 4)

Recent historical studies on gender in Punjab have similarly suggested a fluid understanding of subjectivity as being formed through constant processes of negotiation, accommodation and contestation with available discourses and therefore, agency being understood through specifics of time and location and not simply through pre-established notions of subversion and conformity (Malhotra 2013).

Apart from conceptual shifts in the understanding of autobiography, the protocols of the genre have also varied with its location in specific geographies and time. Life-writings in late-19th and early-20th century in India emerged as hybridised forms that assimilated western models of 'private life', and evidentiary and linear templates of autobiographies with an indigenous repertoire of hagiography, oral traditions, legends and bhakti devotion. A specific feature of these life-writings is an attempt to map the life of the self on to the life of community or nation, that is, 'self-in-society' (Arnold and Blackburn 2004: 20–21). The autobiographical project in 20th century India was simultaneously a project of history writing as well as scripting a newly produced sense of selfhood, a 'history of subjectivation' as well as 'collective memory-making' (Kumar 2012: 481). Autobiographies of public men, such as Mahatma Gandhi and Pandit Nehru assimilated this interiorised self within the nationalist project with ease.[2] This seamless continuity of the self-in-the-making with the nation-in-the-making is however disrupted in Amrita's life-writings. In fact, in women's life-writings of the time, this inhabitation in the nation is rendered uncomfortable and has to be considered through other modalities of enunciation, such as dissent, 'recalcitrance' (Amrita's description of a writer's stance) or 'reluctance' (Orsini's use of this frame to study Mahadevi Verma's autobiographical writings): 'From the Ganges to the vodka, / is the travelogue of my thirst' (Amrita 1994: 45).

Women's enunciations in early-20th century Punjab were facilitated by the emergence of new public and print spheres, access to education, crystallisation of new, "modern" literary cultures and critical public debates on communal and linguistic identities, cultural practices, women's reform, language and aesthetics. The next section traces the emergence of modern subjecthood for women in Punjab, their configurations of the public, both in its material and discursive understanding, their 'strategies of selfhood' (Bhabha 1994: 1–2) and the possible connections with Amrita's imagination of the literary self.

Women's Inhabitation of New Literary Subjectivity in 20th Century Punjab

In an interview with Madhu Kishwar and Ruth Vanita, Amrita remarked on the break with literary tradition in her writing and the shock and outrage that her work caused in the Punjabi literary world. 'But she told us that when she published her first collection of verse in 1936, there were only two known women writers in Punjabi, and they wrote on religious themes' (Kishwar and Vanita 1982: 2). On the other hand, in the work of male writers, 'woman was a flower, woman was beauty, youth, grace' whereas she describes her subject to be 'woman in search of her identity through struggle' (Kishwar and Vanita 1982: 2). Amrita describes her non-conformity with literary and social traditions in a similar vein in *Rasidi Ticket*, 'I have many contemporaries, only I am not contemporaneous' (Pritam 1994:14).

Despite the belief that the few women writing in the early-20th century in Punjab were completely contained within the reform and the nationalist discourses of the time, archival research shows that they inhabited the literary and public sphere in different ways as readers, writers, consumers, editors of periodicals, singers, listeners and participants in oral and written cultures of literature.[3] It is in women's periodicals, a genre that has not received much attention, that one can hear women's voices through their letters, opinion pieces and experimental literary genres, voices that sometimes ran contrary to the constructions of 'idealised' women in the patriarchal, reformist imaginary.[4] Women imagined routes to public life, used 'private' idioms of family, domesticity and motherhood to ask for changes in 'public' policies, demanded mobility and entry into education and professions and envisaged emotional and affective solidarities through print.[5]

Here, two tropes in women's periodical literature are outlined that perhaps laid the groundwork for women's writing that was to emerge later: women's claim to the representation and materiality of their bodies as against the female body being the locus of the colonial, reform, and nationalist preoccupation with women's sexuality and reproduction; and the claim of professional authorship and the rise of the public intellectual.

The discursive battles for demarcating religious identities in 20th century Punjab were also fought over women's bodies, their practices and their relationship to the public sphere, which became new indicators to mark religion, class and caste. Here, too, the periodicals give us an important insight into how women themselves reframed these discursive representations of their bodies into a claim to their corporeal self and concerns about health, sexuality, pleasure, new medical subjecthood and entry into medical professions. The constitution of modern womanhood through the desires of the material body as against the body invested with a moral value by others is a dilemma that continues into 20th century women's autobiographies through the tropes of desire and dissent. The Progressive Writers' Movement and activism brought women's sexuality and experiences of the body into sharp focus through radical critique of conservative structures, for example, in the work of Rashid Jahan (1905–1952), who ripped apart 'norms of respectability for *sharif* women' (Bano 2012: 59).

It is the vocabulary of desire, passion and the haptic that suffuses Amrita's autobiographical writing and creativity, 'On every poem that I wrote, I carried the cross of forbidden desires' (Pritam 1994: 12). Her 'clandestine relationship' with her sixteenth year makes her question parental authority, literary conservatism, rote-learning system, drab middle-class morality and the stratified social system. Creativity itself spews from the contemplation of desire, 'I have found it gushing forth – coursing in the veins and speeding up the flow of blood in my body' (Pritam 1994: 7). The yearning for the intended one and the 'thrill' of his embrace and touch, she says, took elemental root in her being. The transgressive body that is intoxicated and desirous breaks the rules of grammar through dreams and the rules of literary representation through the language of passion. These dream sequences are an important part, especially of *Aksharon ke Saaye*. Despite the prison house of morality that constitutes her very self, writing and experiencing desire become a mode of rethinking that self, carefully charted through self-censorship and the transgressive. Mentioning an incident in which she rubbed Vicks on Sahir's body, she acknowledges, 'the mere contact had magnetically rendered me into a mere woman' (Pritam 1994: 26). The body is thus a site on which cultural forces and 'private' desires are negotiated and 'intellection mediated somatically' (Smith 1994: 271).

Another mode of literary subjectivity that became possible for women in the late-19th and 20th century was a claim to professional authorship and the 'intellectual' work that it involved. The proliferation of print activity, the mobilisation of communities on grounds of caste and religion by urban, educated men gave rise to new 'associational publics' (Bhandari 2007: 269) and public intellectuals and publishers such as Bhai Vir Singh, Harsukh Rai, Dayal Singh Majithia, Munshi Naval Kishore and Ruchi Ram Sahni in Punjab.[6] Literary activity became a powerful medium of social mobilisation and crystallisation of new literary cultures and genres. Inhabiting these print and literary cultures offered new sites to women to achieve legitimacy as 'public intellectuals' apart from middle-class domesticity and marriage. For women like Hardevi, Sushila Tahl Ram, Harnam Kaur, Kamala Satthianadhan and Sarala Devi Chaudhurani,[7] print activism became allied with their social activism and attempts to create early social networks and women's movement in Punjab. Writers like Rashid Jahan, a qualified gynaecologist (her other 'public' engagement), made her strident critique accessible not only through print but also through other popular media, radio and theatre.

This engagement of women as public intellectuals with new institutions of modernity, such as family, marriage, law, and science and emerging literary spheres in the newly-independent nation state was an important legacy for writers such as Amrita Pritam (1919–2005), Qurratulain Hyder (1927–2007), Ismat Chughtai (1915–1991) and Krishna Sobti (1925–2019). Yet, 'the tensions that being a public intellectual and an independent woman entailed' (Orsini 2004: 55) played out differently in their writings and autobiographies. In Amrita's life-writings, her 'recalcitrance' and the daring of her 'pen' become important metaphors through which she claims a creative, individual voice as well as respectability and responsibility to other women as a public intellectual.

> Society attacks anyone who dares to say that its coins are counterfeit. But when it is a woman who dares to say this, society begins to foam at the mouth. It puts aside all its theories and arguments, and picks up the weapon of filth to fling at her. A woman who has suffered an attack can understand it, this attack is not against a particular woman, it is an attack on the whole of the womanhood…. So my story is the story of women in every country and many more in number are those stories which are not on paper, but are written in the bodies and minds of women….
>
> (Pritam 1971: 71)

The burden of public recognition for a woman who chose to live through her pen may not have been easy for she talks about the many years that she spent in taming and 'disciplining' the woman in the tussle between the woman and the writer, and her pen working to integrate the split between the 'public' and the 'private'. 'So often have I nudged myself into an awareness of the woman in me. The writer's role is obvious. But the existence of that other being have I increasingly discovered through my creative works' (Pritam 1994: 26). This act of reassembling the parts of the splintered self, she says, requires 'the distance of years' and a creative search for alternative 'truth' (Pritam 1994: 26). 'In search of that the dust that overlays thought has to be put through a sieve. What is thus sought and obtained is also an aspect of reality' (Pritam 1994: 146). The autobiographical act is thus woven through intentionality, memory, memorialisation and a subjective redefinition of 'reality'.

Amrita's Life-Writing: The Journey from 'I' to 'I'

Commenting on conventional audience expectation from autobiography, Amrita says,

> An autobiography is generally taken to be the gospel truth set in glittering words of gold ... an artefact of self-praise. The basic truth is the writer's own need. This is a continuous process that leads from one reality to another (Pritam 1994:146).

Thus, she draws attention to the self-consciousness and reflexivity of the autobiographical act in which the self is both 'actor and narrator' (Kaviraj 2015: 136), a 'text' for study, always becoming, and subject to re-vision through memory. The stirring of memory to enunciate this self seems like 'doomsday' (Pritam 1994: 7), she writes at the beginning of *Rasidi Ticket*. The attempt is nevertheless made through fixed signposts of locations and dates – of her parents' meeting and marriage, of her birth, her mother's death, her lineage of creativity and rebellion and then her adolescent dreams.

The inadequacy of this empirical and chronological method becomes evident soon enough when it cannot bear the burden of a self dispersed through cultural prescriptions, dreams, social relationships and desires that are nevertheless historically mediated. 'A birth bereft of the I / is like a sin decorating my trayful of offerings' (Pritam 1994: 136). Her autobiography, she says, is the story of her dreams being transcribed and then tossed around (Pritam 1994: 142). The fragmentary and the fluid then become modes of narrativising the self that is decentred by 'the fissures of female discontinuity' (Benstock 1998: 152). Incidents, flow of frames and moving pictures are employed to give narrative coherence, almost like a cinematic technique, a medium that Amrita was closely associated with.

In *Aksharon ke Saaye* and *Kala Gulab*, she describes autobiography as an account of a journey of life as well as a contemplative act, a journey from the embodied to the incorporeal consciousness, which can be psychic, community, sexual or cultural consciousness. It is through this consciousness and her creative act that she says she has tried to salvage her 'self':

> This is a journey from 'I' to 'I'
> a journey from servitude to love

a journey from inertness to consciousness
a journey from word to its meaning
journey from the finite to the unbounded
that is, from the limited to the limitless.

(Pritam 2019: 107)

Navigating through the ideas of truth, reality, history, memory and emotions, Amrita's life narrative is an attempt to re-vision life and thus 'possess it more fully' (Menon 2015: 57).

Love – Affect, Politics, Aesthetics

One of the central tropes through which the self is sought to be more fully possessed is that of love – love as corporeal desire, as creative inspiration, as an act of cultural defiance, as social impossibility projected on to dreams, as life-long friendship, as an emotional and psychic need and as aesthetic practice. These shifting paradigms of love woven through all three narratives give us an idea about what it was to inhabit a time in which the ethics and morality of a nation were being defined anew through cultural practices of intimacy, desire, marriage and family, and 'the affective map of the nation' was being re-drawn through 'a different and complex plane of desire and emotion' (Mazumdar 2011: 143).

For a nation beleaguered by the horrors of partition on communal grounds, the idea of love that crossed borders of religion, caste and creed perhaps provided reprieve in the imagination of a secular India. Amrita recollects her childhood revolt against her grandmother that has bearing on this later imaginary of a liberal India:

I used to notice three glass tumblers kept away from all other pots and pans on a shelf in the corner of the kitchen. These were for use only when Father's Muslim friends were offered tea or buttermilk when they came to visit him. After these tumblers had served their purpose they were scrubbed and washed and put right back in their ostracised niche.

(Pritam 1994: 5)

After her revolt, she says, the utensils ceased to be 'Hindu' or 'Muslim'. 'Neither the grandmother knew nor I that the man I was to fall in love with would be of the same faith as the branded utensils were meant for' (Pritam 1994: 5). In the narration of her life, she makes this 'transgression' almost a metaphorical mainstay for both her life and aesthetic search.

While the literary aesthetics of explicitly sensual love, such as *shringara*, that of defiant love in the *qissas* of Hir-Ranjha, Sohni-Mahiwal and Mirza-Sahiban, and sexually explicit oral songs were available as discursive

77

possibilities in the north-Indian repertoire in the 20th century, 'transgression' became unacceptable when literary convention seeped into practice.[8] By the 'transgressive 1960s' (Gadihoke 2011: 105), Bombay cinema and film songs had made available abundant visual and literary vocabulary of transgressive desire and pleasure, just as it melodramatically negotiated the gap between 'individual' fulfilment and social values, 'Intimacy and desire pervade the frame ... yet mark out their differences in terms of perceived Indian values' (Gadihoke 2011: 141).

The association with Bombay cinema of many Progressive writers and performers (including Amrita and Sahir), who had migrated from literary and cosmopolitan centres across the border, made it an eclectic space where religious, linguistic and caste borders were crossed. The Hindi-Urdu-Punjabi lyrical output by both Amrita and Sahir evinces this border-crossing, as it evinces 'the intertextuality between literature, cinema, music, and the oral repertoire' (Sangari 2007: 272). Love and intimacy expressed in the literary and cinematic space would, however, become an unseemly spectacle when it came to public 'confession', especially by a woman. Having survived this pain, Amrita writes in her autobiographical writings about love that is a social discourse within and outside, a mode of dissent for an individual as well as for the community of women and an emotion tied to history, time and space.

What begins as a physical yearning, 'a consuming fire' (Pritam 1994: 13) in adolescence can only find fulfilment in a dream before it finds embodiment in the form of Sahir. 'I kept putting words together, stealthily touching the form in my imagination of the one I loved ... the intensity of my passion did not carry to the one I loved' (Pritam 1994: 97). Love as an emotion or affect is then re-interpreted as a social inhabitation through the autobiographical act. There is always a 'deep entanglement of materiality and cultural practices with the affective or emotional' (Khan 2015: 612). In this sphere, the narrator knows that love was always destined towards tragedy, 'The beginning of this tale was silence and the intensity of it too was carried out in silence' (Pritam 1994: 116). While she imbues this love with larger socio-mythic dimensions by embedding it in the tales of Urvashi, Menaka, Hir-Ranjha and Mirza-Sahiban, the intensity and corporeal desire is also represented through striking imagistic memories, such as that of her smoking the cigarette stubs left by Sahir.

Mediating between dreams and social reality, she creates a literary subjecthood through images of defiant creativity and memories of pain. Memory can be seen in these life narratives, not only as an instrument of temporal organisation but as a site of enunciation, a careful choice of events to be memorialised in the theatre of the present to perform the self.

In the sea of imagination, my dream swims like fish / When this fish touches the ground, it will be tormented to death / When my dream meets reality, it will go into throes of death / But if you have the hunger, the sea of imagination is immense / I will cast a net of my life, and catch the golden fish of my dreams.

(Pritam 1971: 44)

Love is envisaged as a visibly political act, when she marks her 'emancipation of the being' on 15 August 1967 (Pritam 1994: 83), having crossed social barriers to find companionship with Imroz. 'But what magic was in the key to your house / That when I opened the lock to your door / I saw the line of honour was not before my feet but behind' (Pritam 1994: 143). It is to this politics of dissent that the creative and autobiographical act is also tied. 'The crude realities of my world fell in love with my dreams and out of such an illicit union was born all that I wrote' (Pritam 1994: 141–142). If, according to her, 'recalcitrance' is an essential sensibility required of a writer, so is an aesthetic frame needed that is as recalcitrant.

The frames of history, memory, time, space and affect can be employed as useful modes of analysis of the radical aesthetics of life-writing that Amrita devises. The ruptures in the narrative suspend a homological approach to temporality – that which sunders past, present and future – and foreground questions of the relationship of past life to present injustice and future regeneration. Rather than being instrumentally connected with (life) history, the narrative voice talks across past, present and future to imagine her 'self' as being implicated in the present and being a 'trace' in the future.

My mother's mother and her mother's mother – every woman's mother had looted the sixteen graces in some mutiny against society. Those graces and arts should have passed on from generation to generation. I had to repay that debt to society. How and when I still do not know.... How many more women will, I cannot say.

(Pritam 1994: 28)

She promises to be the '*hujre di mitti*' (soil from Sufi meditative place) which lies beneath the debris of the world, and that will sprout new beginnings (Pritam 2019: 138) in the future. The expansive self connects temporally and spatially to the pain of the Bengal famine, the Quetta earthquake, the freedom struggle, the Second World War, Partition, Vietnam, Bulgaria, Hungary, Germany, Italy and 'others steeped in bloodshed by foreign guns', some 'stricken pale from fear' (Pritam 1994: 59).

A singular, 'personal' voice of testimony of cultural memory that an autobiographical voice is assumed to be is dispersed into the impersonal, 'fictional' voices of characters of poems, stories and dreams, thus confounding the distinction between author, narrator and character and opening emancipatory spaces in the present. In the Preface to *Aksharon Ke Saaye*, she says, 'When I could not call Amrita, I called her Nirmala or Achla, Malika or Karmawali, Ratni, Canny, Meenu or some other name...' (Pritam 2019).

It is in thus providing politically generative spaces for the readers that the three autobiographical narratives spill over their narrative closures, and make sure that neither the end of life, nor its recording in words, will mean the ceasing of political memory. In this sense, Amrita Pritam's life-writing is a 'revolutionary gesture against amnesia' (Smith 1993: 182).

Notes

1 See Udaya Kumar (2012), and Sudipta Kaviraj (2007).
2 See Javed Majeed (2007).
3 This information has been gathered from *Annual Reports on Publications*, *Native Newspaper Reports*, *Reports on Printing Presses in Punjab*, etc.
4 Examples of idealised images of women that reformist literature produced are: Bhai Vir Singh's *Sundari* (1898) and *Satwant Kaur* (1900) in Punjabi, Pandit Shraddha Ram Phillouri's *Bhagyavati* (1887) in Hindi, and *Mirat-ul'u-rus*, or the "The Bride's Mirror" by Maulvi Nazir Ahmad (1869) in Urdu.
5 This analysis is based on a reading of the following women's periodicals in Hindi and Punjabi: *Bharat Bhagini* (Hindi, 1902-4), *Punjabi Bhain* (Punjabi, 1907–1920).
6 Bhai Vir Singh (1872–1957), Ruchi Ram Sahni (1863–1948), Harsukh Rai (1816–1890), Munshi Naval Kishore (1836–1885), Dyal Singh Majithia (1848–1898).
7 Hardevi was the author of travelogues *London Jubilee* and *London Yatra* (1888) and some prose tracts. Sushila Tahl Ram was the author of the first English novel from Lahore, *Cosmopolitan Hindustani* (1902). Harnam Kaur was a co-editor, along with Takhat Singh and Bhai Vir Singh, of *Punjabi Bhain* (1907–1918), a monthly in Punjabi, published from the Sikh Kanya Mahavidyalaya, Ferozepur. Kamala Satthianadhan was a writer and editor of *The Indian Ladies Magazine*, published in Madras from 1901 to 1918 (under her editorship) and later from 1927 to 1938. Sarala Devi Chaudhurani (1872–1945) was the daughter of Swarnakumari Debi (Rabindranath Tagore's sister) and editor of *Bharati*, a monthly journal, from 1895.
8 Refer to Orsini (2007), Jeevan S. Deol (2007), Raheja and Gold (1994) for a detailed discussion on how these traditions were reworked over time and through the prism of 20th century cultural politics.

References

Arnold, David and Stuart Blackburn, eds. 2004. *Telling Lives in India: Biography, Autobiography, and Life History*. Delhi: Permanent Black.

Bano, Shadab. 2012. "Rashid Jahan's Writings: Resistance and Challenging Boundaries, *Angaare* and Onwards", *Indian Journal of Gender Studies* 19, no. 1: 57–71.

Benstock, Shari. 1998. "Authorizing the Autobiographical", in Smith, S. and Watson, J. (eds.), *Women, Autobiography, Theory: A Reader*, pp. 145–155. Wisconsin: University of Wisconsin Press.

Bhabha, Homi. 1994. *The Location of Culture*. London: Routledge.

Bhandari, Vivek. 2007. "Print and the Emergence of Multiple Publics in 19th Century Punjab", in Sabrina Alcorn Baron, Eric N. Lindquist, and Eleanor F. Shevlin (eds.), *Agents of Change: Print Culture Studies after Elizabeth L. Eisenstein*, pp. 268–286. Massachusetts: University of Massachusetts Press.

Bruno, Giuliana. 2002, rpt. 2018. *Atlas of Emotion: Journeys in Art, Architecture and Film*. New York: Verso.

Cohn, Bernard. 1985. "The Command of Language and the Language of Command", in Ranajit Guha (ed.), *Subaltern Studies: Writings on South Asian History and Society*, vol. 4, pp. 276–329. New Delhi: Oxford University Press.

Deol, Jeevan S. 2007. "To Die at the Hands of Love: Conflicting Ideals of Love in the Punjabi Mirza-Sahiban Cycle", in Francesca Orsini (ed.), *Love in South Asia: A Cultural History*, pp. 142–158. Cambridge: Cambridge University Press.

Gadihoke, Sabeena. 2011. "Sensational Love Scandals and Their After-Lives: The Epic Tale of Nanavati", *BioScope* 2, no. 2: 103–128.

Gusdorf, Georges. 1980. "Conditions and Limits of Autobiography", (1956) in James Olney (ed. & trans.), *Autobiography: Essays Theoretical and Critical*, pp. 28–48. Princeton: Princeton University Press.

Kaviraj, Sudipta. 2015. *The Invention of Private Life*. New York: Columbia University Press.

Khan, Razak. 2015. "The Social Production of Space and Emotions in South Asia", *Journal of the Economic and Social History of the Orient* 58, no. 5: 611–633.

Kishwar, Madhu and Ruth Vanita. 1982. "Stories Written on the Bodies and Minds of Women: Amrita Pritam's Life and Work", *Manushi*, no. 10: 2–11.

Kumar, Radha. 1993. *The History of Doing: An Illustrated Account of Movements for Women's Rights and Feminism in India, 1800–1990*. New Delhi: Zubaan.

Kumar, Udaya. 2008. "Autobiography as a Way of Writing History: Personal Narratives from Kerala and the Inhabitation of Modernity", in Raziuddin Aquil and Partha Chatterjee (eds.), *History in the Vernacular*, pp. 214–248. New Delhi: Permanent Black. e-edition 2012.

Lejeune, Phillipe. 1982. "The Autobiographical Contract", (trans. R. Carter) in Tzvetan Todorov (ed.), *French Literary Theory Today: A Reader*, pp. 192–222. Cambridge: Cambridge University Press.

Mahfil Staff Reporter. 1968–69. "Of Pain and Protest", *Mahfil* 5, no. 3, Amrita Pritam Number (1968–1969): 1–3.

Majeed, Javed. 2007. *Autobiography, Travel and Postnational Identity: Gandhi, Nehru and Iqbal*. Basingstoke: Palgrave.

———. 2013. "Miracles for the Marginal? Gender and Agency in a Nineteenth Century Autobiographical Fragment", *Journal of Women's History* 25, no. 2: 15–35.

Mazumdar, Ranjani. 2011. "Aviation, Tourism and Dreaming in 1960s Bombay Cinema", *BioScope* 2, no. 2: 129–155.

Menon, Ritu. 2015. "Pentimento: The Self Beneath the Surface", in Anshu Malhotra and Siobhan Lambert-Hurley (eds.), *Speaking of the Self: Gender, Performance, and Autobiography in South Asia*, pp. 56–71. Durham and London: Duke University Press.

O'Hanlon, Rosalind. 1988. "Recovering the Subject: Subaltern Studies and Histories of Resistance in Colonial South Asia", *Modern Asian Studies* 22, no.1: 189–224.

Orsini, Francesca. 2004. "The Reticent Autobiographer: Mahadevi Varma's Writings", in David Arnold and Stuart Blackburn (eds.), *Telling Lives in India: Biography, Autobiography, and Life History*, pp. 54–82. Delhi: Permanent Black.

Pascal, Roy. 1960. *Design and Truth in Autobiography*. Cambridge, MA: Harvard University Press.

Pritam, Amrita. 1976, rev. 1991, rpt. 1994. *The Revenue Stamp*. Trans. Krishna Gorowara. Delhi: Vikas Publishing House. e-edition.

———. 1968, rpt. 1971. *Kala Gulab*. New Delhi: Star Publications.

———. 2001, rpt. 2019. *Aksharon ke Saaye*. New Delhi: Rajpal.

Raheja, Gloria Goodwin and Ann Grodzins Gold. 1994. *Listen to the Heron's Words: Reimagining Gender and Kinship in North India*. Berkeley: University of California Press.

Rhodes, Jacqueline. 2005. *Radical Feminism, Writing, and Critical Agency: From Manifesto to Modern*. Albany: State University of New York Press.

Sangari, Kumkum. 2007. "Love's Repertoire: Qurratulain Hyder's *River of Fire*", in Orsini (ed.), *Love in South Asia: A Cultural History*, pp. 259–285. Cambridge: Cambridge University Press.

Smith, Sidonie. 1993. *Subjectivity, Identity, and the Body: Women's Autobiographical Practices in the Twentieth Century*. Bloomington: Indiana University Press.

———. 1994. "Identity's Body", in Kathleen Ashley, Leigh Gilmore, and Gerald Peters (eds.), *Autobiography and Post-modernism*, pp. 226–292. Amherst: University of Massachusetts Press.

———. 1998. "Performativity, Autobiographical Practice, Resistance", (1995) in Smith, S. and Watson, J. (eds.), *Women, Autobiography, Theory: A Reader*, pp. 108–115. Wisconsin: University of Wisconsin Press.

Smith, Sidonie and Julia Watson. 1998. *Women, Autobiography, Theory: A Reader*. Wisconsin: University of Wisconsin Press.

———. 2001, rpt. 2010. *Reading Autobiography: A Guide for Interpreting Life Narratives*, Second Edition. Minneapolis and London: University of Minnesota Press.

Stanton, Domna. 1998. "Autogynography: Is the Subject Different?" (1984) in Smith, S. and Watson, J. (eds.) *Women, Autobiography, Theory: A Reader*, pp. 131–144. Wisconsin: University of Wisconsin Press.

9

DESIRE, LOVE AND SPIRITUALITY

Transformation of the Self in Amrita Pritam's
Writings

Yadwinder Singh
translated by Harmeet Kaur Jhajj

Punjabi literary circles are replete with diverse viewpoints about Amrita Pritam. This often happens when the persona of a writer becomes more charismatic than her writings. One of the perspectives divides Amrita's literary career into two periods. In the initial period, she challenges the constraints of patriarchy while in the later period, her idiom becomes spiritual. An alternate interpretation points to an initial defiance of patriarchy, eventually leading to encasement in that very framework.

At the surface level, this interpretation appears to be pertinent but the matter is not so simple and straightforward as it appears. This chapter seeks to explore if there is any relationship between Amrita's progressive outlook, her feminist approach and her spiritual identity. It examines if Amrita comes in conflict with or faces a dilemma in the two periods in her writing career, and if so, what are the convergences? Is it adequate to skim the surface of her writings by casting a cursory glance or need one read between the lines as Derrida suggests one must while decoding a text? What could be the reason behind the discourse or form of her writings remaining the same while the content of the writing keeps changing? Why is it that her language remains the same right from the beginning of her creative period till the very end? It is essential to understand the fundamental core of her persona and her creative self, the relationship between the two, and to ponder over whether her writings can be read as a reflection of her persona.

It is true that writing cannot be separated from the writer. But every piece of writing has a connection with the outside world, too. The world does not endorse self-conceived meanings, but the perspective of the writer brings everything within the ambit of meaning. Hence, it becomes important to see how the writer constructs the self from her inner turmoil arising out of a conflict with the outside world. On the other hand, it is also important to understand how the self-image of the author is associated with her creative

DOI: 10.4324/9781003214656-16

impulse. Hence, it is pertinent to begin the discussion from the point where Amrita herself talks about her creative process and its relationship with the outside world. In her earlier autobiography, *Kala Gulab* (*Black Rose*), Amrita addresses the framework of her creativity and the construction of the self –

> (My) Beloved, of my imagination
> It seems to me
> My whole life
> Is a letter I wrote you.
> Every heartbeat is an alphabet.
> Every breath, a syllable's measure
> Each day, a sentence
> And my whole life, a letter.
> Were this letter to reach you
> It would have ended my abject reliance on language
> But
> Till date
> No words in any language
> have fallen deep enough in love with thoughts
> To write this entire letter
> It is because of this dependence
> that
> All the poems that I have written –
> All the stories, novels,
> Seem only a few phrases of this letter
> Not the whole letter.
>
> (Pritam 2002: 12)

This poem may be read as a confessional statement about her writing or be interpreted as the hidden door to enter the chamber of her creative process. In this poem, she visualises the framework of the self as well as expresses her view of the outside world. There are three salient points in this poem. First, Amrita regards the entire range of her work simply as a missive to her beloved – with all the novels, stories and poems being only a few phrases of this letter. Secondly, she clearly addresses this poem to a beloved who is not a real but an imagined being, and her writings are an attempt to reach this imagined being. Thirdly, imagination stems from thought. It is possible to conceive the imaginary but impossible to attain it. Consequently, this letter (or poem) that symbolises Amrita's creative world remains incomplete.

This poem can be instrumental in understanding both the mystery of Amrita's personal self and of her creative world. A relevant question that emerges from this poem is how Amrita confronts and further resolves these three – desire, love and spirituality. These symbols are important milestones in the construction of her self and her creativity. Keeping these as a central concern, this chapter is an attempt to establish a dialogue between Amrita's personal self and her creativity.

French psychoanalyst, Jacques Lacan talks about three phases associated with the human self in his 'Mirror Stage Theory'. According to him:

> Between the ages of six and eighteen months the infant begins to recognise his/her image in the mirror, and this is usually accompanied by pleasure. The child is fascinated with its image and tries to control and play with it. Although the child initially confuses its image with reality, he/she soon realises that the image has its own properties, finally accepting that the image is their own image – a reflection of themselves.
>
> (qtd. in Homer 2005: 24)

Fascination with one's own reflection in the mirror is the initial stage of the journey that leads to love with another in the future. Enamoured with one's own reflection in the mirror, the child wants to play with it. One wants to hold and control it but gradually realises that one cannot exercise any control over it. Failure to do so pushes one towards the domain of language. Language now replaces the image. The child begins to nurse the illusion of completing one's self-image by associating it with that of another. This is the second condition of the mirror-stage which Lacan calls symbolic (1988: 29). One may think that one has created language but one tends to forget that language too constructs one and plays a significant role in the development of the human self. Lacan believes that the human unconscious is akin to the process of language construction. Being itself an incomplete creation, language is incapable of grasping the complete meanings of human life. Hence, reality can never be accurately translated into language. The third link in Lacan's theory is the real world. One wants to understand the mystery around oneself and for this, one must rely upon language. Language transforms reality into symbols. Whatever one knows of this world is through language discourse. That which remains outside the purview of this discourse compels one to be in constant search of it. The sense of regret and sorrow of not knowing that which remains outside the image and language causes a crisis of self-identity. Lacan theorises it as the Real (Homer 2005: 81).

To understand the mystery of Amrita's creativity, a focus on Lacan's three phases regarding the human self is crucial. Before a child enters the world of language, many images form and dissolve in one's unconscious. A child's perception of reality becomes possible through these images. A child's curiosity to know one's own self too arises when one looks at one's reflection in the mirror. It is this reflection that enables one's consciousness about one's difference from others. However, the reflection does not have a stable form and the child easily swaps one reflection with another (Lacan 1977: 4). Lacan regarded the experiment conducted by the Austrian zoologist, Konrad Lorenz, upon the eggs of the duck as a model for image construction in a child. Before the eggs hatched, Lorenz placed his shoes near them. The newly hatched ducklings associated the shoes with the imagined image of their mother. Wherever Lorenz went wearing those shoes, the ducklings followed him, thinking the shoes to be their mother. Lacan postulates that a child continues to befool oneself with the image formed in early childhood (online).

With reference to Amrita, it is important to know which of her childhood images constitute the metaphors of her life. Amrita has used the symbol of the dirt of one's body for her self-image in several writings. While talking about her early life, she writes:

> My mother took extreme care to never dishonour the patriarchal authority of my father. However, I always felt, right from my childhood, that just as Parvati created Ganesha from the dirt of her body, similarly my mother kneaded all her bitterness, all her unhappiness, all her resentment, and all her anger when she created my form and she herself was able to purge herself of every scrap of resentment.
>
> (Pritam 2002: 60)

It is possible to identify two fundamental bases of Amrita's self-image. The first is the myth behind Ganesha's origin. Parvati would suffer pangs of loneliness due to the frequent absences of Lord Shiva from home. To rid herself of this loneliness, she gathered the dirt from her body, sculpted a statue from it, and brought it to life. Due to his unique origin, Ganesha is different from other children as he belongs to his mother alone. The father has no role to play in his creation.

Amrita's comparison of herself with the human figure constructed with the dirt of her mother's body without any contribution from the father is significant in understanding the framework of her self-image and the subsequent emergence of her unconscious in her writings. The base of this unconscious is connected to the family. Taking Sigmund Freud's theory of the Oedipal Complex as the base, Lacan connects the family to the Law of the Father or Oedipal Law. Lacan is of the view that being born of a mother is the natural birth of a child, whereas becoming proficient in the Law of the Father is a child's social birth (Homer 2005: 59). When Amrita talks about her mother who could not oppose her husband her entire life and vented her frustration by pouring the whole of it into the being of her daughter, Amrita is unconsciously refusing to be moulded by the Law of the Father.

The social signification of dirt is the second premise of this tale. In the context of Punjab, there are several socio-cultural references to the dirt of the body and that of the mind. Dirt of the body refers to grime and sweat while that of the mind indicates moral depravity. It is vital to understand why Amrita expresses her self-image through such a socially unacceptable image. One conscious reason is that she makes clear her protest of being unauthenticated by patriarchy through the image of dirt. One can observe an imperceptible and unconscious emotion behind this which is linked to the attribution of meaning to her sense of being unauthenticated. Behind this unconscious feeling, the form of her self-image is no longer dirt alone. In her poetry, this self-image gets transformed into several other images and an important image amongst these is that of the phoenix. In her poetry, the symbol of dirt gets transformed into the mythical phoenix that rises from its own ashes.

In social environment, the meaning of the dirt of the body is something that is devoid of quality. Dirt must assume the shape of a human figure (Ganesha) to acquire meaning. Just as dirt, despite having negative connotations, acquires a positive meaning when it takes the shape of Ganesha, similarly Amrita, too, is in search of a meaning for her existence. It is imperative that she construct a social image of herself to attain this goal, but the problem is that this social context is tied to the laws of patriarchy. The issue before Amrita is that she must give expression to the purpose of her existence through words despite the suffering and heartbreak that her vocal and demonstrative protest against patriarchy's repressive societal practices cause her. The unconscious desire of Amrita's self-image culminates in the process of transformation from the unacknowledged and insignificant existence of the dirt of the body into the phoenix that consumes itself in flames to illuminate the world, thus rising from its own ashes.

> The Phoenix shall sing the *deepak raga*, song of the lamp
> And consume itself in the flame of love
> The destiny of this song is ashes
> Salute to the passion of the Phoenix.
>
> (Pritam 2019: 88)

In this way, her own intense longing gives rise to self-contradictory self-images – the socially unacknowledged body-dirt and the ambitious desire of acceptance by society even if that acceptance is at the cost of consuming oneself in the fire of one's own passion to illumine the world. This conflict makes her a split personality – on the one hand, she suffers untold anguish on account of voicing her protest, and on the other, she aspires and yearns to protest. Heidegger in *Being and Time* says that the crisis of human existence results from the tussle between a human being's present situation and an imagined future (Homer 2005: 20). Amrita's self-image, too, reflects this dilemma of her soul. Her self-image is torn between her present situation (body-dirt) and her desired future (the Phoenix). Body-dirt or ash reflects her imperfect existence and her fragmented self. A sense of completion lies in becoming either Ganesha or the Phoenix.

Lacan says that a child's presumed self-image is proof of its being regarded as complete. However, this sense of perfection is only an illusion. Labouring under the illusion of her complete self, all the things and persons become 'other' for the child. The main reason behind this is that any perception of the self is possible only by setting oneself apart from the others (Homer 2005: 21).

The crisis of human beings is that, on the one hand, one considers one's self-image to be perfect while on the other, one's imperfect identity does not allow one any peace. Consequently, one's self-image begins to look for the meaning of its existence in the love of another person. There are many instances in Amrita's writings that point toward attempts to conjoin her unfulfilled desires with another person in the hope of constructing a complete image. Recounting an incident of her childhood, she says that once in her innocence she asked her father what God looked like; to which her father replied that one had to walk on the path shown by the Guru to attain God. He showed her the pictures of the ten Gurus and asked her to visualise any one of them. She says:

> It is not possible to visualise ten faces. I would have to choose one of them. I would take up one picture, then another but again and again my eyes would be drawn to the pictures of the sixth and the tenth Guru – both were in the prime of their youth, bespeaking valour, a shining horse and a falcon perched on one arm.
>
> (Pritam 2002: 13–14)

Instead of visualising the picture of the first Guru, Guru Nanak Dev like most other children, Amrita would dwell on the images of the sixth and the tenth Gurus. There are two possible reasons behind this choice. The first is her conscious desire to prove herself as different, perhaps even better than other, ordinary children. (The image of the phoenix rising from its ashes is a revelation of this desire.) Secondly, the adjectives used for the pictures of the sixth and the tenth Gurus ('in the prime of their youth, bespeaking valour, a shining horse, and a falcon perched on one arm') are a manifestation of her unconscious desire.

It is this unconscious desire that leads her imagination to the second symbol discussed in this chapter – love. There are two more milestones ahead in this journey from imagination to love. First, the knowledge of the self being incomplete and second, the desire to attain fulfilment through union with another. Lacan says that the idea of a complete self is pure imagination and it is impossible for a human being to ever have a complete self. It is a hide and seek between image and word. One remains preoccupied in this game of image and word throughout one's life. The human self is constructed by seeing its reflection in the mirror and expressing itself in language. On the other hand, the pain of the memory of having remained a part of the mother's body for nine months challenges a human's notion of one's complete self. It is this sense of incompleteness that attracts one towards another person.

Amrita's journey from desire to love is her journey from the self to the other. In the course of this journey, Amrita's search results in her self-image swapping places with the image of the other. Her dreams as recorded in her writings offer the possibility of gauging the intensity of this journey. Her self-image assumes many shapes in her dreams; the first of which is that of Rajan. Describing one of her dreams, Amrita writes, 'One night the prince of my dreams said to me, Listen, don't recount dreams of me to others. And, from now on I shall come to you in disguise' (Pritam 2002: 14). Amrita goes on to say that from that moment onwards the image of the sixth Guru was replaced by that of the young man, Rajan, in her dreams. Freud says that often in our dreams the imagined images keep changing their shapes; they merge with each other and later it is not possible to segregate them and bring them back to their original forms. Despite this, these images have a common element which brings them within the ambit of meaning (Homer 2005: 43). Many a time, the image in our dreams is transformed. In other words, it is the desire to convert imagination into reality. That Rajan replaces the sixth Guru in Amrita's dream demonstrates her desire to transform the image of the sixth Guru in her imagination into a realistic image – that of Rajan.

In dreams, it is not just images that blend and mingle; emotions like anger, fear, hatred and love, too, assume the form of an allegory. This allegorical narrative emerges also from the mental drill to invest the incomplete self with meaning. In many of her works like *Kala Gulab* (*The Black Rose*), *Hujre di Mitti* (*The Soil of the Cloister*), *Darveshan di Mehndi* (*The Dervishes' Ecstasy*), *Lal Dhaage da Rishta* (*The Bond of the Red Thread*), etc. Amrita narrates many dreams which seem like allegories. In one such dream, she sees a bare-bodied Rajan, the prince of her dreams, sitting far away on a bed. The white shirt that he has taken off is lying near him. Suddenly, the image of her father raising his finger at Rajan rises in front of her eyes (Pritam 2002: 22).

Among the many mysteries behind Amrita's creative process, one lies hidden in this dream allegory. Amrita first draws a restrictive boundary line in her writing. Her father raising his finger at Rajan in this dream represents this restriction. The basis of this restriction is obedience to the Law of the Father. The world of unfulfilled desires symbolised by the image of Rajan with his naked torso lies behind such opposition of restrictive patriarchal rules. Central to her writings is the desire to transform the world of restrictions into the world of desires. In her early poems, this duality between restriction and desire can be clearly identified.

> Your sorrows and mine, and scores of other such sorrows
> Your tears and mine, and tears of so many others

This journey seven years long, not just we who traverse
Lakhs like Sassi and Punnu suffer blisters on their feet in deserts
At the feet of every Sohni
A spring cascades today too
On the soles of every Sassi's feet
Blisters writhe in pain today too.

(Pritam qtd. in Kaur 2013: 146)

There are two more dreams similar to this which help us understand what she is longing for. In the first dream, she is held captive in a fort and a crowd gathers outside. The crowd is thirsty for her blood and there is no way to escape. In this state of panic, the sky becomes visible to her from the fort and suddenly she starts growing taller and taller till she reaches the sky where it is impossible for those wanting to kill her to reach her. In the second dream too, she is running to escape from a crowd. Suddenly she sees a river in front of her. Gingerly, she puts her feet in and is amazed to discover that she could walk on water. The crowd is standing on the bank of the river and can cause her no harm at all (Pritam 2002: 19–20).

The common element in these dreams is her 'self' leaving the ground and soaring up in the sky or walking on water. The ground symbolises the earth, the sky represents the heaven and water the netherworld. The ground represents her current situation, the sky and water signify a possibility to escape her present. The crowd outside the fort and on the banks of the river could be her critics and detractors – those who belittle, denounce, condemn and censure her. She cannot deal with them on the ground, hence she explores the possibility of a new world through the symbols of the sky and the water. This possibility plays out on the plane of her mind and represents the shield of security that she conjures up to escape her current undesirable situation.

This can also be called the world of romance, where she feels secure; and it is this world that is the foundation of Amrita's creativity. It creates its own symbolic reality and gradually this imagined reality begins to dominate her work. The presence of this duality in the framework of Amrita's self becomes the focal point of her creative work. Hence every opposition she encounters is coloured with the brush of romance and even her progressive literature does not remain untouched by it. Her poems in the anthology *Sunhede* (*Messages*) for which she won the Sahitya Akademi Award sound the clarion call of creating a world that is uninhibited in matters of love. In her most celebrated poem on the partition of Punjab in 1947, 'Ajj Aakhaan Waris Shah nu' ('To Waris Shah'), she symbolises the tragedy of partition through the love legend of Hir. Even later, though the subject and tone of her writing changes from revolutionary to spiritual, the colour of romance remains intact, and even dominant, throughout. Nor is her language free from the hues of romance.

It is important to understand that this is not simply a case of Amrita's work gaining popularity or the adverse public reaction it evoked, or its corrosive impact on her psyche. What is important is the manner in which she confronts the questions she is faced with. Romance is an important strategy in Amrita's construction of language and it is through romance that she not only confronts the issues of her time but also forms the strategy to free herself from them. When she cannot change her surroundings according to her perspective then this strategy often becomes a part of her creative process. Her creativity passes through a kind of imagined reality.

In the poem quoted at the beginning of this chapter, Amrita says that her entire work is akin to a letter addressed to the beloved. She also says that this letter is incomplete because language is incapable of doing justice to one's emotions and can never fully express the self. From this perspective, it is clear that the self can never be made complete through a union with another. A conflict remains forever present in the very concept of love; a conflict which is often neglected.

Amrita desires to make perfect her self-image by demanding someone who could approximate the image of her imagination. This demand cannot be fulfilled. One reason for this is that the other, whether it is Rajan (a figment of her imagination), or Sahir Ludhianvi (her epic, unrequited love) or Imroz (her lifelong companion), with whom Amrita desires to attain fulfilment are themselves incomplete; imperfect. It is possible that their own imagined reality is associated with someone other than Amrita. Lacan says that two people loving each other means that there are four people involved in the process. Both have one more image present in their individual imagined realities apart from that of their beloved. This is the 'other' whose presence is engraved on the mental plane but who does not exist in reality (Homer 2005: 88).

In another reference, Amrita mentions a dream in which she begins to gain a mature understanding of the foolish nature of love. In one of her dreams, she emerges from the illusion of being the only desire of her beloved. She realises that loneliness is the central point of her life:

> That night I saw him in my dream and her also, whose name is now linked with him. In her curly hair I pinned a rose myself. The same flower that he had once pinned in my hair. It's been some time since I read this – 'If I had to describe my life in one word; I should use the word loneliness twice. That day I understood how the entire expanse of a tree is contained in a little seed. That day I came to know that my entire life is not a letter, not a paragraph, not a sentence, it is a word, only one word – loneliness'.
>
> (Pritam 2002: 27–28)

This long and tormenting journey through loneliness is the third milestone in her existence as well as in her creative process which has been termed 'the romance with spirituality'. When Amrita reaches this milestone, she gains an insight that it is impossible to become complete through union with another self because the other self is also incomplete. She realises that the imagination which she converts into writings in the form of letters cannot be fully embodied in language. As this belief deepens, her writing begins to adopt the medium of spirituality. She is now in search of the 'One' who contains the image of a complete self. From this point, her spiritual journey begins to seek a union with that imaginary image which alone is believed to be complete in the entire universe. In her writings, this journey begins with her book *Hujre di Mitti* (*The Soil of the Cloister*). She pens the following lines at the beginning of this book:

> The pen broke the sequence of songs today
> What height has my passion scaled today?
>
> (Pritam 2002: 118)

An important point in this reference is that though language cannot give complete expression to the self, yet language is still the best option available. Despite being imperfect, language is the only medium to attempt any expression at all. This lends an enigmatic quality to Amrita's writings. Her creative exercise undergoes two changes when she sets out in search of spirituality. First, there is an increased use of fantasy in her writing. Now Osho and Sai become the foundation of her fantasy. Like her previous writing, the work of this period is also constructed upon her dreams – the difference being that in the writing of this period, the prince of her dreams is replaced by her mystical experiences. To give expression to these experiences, she has to take recourse to fantasy. It goes to the credit of fantasy that it can create an illusion of something that does not exist. God is also such an idea, which though intangible, yet can be most deeply felt and experienced. To give expression to this idea, Amrita's language begins to centralise on abstract contents like astrology, mysticism, rebirth, etc. yet the form of romance remains intact in her writing as before.

The second transformation in her writings is that the social context moves to the margin. Societal restrictions and patriarchy which had formed the subject matter of her initial writing find no place in her later work. In this period, Amrita begins to see every occurrence and everyone's behaviour through the lens of spirituality. The change in her creative process can be best understood in the context of her observation about revolution:

> History could never penetrate the soul of revolution. It has been using this word for every violent incident. That's why I want to talk about this word. The soul of revolution is in the fragrance of the seed that blooms in the conscience of man. It is not concerned with wresting power. It has nothing to do with pillage or plunder.

Its only purpose is to completely transform the weight of our innate nature and to convert it into spirituality. This revolution originates in passion. The germ of revolution is in the passionate longing of love.

(Pritam 2002: 168)

In this stage of her creative journey, Amrita is in search of that elusive thing which language is incapable of expressing. With reference to Osho, Amrita calls it the unknowable – that which is beyond knowledge. Osho mentions three stages of knowledge – that which is known, that which is unknown, and that which remains unknowable. The known has already been perceived. That which is known today, need not have been known always. At some point in history, it may have been unknown. Similarly, the unknown is what we do not know today but may learn about in the future. The unknowable is different from both – something that eludes comprehension and shall always do so. It has never been known, nor will be; indeed, nor can ever be.

Lacan calls this situation the 'Real' that remains beyond the purview of language. It keeps teasing one's memory. The more we try to erase it, the deeper it gets embedded in one's unconscious. The search for what refuses to be expressed in language despite repeated attempts is intensified. Like language, desire too is a string of countless interpretations and meanings. Neither meaning nor desire ever attains fulfilment (Homer 2005: 84). The fulfilment of a desire gives birth to more desires. Mirza Ghalib explains this paradox succinctly in one of his verses, 'Thousands of desires, each worth dying for / Many of them I have realised, yet I yearn for more'. It is this skein of desires that constructs one's unconscious (online).

Desires, too, keep transforming themselves like symbols in the human unconscious. This transformation alternatively becomes desire, or love or spirituality. Amrita's desire creates the image of Rajan while her love for Sahir transforms this image into words. The truth about the imperfection of love sets her on the path of spirituality. When she reaches this point, it dawns upon her that the God experience, which is the ultimate reality, is beyond the realm of human expression. The quest of this absent entity or element sets her writing on the trail of that sign which does not have any final signification. The unconscious sustains itself in this over-confident hope that someday or the other this desire will be fulfilled. But in reality, this never transpires.

This unfulfilled desire forms the grounds for Amrita's creative world. Despite knowing that words fall short and cannot do justice to express what is in her heart, she continues to write. She wants to give expression to everything that forms a part of her half-lived experiences with the result that the romantic framework in the body of her work becomes all the more complex; to the extent that she begins to colour even tales of astrology, rituals and past lives with romance. The reality of the outside world does not match her dreams; and the world of dreams can only be created by sidelining this fact. Amrita feels secure in the cocoon of romanticism that she weaves around herself, and it is this that has imparted such an aura to both her personality and her writings.

References

Homer, Sean. 2005. *Jacques Lacan*. London and New York: Routledge.

Kaur, Veerpal. 2013. "Geetkar Amrita Pritam: Ik Adhyan", in *Khoj Patrika: Amrita Pritam Vishesh Ank*, ed. Rajinder Lahiri. Patiala: Punjabi University: 143–148.

Lacan, Jacques. 1977. *Écrits: A Selection*, trans. A. Sheridan. London: Routledge/Tavistock.

———. 1988. *The Seminar of Jacques Lacan, Book II: The Ego in Freud's Theory and in the Technique of Psychoanalysis 1954–1955*, ed. J.-A. Miller, trans. S. Tomaselli. Cambridge: Cambridge University Press.

Pritam, Amrita. 2002. *Kala Gulab te Hujre di Mitti*. Delhi: Shilalekh Publishers.

———. 2019. *Kaagaz te Canvas ton Pahilan*. Delhi: Shilalekh Publishers.

https://www.simplypsychology.org/Konrad-Lorenz.html (accessed on 25.11.2021).

https://www.rekhta.org/ghazals/hazaaron-khvaahishen-aisii-ki-har-khvaahish-pe-dam-nikle-mirza-ghalib-ghazals (accessed on 25.11.2021).

10

THE ENCHANTMENT OF THE 'MAGICIAN' SAHIR

Jung Bahadur Goyal
translated by Hina Nandrajog

Most people spend their entire lives in dull ordinary routines in accordance with the norms and customs prevalent in their times. Only in rare ages of human history are a handful of people born who erase existing lines to etch bold new strokes; such people have the courage to follow their hearts. They create something unique and lead fulfilled, distinctive and authentic lives. Their charisma and uniqueness become legendary even while they are alive, and people begin to take greater interest in their personal lives rather than in their work. For example, in England, it became a fashion to walk with a limp to imitate Byron. Balzac's extravagance and his romantic liaisons were more the talk of the town than his distinct style of writing. People enjoy anecdotes about George Bernard Shaw's wit to this day. Similarly, the magic of Amrita Pritam's charismatic personality, her lifestyle and her tales of romance continue to thrill people even today.

Amrita's critics are as hostile as her admirers are loyal. But the surprising thing is that her critics cannot help but praise her in the end, while her admirers cannot eschew subdued criticism of her. This amalgamated response of love and hate is evidence of the full-bodied and meaningful life that Amrita led. Swami Vivekananda defined the concept of an immortal person as one who is forever alive in the memories of people. Amrita left this world in 2005, but she is alive in the hearts of people even today; they still talk about her, tell tales about her, and write novels, stories, essays and poems on her life; plays are enacted on her and preparations are afoot to make a film on her life. As the time duration grows longer, the myth that is Amrita Pritam becomes increasingly more enigmatic, to decode which will be an interesting experience for future scholars.

A living and breathing poem by herself, Amrita did not merely write poetry, she verily lived it. Imbued with poetry, every pore of her being – her breath, her words, her glances, the movement of her fingers, her deportment,

DOI: 10.4324/9781003214656-17

her laughter, her anger and loss – all held echoes of the melodies of poetry. She was a literary mendicant who had attained the 'word' with the intensity of her meditation. Such an ability is possessed only by such a one as Michael Angelo, the touch of whose hand could bestow eloquence upon a slab of stone. Such a talent is only found in a Van Gogh who sketches a line with a pencil and it begins to dance.

Amrita's poetic journey began early in life. Once, while her father was immersed in composing a poem, she asked him what he was thinking about. He told her that he was writing a long poem called 'Vairag de Bain' ('Dirges of Separation') and had got stuck on the second line:

> beda gheriya manjh di dhaar andar, / The boat is caught in a whirlpool
> lokkin aakhde ne iththey thaa koi nahi. / People say no banks lie close by.

He was not satisfied with the word 'people' and was searching for a substitute. He was still grappling with the issue when Amrit Kaur came to him and told him to write 'taaru aakhde ne iththey thaa koi nahi' / 'swimmers say no banks lie close by'. Amazed at his eight-year-old daughter's use of such an apt word, Giani Kartar Singh Hitkari became convinced that she had a natural talent for poetry.

The death of her mother when she was only 11 years old was a traumatic experience for Amrita that splintered her entire personality. Her religious belief was shaken. She was compelled to give in to her father's diktat to pray, but did so sullenly. While wandering among the debris of the ruins of spirituality, as she would climb on the rooftop and gaze at the moon, she would imagine her mother's name 'Raj' written on its page – and then who knows how, the alphabet 'n' got suffixed to it to make it 'Rajan' – the prince of her dreams. When she slept at night, Rajan would enter her dreams by crossing all walls and doors. She would imagine playing with him, visualise herself reciting poems to him or see him paint her portrait in the dream. Her Rajan was a poet as well as a painter. Amrita used her father's lessons in the basics of poetic metre, taught to encourage her to write devotional verse, to write her first romantic poem at the age of eleven – 'Rajan de Naam' ('Addressed to Rajan'). But her poem was torn up by her father who discovered it accidentally and was furious with her for writing romantic verse instead of religious poetry.

Lonely after her mother's death, Amrita moped around the house all by herself. Her father advised her to immerse herself in studies. She took the exams for 'Middle' in 1932, and also cleared 'Budhimani' exam with only a month and half for preparation. In 1933, she also cleared the difficult exam of 'Giani' with a first class. She was not even 14 years old then. Her father is believed to have said that after clearing this exam she became so immersed in serving her mother tongue, Punjabi, that she even forgot to eat and drink. In 1935, they stayed in Dalhousie for three months and Amrita wrote several poems there which encouraged her passion for writing.

After his wife's death, Kartar Singh Hitkari had shifted to Lahore with his daughter. He had become aloof and distant. Even before his marriage, he had been an ascetic and had become a devotee at Sant Dayal ji's dera. Perhaps he had accepted the ties of marriage as per some divine command only to gift the world with an 'Amrit' – or nectar!

Later, in her autobiography, *Rasidi Ticket*, Amrita Pritam writes:

> Love and Asceticism pulled him in two opposite directions. There were several moments when I would break down. I could not decide whether I was acceptable to him or not acceptable. I felt my own being to be both wanted and unwanted at the same time. I kept writing poetry; I think to become as loved in my father's eyes as I was unloved.
>
> (Pritam 1998: 11)

Amrita was still enveloped in loneliness when she stepped on the threshold of youth. Her mother was dead, she had no friend or companion, she was not allowed to step out of the house and her father was totally immersed in writing and lived and breathed among books. Amrita says that she was like one of the books lying at home – a book with blank pages. In such an environment, she created a parallel universe, a world of dreams, in which she felt very safe. In her autobiography, she talks of how she viewed the sixteenth year of her life:

> I did not have a natural relationship with my sixteenth year, it was a clandestine relationship. In this year, every familiar thing becomes tight and stifling like the clothes on one's body... there are so many taboos and dos and don'ts in the environment, in the air one breathes that an opposition begins to smoulder in one's breath.... My acquaintance with the sixteenth year was like an unfulfilled love affair, the ache of which lies forever crouched inside one; and that is why that sixteenth year is somewhere or the other mingled with each year of my life....
>
> (Pritam 1998: 17)

Once Balwant Gargi asked her whom she loved. She is believed to have answered, 'Myself, I am in love with myself'. It was the magic of her sixteenth year trapped in her imagination that made her fall in love with her own image for the rest of her life. In this phase of life, not just one's own, even the face of the beloved in one's imagination appears to be the most beautiful one. One falls in love with one's own image in the mirror. Lou Andreas-Salome, Russian psychoanalyst who has done extensive research on narcissism, says that there are some personalities whose entire image cannot be represented adequately within the limits of a mirror. Such people view the entire world as a mirror in which they see their 'self'. Amrita's creative journey is from her 'self' to a larger 'self'. From the finite to the infinite. She says that it makes no difference if the beautiful image is the face of a beloved or a picture of the earth; this is the relationship of the sixteenth year of the mind with imagination, and for her this relationship is an enduring one. She says:

> My sixteenth year is still mingled with every year of my life. Only now its face is not strange; it has become most familiar. Even now, everything around me appears narrow and constricted like the clothes on the body, lips crack with the thirst for life, one wants to touch the stars in the sky with one's hands and if there is any injustice committed against anyone anywhere in the world, my breath begins to smoulder in revolt against that.
>
> (Pritam 1998:17–18)

At the age of 17, she was married to Pritam Singh Kwatra. In her autobiography, the only thing she says about her in-laws is that they were all good people, but it appeared that fate had signed off on their destiny capriciously. This marriage was a meeting of the body, not the mind. Her pain and the sorrow of her married life can be felt in her poem, 'Kumari' ('Virgin'):

> When I stepped on our marital bed
> I was not one – but two
> One married with full rites, and another an utter virgin
> To cohabit with you
> I had to murder the virgin
> I did murder her.
>
> (Pritam 2018: 47)

A sense of loneliness had been etched in her fate. Like a curlew separated from its flock, her mind did not find serenity. However, even if her outward, societal life was empty, her inner life was filled with dreams, thoughts, feelings and images. She wrote prolifically and soon acquired a reputation as a noted Punjabi poet. She had many literary contemporaries, but she did not regard herself as her own contemporary. She was living in the fourth decade of the 20th century, but her imagination belonged to some other century which was yet to come in the future. In one of her poems, Amrita says:

> There are many contemporaries
> Only 'I'

am not my contemporary ...
Without 'I' my birth
is a symptom
of a crime in the disc of a full moon ...
A sliver of flesh
trapped in flesh ...

And on the tongue of this flesh –
Whenever a word comes,
committing suicide
Or escaping suicide –
It drops on a page,
and is murdered.

(Pritam 2018: 53)

To find liberation from the silence and loneliness in her life, she consulted Dr Latif, who was a Professor of Psychology at Forman Christian College, Lahore. She told him that she had no problem in her married life, but she did not feel herself to be alive. He asked her if she loved anyone to which she replied in the negative. When he asked her what she wanted, she said that she wanted to go away somewhere, perhaps to Preet Nagar. He advised her against that saying that she would lose her 'self' there and it would be better for her to immerse herself in some hobby. Amrita abandoned the plan of going to Preet Nagar and took up a job of a sitar player as a casual artiste in Lahore Radio Station. After some time, she began to present Punjabi programmes.

Preet Nagar used to host a literary fest every *phagun*, the spring season, in which not just Punjabi writers but writers in other languages also used to participate. Amrita attended the annual fest in 1943. Noted Urdu poet, Sahir Ludhianvi also came from Lahore to attend the programme. His poetry was very popular those days. Amrita stayed at Gurbaksh Singh Preetlari's house and the rest of the guests had been put up in a school building. Amrita and Sahir neither knew nor recognised each other. When the mushaira began at night, the sky was laden with clouds. Amrita read a heart-rending poem on a drought-stricken Bengal which was much appreciated. When Sahir began to read his poetry, Amrita was enraptured with the magic of his words. She mentions her first meeting with Sahir in *Rasidi Ticket*:

At that time I only heard his voice and it seemed that the air in which his voice had mingled ... that air had become fragrant. God knows which Kalidasa suddenly sent rains that it rained non-stop for two days and nights. The third day, all of us, whoever had gone to that village, set out to return home. The track of the village had

99

been submerged in water. We had to walk about five miles on the embankment of fields and then from Lopoke village we would have got a bus to take us back to Lahore.

(Pritam 1998: 19)

Amrita was acquainted with most of the fifteen-odd people in the group, but she did not know Sahir at all. He was still a stranger to her then. When she saw the silhouette of Sahir's body in the 'soft glow of the sun' she walked in the shadow of his body, and it was as if she had 'wrapped that shadow around her body'. For the first time in her life, Amrita felt that she had been 'walking in his shadow ... from a past life'.

She saw a glimpse of the Rajan of her dreams in Sahir's shadow and was forever enraptured. But upon reaching Lahore, they went their different ways. Once she asked someone, 'If someone calls Sahir, will he come?' 'If you call him, he will drop everything and come'. 'Ok. Tell him sometime....' Amrita only said this much. She says, 'That fortunate day soon arrived, when his feet crossed my threshold for the first time' (Pritam 1998: 20). She goes on to say that she would wait for weeks and months for some conference where 'I would hear his voice, and when he would come sometimes, even my black nights would spread silver moonlight under the feet of my dreams' (Pritam 1998: 19). Later she writes:

One day he came and he had a piece of paper in his hand, with his poem written on it. He read the poem and then giving the paper to me, I don't know why he said, 'The place that is mentioned in this poem, I have never seen, and the girl mentioned in the poem, she is no one....' When I tried to return the paper, he said, 'I have not brought it to take it back.' This was the moment that sewed a golden fringe to my dark clouds ... the stars in the sky throbbed like my heart in the night; and after that whenever I wrote any poem, it seemed as if I were writing a letter to him.

(Pritam 1998: 19)

Then began a string of meetings between Amrita and Sahir. Whenever they met, their lips said nothing, only their silence spoke to each other. Amrita felt that a shard of her own silence would sit in the facing chair and then depart. He would silently go on smoking cigarette after cigarette, smoke about half of it, stub it in the ashtray, then light a fresh one. After he left, only cigarette stubs would remain in the room. At times, Amrita wanted to touch his hand but custom held her back. After he left, she would gather all the stubs and keep them in her almirah. Then she would take out one at a time, sit alone and light it all by herself. When she held the cigarette stub in her fingers, she would feel as if she were touching his hand. She says, 'That is the first time I got into the habit of smoking. Every time I lit a cigarette, I felt – he is close by. As if he appeared like a genie in the smoke of the cigarette....' (Pritam 1998: 27).

Years later, Amrita Pritam depicted this feeling in her novel *Ik si Anita* (*There was an Anita*) and also in a poem:

> Time grabbed a twig
> And wrote an account
> ...
> Life burnt like a cigarette
> The scent of my love –
> Mingled with your breath
> And with the breeze.
>
> Look, let this stub
> Drop from your fingers
> Lest the heat of my love
> Singe your fingertips.
>
> No sorrow in life now
> Conserve this fire
> I pray for the hand
> Light another cigarette now.
>
> (Pritam 2019: 160-161)

Sahir, too, would be impatient to get a glimpse of Amrita. He would often stand at a wayside kiosk near Amrita's house, smoking a cigarette or drinking a soda water in the hope that she would open a window and glance outside and he would be able to gaze at her. He moulded the experience of his first meeting with her on that rainy night in Preet Nagar and his romantic feelings for her in a beautiful poem that became a hit song in the Hindi film *Barsaat ki Raat* (*That Rainy Night*).

> Never shall I forget
> That rainy night
> When I met an unknown beauty
> That rainy night
> ...
> She who dwells in my songs
> An image was she
> The imagination of youthful dreams
> Was she
> She who descended from the skies
> That night of nights

101

Never shall I forget
That rainy night. (online)

After the partition of India, both Amrita and Sahir came to settle in India. She first came to Dehradun with her husband, and later moved to Delhi.... Sahir also came to Delhi from Lahore in 1949 because all his friends and companions had come to India. One day he came to meet Amrita and told her that he was going to Bombay in search of livelihood. He asked Amrita for some poems and her photograph. After that, in Amrita's words, 'Newspapers and books became postmen, and my poems were my letters – to him' (Pritam 1998: 20).

One day, she received a letter from him:

> I was listening to the radio just now and heard your voice. I felt as if you were close to me. Then the voice stopped, and I realised that you were nine hundred miles away.... Then my heart said to me, 'Those who are close to one's heart, they are not far at all'.
>
> (Pritam 1998: 28)

Both felt close to each other. The letters that Amrita wrote to Sahir took the form of poems. These missives of love were strung together in a book *Sunhede* (*Messages*). In Kalidasa's *Meghdoota* (*Cloud-Messenger*), the yaksha sends love letters to his beloved yakshini through clouds as couriers. And Amrita sent her sweet messages through her book. This book won her the prestigious Sahitya Akademi award in 1956, but rather than feel happy she was perhaps more saddened that the one for whom the messages were intended had not read them.

The embers of Sahir's memory remained kindling in Amrita's heart, although she met an artist named Imroz around 1957. Sahir never came to Delhi specifically to meet Amrita. But if he came to Delhi for any work, he would certainly meet her. Amrita, too, always kept looking for reasons to visit Bombay. Once she went there to read her poetry. Sahir was also present. After the mushaira, fans surrounded Sahir to take his autograph. When he became free, Amrita extended her hand and said, 'Autograph please'. Sahir smeared the ink from his pen on his thumb and pressed it on her palm. He said, 'I have put my signature on your palm. Whenever you want, you can redeem this pledge' (Pritam 1998: 30).

Amrita was a self-respecting woman. She did not want any favour in return for her love; she only wanted her love to be reciprocated. Her return plane ticket was booked for that very evening. At Sahir's insistence, she stayed back in Bombay at his place for three days. In those three days, they only kept looking at each other as one looks at a wall.

Later Amrita wrote a story called 'Eh Kahani Nahin' ('This is not a Story'). The story had two characters – 'A' (Amrita) and 'S' (Sahir). In *Rasidi Ticket* she describes a scene from the story when the two of them sit, looking at each:

> S looks at the diamond ring in A's finger as if asking, 'What shall I do with this legal thread wrapped around your finger?' A looks at her finger and laughs softly, as if saying, 'Just say the word once, and I shall prise open this legal binding with my nails, and if my nails cannot open it, then I shall bite it off with my teeth.' But S remained silent and A also stood silently. Just like roads keep standing at one place even when they travel, they too kept moving, standing at one place....
>
> (Pritam 1998: 35)

Later Amrita wrote: 'It was the silence of Sahir that the years of my life could never fathom. And perhaps he could not understand it either. Wherever one tried to move the iceberg of silence from, it did not melt' (Pritam 1998: 35).

Amrita's love for Sahir was as deep as the ocean's attraction to the full moon, and it led to a volcano of emotions erupting inside her. Sahir could write songs and poems about love, but could not immerse himself in it. He appears to be like Paul Morel, the protagonist in D.H. Lawrence's English novel, *Sons and Lovers*, who was caught in the throes of Oedipal love and was incapable of a fulfilling relationship with a woman; his mother seemed to be his only refuge.

After Amrita had stayed for three days in Sahir's house, Sahir took the cup from which Amrita drank tea for the last time before she left and, without rinsing it, placed it in his drawing room. When Amrita took her leave from him, he wrote a poem which he used in a film produced by Bharat Bhushan, *Dooj ka Chaand* (*The Crescent Moon*).

> O those who leave the gathering
> How can I blame you
> You, householders all
> I, a vagrant and notorious.
> ...
> You pretended love for a couple of days
> We socialised for a couple of days
> A good time we spent and
> It was all fun and enjoyable
> Now what use talking about that
> Time is up and the fun is over
> My friends, the goblet is empty.... (online)

In the last days of 1960, once when Amrita was about to call Sahir, her eyes fell on the front page of the weekly *Blitz*. The headline proclaimed, 'Another woman has entered Sahir's life – the singer, Sudha Malhotra' (Pritam 1998: 35). Amrita turned to stone. When the new year dawned, a broken-hearted Amrita welcomed it by saying:

> As if the earth has read
> A sad missive from the sky,
> So has the new year come!

(Pritam 2019: 165)

She had just written this poem and kept it away when the renowned dramatist, Balwant Gargi came to meet her. He records their meeting in his essay, 'Amrita Pritam' thus:

> I picked up the papers. 'What have you written this poem about?'
> 'About the new year ... best wishes for a new year for him.'
> 'Whom?'
> 'Him.'
> I looked into her eyes. A cold ember flickered in her eyes.
> 'You still think about him?'
> 'Yes. I don't know why. Although I understand that I have no relationship with him now. But his breath is mingled in the blood coursing through my veins. I don't know how it has mixed with my blood like poison.... I have no attachment for him, no love, in fact, I hate him ... or perhaps it is not even hate.... Then what kind of a feeling is it? A helpless, bitter feeling ... as if I have plucked and eaten a half-raw mango and the bitter taste of the mango pit lingers in my mouth. There is a strange taste on the tongue.'
> 'Why do you remember him so much?'
> 'I don't. Not at all. I don't think of him at all. I think, it is good that one chapter of my life has come to an end.'
> 'Whenever I meet you, you speak of him. If you have no feelings for him, then why do you think about him? Your new story "Malaah da Phera" ("The Boatman's Round") is about him only. This poem may also be about him....'
> Then she recited the poem to me.
> 'What have you titled it?' I asked....
> 'Saal Mubarak' ('Happy New Year')....
> 'Why don't you take off these torn old clothes of your past and throw them away?'
> 'How can I take them off and throw them away? I myself am only a torn rag....'

(Gargi 2014: 30-31)

Sahir dwelled in the breath of Amrita, so she says:

> I said all that I had to
> Yet a sigh whispers of you!
> A phulkari of radiance imbues the air
> Who will fill in the pattern....

(Pritam 2019: 148)

Her plea for love seems to have been heard by God and Imroz entered her life like a boon....

[Note: Sahir Ludhianvi was the pen-name of Abdul Hayee; 'sahir' means 'magician' in Urdu.]

References

Gargi, Balwant. 2014. "Amrita Pritam", in Jasbir Bhullar (ed.), *Hauz Khas da Booha*, pp. 13–31. Chandigarh: Lok Geet Prakashan.

Ludhianvi, Sahir. 1950. "Zindagi bhar nahi bhoolegi", https://www.rekhta.org/geet/zindagii-bhar-nahiin-bhuulegii-vo-barsaat-kii-raat-sahir-ludhianvi-geet (accessed on 21 December 2021).

———. 1964. "Mehfil se Uth Jane Walo", https://www.rekhta.org/geet/mahfil-se-uth-jaane-vaalo-tum-logon-par-kyaa-ilzaam-sahir-ludhianvi-geet (accessed on 21 December 2021).

Pritam, Amrita. 1976, rpt. 1998. *Rasidi Ticket*. Delhi: Shilalekh Publishers.

———. 1981, rpt. 2018. *Kagaz te Kanvas*. Delhi: Shilalekh Publishers.

———. 1986. *Ik si Anita*. Sirhind: Lokgeet Prakashan.

———. 2006, rpt. 2019. *Kagaz te Canvas to Paihlan*. Delhi: Shilalekh.

Source

The chapter is excerpted from Goyal, Jung Bahadur. 2018. "Main Tainu Pher Milangi", *Muhabbatnama*. Amritsar: Singh Brothers: p. 212-248.

Figure 11 Ardour Incarnate: Amrita and Sahir

Figure 12 Unique Companionship: Amrita-Imroz

Part III

GENDER, NATION, SOCIETY

11

CULTURES OF HONOUR, CULTURES OF TRAUMA

A Reading of Amrita Pritam's *Pinjar*

Ritika Verma and Anjali Gera Roy

As per official sources, an estimated 50,000 Muslim women were abducted in India and the corresponding number of Hindu and Sikh women in Pakistan was 33,000 (Menon and Bhasin 2018: 70). While the alarmingly high statistics corroborate the thesis that in national and civil wars women's bodies have always been contested sites of power, women's specific experience of violence in Punjab, including their abduction by men of rival communities and their recovery by the newly-formed states in their self-appointed role as their *mai baap* (Das 1996: 1512), needs to be understood in light of the code of *izzat*[1] prevalent in Punjab. Such a construction, in addition to the official discourse's repression of memories of Partition over those of independence, also leads victims' families to become complicit in silencing their experiences and magnifies the difficulties of recovering women's history. Not surprisingly, having internalised the same notions of *izzat*, often women themselves chose to remain silent. Feminist historians (Menon and Bhasin 2018; Butalia 2017), sociologists (Das 2007) and literary scholars (Didur 2006) who have engaged with the traumatic experience of Partition violence on women have unravelled the complex ties between gender, nationality and patriarchy. However, decades before Partition scholarship brought to light the testimonies of abducted women, social workers (Nehru 1949; Kidwai 2004) and writers had called attention to the gendered nature of violence and the complex responses of abducted women to this act of restorative justice.

In this context, the essay employs the theoretical framework of literary trauma studies to argue that Amrita Pritam's *Pinjar* (1950) provides one of the earliest responses to the interplay of historical and structural trauma of women that resulted in their silencing. The novel's framing of the fate of the 'cursed daughters of Punjab'[2] – Pooro, Lajo and others – before and after Partition within Punjabi cultures of honour collapses the 1947 violence on women's bodies with earlier forms to foreground the

DOI: 10.4324/9781003214656-19

disruption of pre-Partition norms and codes. Focussing on the novel's inter-related use of content and form to achieve this purpose, this chapter analyses in particular how the representation of Pooro's fragmented self, the liminality of her dreams post-abduction, the figurative device of metaphor and the use of intertextuality highlights the traumatic position of women within Punjabi patriarchy in the light of the analytical category of *izzat*.

Trauma, Gender, Partition

A focus on the gendered dimension of Partition complicates our understanding of the event's traumatic consequences. Both the abduction of women and their recovery by the newly-independent nation states are linked in complex ways to pre-Partition norms and codes of honour, and to the project of nationalism and nation building. During the violence of Partition as well as in the Central Recovery Operation, women's bodies became metonymic of the nation (Menon and Bhasin 2018; Butalia 2017). Multifarious forms of sexual violence inscribed a permanence to women's sexual appropriation, devalued their role as nourishers and by extension made the nation symbolically sterile and stigmatised (Menon and Bhasin 2018; Kakar 1995). In addition to the scale of violence by the Other, the deeply entrenched male code of honour further put women in a doubly disadvantaged position. With reference to the Punjabi community, Mucina notes that '*izzat* is embedded within a collectivist notion of one's responsibility to family and community and the preservation of the family "honour" and reputation' and an almost sacred emphasis is laid on the preservation of honour with specific genders ascribed with specific sets of 'boundaries, roles and responsibilities' (2018: 427). This invariably becomes a bio-political tool for disciplining women's bodies as their transgression translates into a loss of family and community honour. During Partition riots, these tenets were taken to their logical extreme and became a justifiable reason for men to kill women of their families. Several women chose death, either at the hands of their kinsmen or through suicide, as a respectable alternative to a life of dishonour with the enemy. Interestingly, such women were not thought of as dead, rather they were said to have embraced *shaheedi* – martyrdom, thus becoming worthy of veneration as opposed to those women who survived.[3]

In addition, the Central Recovery Operation launched in the aftermath of Partition to rescue and recover abducted women to their *legitimate* (emphasis added) families came as a further onslaught of trauma. Though conceived as a humanitarian project, it was nevertheless rooted in the notion of nation as a masculine entity. Just as in abduction, here again women's bodies become the site of national honour so that restoring glory to the nation necessitated physically relocating women into the domain of purity that was their original family even if this implied a show of force. In addition, it was also necessary to defend the Indian state's political ideology of secularism and its positioning of itself as a responsible, civilised government.

The framework of trauma theory offers a useful paradigm for situating women's experiences of Partition in Punjab within a larger tradition of women's experiences in the established Punjabi codes of honour. However, the understanding of interplay of historical and structural trauma that the project at hand demands resists a neat analysis to the Caruthian model[4] alone, conceived as it is primarily in response to the Holocaust as the traumatic event *exemplar*. Imposition of a universal model without consideration of the cultural, political and material conditions of trauma results in an oversimplified, even inaccurate, account of trauma.[5] We argue that Veena Das's body of work that is primarily rooted in her anthropological and literary engagement with the Partition inaugurates a form of trauma theory that inheres in the Indian condition and provides an entry into the gendered nature of Partition trauma. The framework also provides the conceptual tools that enable the study of alternative forms of women's trauma such as that depicted in the novel.

A traumatic experience – such as abduction – produces a breach in what Veena Das calls 'the relation between the subject and the world' (2007: 4). Since the subjectivity of an individual continually remains in a state of formation, events of extreme violence threaten the limits of the familiar world, thereby casting the subject in the middle of world-annihilating doubt. Events of violence fragment the world whereby they permit only a particular manner of inhabiting the fragmented world. 'What it is to pick up the pieces and to live in this very place of devastation?' (Das 2007: 6). An extraordinary event seeps into the ordinary such that the extraordinary and the ordinary become inextricably entwined. Life, in the aftermath of a violent extraordinary event, can only be recovered through a 'descent into the ordinary' (Das 2007: 7). Therefore, consequences of trauma need not necessarily be explicit, inviting immediate recognition. Instead, they might be subtle, folded into ordinary everyday lives. Das's examination of trauma collapses neat distinctions between trauma as a sudden, unexpected event and as an insidious phenomenon by exhibiting that the suddenness of the extraordinary traumatic event is entwined with the ordinariness of everyday life.

Testimony to the Trauma of Gender

Pinjar frames women's traumatic experience in Punjab during Partition within their ordinary, everyday experiences in the deeply entrenched Punjabi culture of honour. Exhibiting a complex entanglement between historical and insidious trauma, Amrita asserts that the very condition of being a woman in a patriarchal society is traumatic. Situating the figure of 'abducted woman' in widely different contexts – of pre-Partition Punjab and of Partition – the novel critiques nationalist and sectarian arguments about gendered violence of Partition being an outcome of rival religious identities. Just like women's bodies become the site of violence in patriarchal displays of power, including that of Partition, for Amrita, abduction is an embodiment of patriarchal, and not communal, anxieties. To abduct a woman is to rupture the sacred boundaries of family and community – or in the case of Partition, of a nation's – *izzat*. To avenge such a loss of honour involves a similar abduction of a woman of the other group. Further, the recovery and restoration of abducted women also represents an attempt to allay anxieties of the newly-formed nation states, themselves imagined as masculine entities. Thus, through the juxtaposition of abduction in the two different contexts, the novel suggests that the trauma inflicted on women during Partition is, above all, a reinforcement of patriarchal gender dynamics in a communally charged situation.

By invoking Waris Shah at the beginning of the novel, Amrita situates Pooro – and other women characters – in the Punjabi historical tradition where women's bodies figure only as symbols of honour in the male power play of vendetta, whether familial, communal or national. The reference is to the wailing of the eponymous protagonist of Waris Shah's tragic romance, *Hir*, who was married against her wish by her parents to protect family honour. In his version of the story, the star-crossed lovers meet a fatal end after Hir is poisoned by her family; and finding his beloved dead, Ranjha also embraces death. The bodies of these 'daughters of Punjab' are to be either preserved according to prescribed mandates, carefully conforming to the rites of passage in a woman's life, or to be violated through rape or abduction. Whether in the case of Hir's transgressive love for Ranjha, Pooro's abduction and the abduction and rape or recovery and restoration of women like Lajo, the central concern that remains is of legitimacy, of where the body rightfully belongs. Using the device of intertextuality to signify the recurrence of trauma as 'textual echoes' (Whitehead 2004: 82–85). Amrita, thus, traces a genealogy of women's trauma in Punjabi patriarchy from the legendary Hir to pre-Partition victims like Pooro to the abducted and recovered women during Partition. In this context, neither was Pooro's abduction an isolated event of revenge nor Partition a temporary madness.

Pinjar narrates the story of Pooro's abduction by Rashida, her subsequent marriage to him and interaction with the worlds of other women during her stay in Sakkar, and the final amplification of her experience of abduction in the frenzy unleashed by the sudden intrusion of Partition. Pooro is the daughter of the *Sahukars*, a respectable and wealthy family of Chatto village in Punjab. In giving a brief biographical context to the family's history, Amrita firmly situates the narrative in Punjabi culture of honour:

> They had seen bad days and at one time been compelled to sell their kitchen utensils on which the name of their forefathers were engraved. Pooro's father and uncle could not bear any more *disgrace* (emphasis added). They left the village and went to Thailand. [...] Then her father came back, cleared the mortgage on the house

[...], saved his ancestral home from attachment to creditors and so wiped off the *disgrace* (emphasis added).

(Pritam 2015: 2)

Even in a far-off land, the family remained tied to its roots to the ancestral home in Punjab and to its code of honour that went beyond the living members to the past generations of ancestors.

This is the tradition within which the circumstances of Pooro's abduction and her successive life is to be understood. While the males of the family had fulfilled their obligation by salvaging the material symbols of family honour, Pooro was tasked with protecting the honour with her body that now rightfully belonged to her fiancé Ram Chand. By the same token, the *Shaikhs* make Rashida pledge on the Koran that he would abduct her before her wedding to avenge *their* honour. Back in the days when the *Sahukars* were moneylenders, they had mortgaged the *Shaikhs'* house against a sum lent to them. When the *Shaikhs* failed to pay the money back, not only did the *Sahukars* forcibly evacuate them from their house, Pooro's uncle also abducted Rashida's aunt and kept her in his house for three days with the knowledge of her grandfather. Despite his reluctance, therefore, Rashida abducts Pooro as her wedding preparations are underway. As an abducted woman, Pooro's body becomes a medium of transgression of established moral boundaries and thus of family dishonour. Consequently, by the logic of an eye for an eye, the honour of the *Shaikhs* stands restored.

Upon her eventual escape, it is this transgressed body that Pooro's family shuns. Her father responds thus to her entreaty to take her along with them to Thailand: 'Who will marry you now? You have lost your religion and your birthright. If we dare to help you, we will be wiped out without a trace of blood left behind to tell of our fate' (Pritam 2015: 22). He is the patriarch responsible for upholding the family honour even if that necessitates leaving his daughter to her fate in the hands of the enemy. Her mother, on the one hand, struggles to restrain her cry lest she is heard, and on the other, joins her husband in his decision citing family honour and fear of death at the hands of the *Shaikhs*, 'Daughter, it would have been better if you had died at birth! If the *Shaikhs* find you here they will kill your father and your brothers. They will kill all of us ...' (Pritam 2015: 23).

Pooro's mother's act of hardening her heart in order to carry out what is deemed rightful by tradition serves as a precursor to the events during Partition when the bodies and lives of women were offered at the altar of honour on a massive scale. The act also lends a finality to Pooro's loss that structures her subsequent life: 'Now she had no hope, nor any fear. What more could anyone take from her than life? The thought dried up all her tears' (Pritam 2015: 23). Pooro is then married to Rashida, converted to Islam and conferred the name, Hamida. Significantly, Rashida's decision to relocate to Sakkar from Chatto does not elicit any response from Pooro.

113

Her affectual ties with the ancestors and the ancestral village is bound to her occupation of the established position within the traditional moral order, signified by her place as the chaste daughter in the natal family. With her bodily transgression of the borders of the family, she is inevitably placed outside the borders of ancestral and community kinship relations.

In Sakkar, her interaction with other women brings forth further figurations of the code of *izzat* and the manner in which it structures their lives. Kammo, a destitute abandoned by her father after her mother's death and treated miserably by her aunt, finds the warmth of motherly love and companionship in Pooro. However, her aunt, having heard rumours of Pooro's elopement, fears that Kammo would do the same and bring dishonour to her family. Threatened by dire consequences, a helpless Kammo is thus forced to sever their relationship. Taro, a sickly woman ill since her wedding day, reveals to Pooro in one of her fits that her husband was already married and her status in his house was of 'a common prostitute' (Pritam 2015: 46). If her in-laws silence her saying that they feed and clothe her, her parents also leave her to her fate as evident in her mother's words, 'It's up to her husband to treat her as he likes. It's a man's privilege' (Pritam 2015: 47). In contrast to Kammo and Taro, the mad woman presents a defiance of the bonds of honour by running about in the lanes of Sakkar with a naked bosom, laughing hysterically in the face of established morality. However, in her death (she is raped and left to die in labour) she is appropriated as a symbol in the contestation of religious honour. Incensed by Pooro's adoption of the mad woman's infant son, the Hindu leaders of the village, relying on hearsay that the madwoman was a Hindu, concur that her son rightfully belongs with them instead of the Muslim Hamida. Notwithstanding Rashida's pleas, they forcibly take him away from Pooro only to return him at the brink of death.

Much of the devastating impact of the prevalent honour code is explored, however, through Pooro's narrative. As such, the third-person narration of her trauma demands a closer understanding. Concurrent with Das's claim, the trauma of abduction produces a breach in the relation between Pooro and her world, disrupting her sense of self and fragmenting the familiarity of her world. She is not her own individual self, rather a fragmented self indelibly marked by the transgressive act of the body. Her being is torn between Pooro and Hamida with her world oscillating between that of honour lost through the abduction of a daughter and of honour reclaimed through revenge. She, thus, continues to live with Rashida as a non-being 'without a shape or a name' (Pritam 2015: 25). Pooro inhabits a split self – 'She was Pooro by the day and Hamida by the night' (Pritam 2015: 25). Her life 'acts out' the split in ordinary activities of everyday life. In Sakkar, as Rashida's wife Hamida, a Muslim, she is debarred from touching Kammo's pitcher of water lest it be polluted. As Pooro, she yearns to shower maternal affection on Kammo with whom she feels a bond of sisterhood. It is as Hamida that she develops a friendship with Taro and finds access to her traumatised

114

world. The concern she feels over the loss of Rashida's crops swiftly evolves into a sense of pride as she learns that it could be her brother who had set fire to the crops to avenge his sister's honour. In Rattoval, while accompanying Rahima's mother, she is overcome with a sense of loss for the world she was promised as Pooro – to enter Rattoval in her bridal palanquin, welcomed with songs as Ramchand's wife. Instead, with the reminder of dishonour writ on her body in the tattoo bearing her new name all she can say to Ramchand was that Pooro had long been dead, thus signifying a collapse of the world that Pooro inhabited. And yet post-Partition when the convoy from Rattoval passes through Sakkar, she resolves to meet him one last time; and in replying to his question if she was indeed Pooro, she makes to him the only complaint she could as both Pooro and Hamida, 'Do you still wish to know?… Her tone was charged with recrimination' (Pritam 2015: 90). In making this complaint, she speaks from the liminality that her trauma had pushed her into – neither Pooro nor Hamida. She was neither a daughter, nor wife nor lover; her body had become a commodity caught in the transaction of honour.

If a mere symbolic presence in the structure of morality engenders a fragmentation of her being, this split-self is most poignantly enacted in her dreams. Dreams, or rather nightmares, are significant in psychoanalytic accounts of trauma as they signal the psyche's return to the original encounter in an attempt to experience trauma in the present. In *Beyond the Pleasure Principle*, Freud argues in relation to war veterans that their dreams exemplified a repetition compulsion, characteristic of traumatic neuroses, in a bid to belatedly 'master the stimulus' (Freud 1990: 25) by retrospectively developing anxiety against it. Caruth draws upon Freud's notion of *nachträglichkeit*, or belatedness, to suggest that dreams, in addition to hallucinations and intrusive thoughts, are the belated experience of traumatic recall that bears a referential relation to the originary event of the past. In other words, dreams are an enactment of past trauma in the present. Pooro's dreams simultaneously bear a referential relation to her abduction and the manner in which it has shaped her present, and betray an attempt to reclaim a pre-traumatic lost world. A presence simultaneously as a body within the tradition of honour and as a being outside of its constraints. It can then be argued that just as her waking life is shaped by the trauma of abduction, her dreams also gesture to the liminal position it has rendered her to.

After her abduction when she awakens to find Rashida sitting beside her, apologising for his sin, Pooro lets out a cry of agony and falls unconscious to have her first dream:

> She dreamed she was in a cave. A black bear was combing her hair with his claws. She shrank in size, while the bear grew bigger and bigger. The bear took her in his shaggy embrace….
>
> (Pritam 2015: 13)

The black bear personifies Rashida and again marks her presence in the interstice created by the sudden fragmentation of her world. Earlier, when she had informed her friends about Rashida watching her, they had jested that she was lucky not to have fallen prey to a bear for it carries a woman to its cave and behaves with her as its wife. Now that she had indeed been abducted and housed by Rashida, she visualises him as a bear. Her being, along with her familiar world, gradually undergoes erasure as the bear as the medium of her dishonour grows in size implying the imposition of a new world that will place her outside the borders of her natal family. The reference to 'shaggy embrace' underscores the symbolic significance her body will come to possess in the process of transfer from the chaste daughter to the bearer of family and community dishonour. The unspeakable dread of an impending future culminates linguistically in the ellipsis that marks the end of the dream.

The event of abduction returns to haunt her dream again after the night she saves and adopts the mad woman's son. Unlike immediately after her abduction, though, now the event as it appears in her dream carries a literality about it before merging the selves of Pooro, Rashida's aunt, and the mad woman:

> She dreamt of Rashida galloping away with her lying across the saddle; she dreamt of his keeping her in a gardener's hut for three nights and days and then throwing her out; she dreamt of her turning insane and running about the village lanes with a life quickening in her womb ... and then giving birth to a child under the shade of a tree. The child was exactly like Javed. It tugged at her breasts and tried to suck with its toothless gums. It howled because there was no milk.
>
> (Pritam 2015: 56)

In visualising the mad woman's son as her own son Javed, Pooro repeats the conflict and anguish she had experienced in his birth. She thinks of him as being carved of her flesh and blood and the only being in all the world that alone belonged to her. Nevertheless, he was an embodiment of her trauma, a continual reminder of the world she lost and the life thrust upon her. What strikes one in this description is that the fear implicit in the previous dream has made way for an ambivalent acknowledgement of the position of her body in the imposed structure. Motherhood as a feeling is integral to the characterisation of Pooro. However, temporarily, she becomes the mother Kammo never had. She consumes white cumin seeds with milk so that her breasts fill with milk for the mad woman's son. During her brief stay at Sakkar, she cares for Lajo as her daughter. Yet, in the dream, her breasts are devoid of the nourishing life force, thus implying a subtle contestation of the enforcement of motherhood upon her. In addition, in dreaming of being kept by Rashida for three days, she becomes one with Rashida's aunt who was similarly abducted and housed by Pooro's uncle for three days. There is, thus, a dismantling of the patriarchal concerns of revenge and honour through a shared identification of their status as victims. Pooro's slippages into the mad woman and Rashida's aunt transcend her individual trauma to become an authorial commentary on the trauma that besets the entire community of women.

Contrary to such dreams that are overtly traumatic are the dreams that have the quality of what Freud calls wish fulfilment and yet they are a testament to the impossibility of return to Pooro's life and world. She dreams of her friends' and parents' house. Of her young brother who had set fire to the whole world to avenge the injustice done to her. The most telling of these, however, is the one she has on the way to Rattoval:

> She dreamed that she was on an embroidered cushion inside a silver palanquin. Her arms were weighed down with bangles; her palms were dyed red with henna. The palanquin lurched sideways and her *dupatta* slid off her head. When she adjusted it, the tassel-bells on her arms jingled.
>
> (Pritam 2015: 73)

Awakened by Rahima's aunt, she wakes up to reality to discover all traces of marital bliss disappear. As they resume their journey, she again lapses into her dream:

> The sound of pipes and drums came to her ears and all at once the palanquin was surrounded by bands of pipers and drummers.... That must be Rattoval where they were welcoming the new bride.... The girls were singing.... A woman lifted her bridal veil.... Then somebody placed a crying child in her lap.... The more the child cried, the more the women laughed; it would bring good luck to the groom.
>
> (Pritam 2015: 74)

Interestingly, the sounds Pooro hears in her dream are all from the real world. The sound of the child's cry is that of her younger son and of the pipers and drummers of a band of musicians in a procession. The impingement of the real upon the dream through the sounds as well as in the aunt's interruptions of her dream sequence to draw her attention to matters of Hamida's world, frame her in the interstices of the two worlds that cannot merge together, even though they intersect. Without the legitimacy of marriage, there is no welcome for the beloved.

The two worlds intersect again in the circumstances surrounding Partition, before finally becoming separate. This intersection also creates

117

the spatio-temporal horizon in which Pooro's trauma of abduction recurs on a massive scale as several women on both sides of the border are rendered *pinjars* (skeletons). The metaphor becomes significant as a device that enables Amrita to connect the continuum of insidious trauma suggested through the characters of Pooro, Kammo, Taro and the mad woman with the historical trauma of Lajo. Ram Chand's sister and Pooro's sister-in-law, Lajo was one of the many women abducted when their *kafila* was attacked by the Muslims. What Partition did, however, was temporarily suspend the code of honour and allow skeletons like Lajo the semblance of a life. Thus, contrary to Lajo's expectations, her brother and husband indeed return to Pakistan to fetch her back. Upon Pooro's request that Lajo always be treated in a respectable manner back in her house, her brother looks down ashamed, understanding the implications of his sister's plea. However, such a suspension of honour codes did not necessarily guarantee a *normal* (emphasis added) life. If Lajo herself was to be taken as a metaphor for women abducted during Partition, she recurs in Rajinder Singh Bedi's short story 'Lajwanti' to shatter assumptions of a normal, pre-Partition life for recovered women.[6] As feminist scholars have shown, the complex relationship between women's bodies and national honour necessitated that they be restored to their legitimate families, at times even against their will. Systematically deprived of agency in the process of recovery and rehabilitation, women's identity both during and after Partition remained in a continuous state of flux. Amrita mounts a critique of such appropriation through Pooro's decision to stay back in Pakistan, an action that makes her the literary spokesperson of thousands of women abducted during Partition who resisted the second trauma of displacement in the garb of recovery (Datta 2008: 19). With the flame of revenge still burning in him, her brother urges her to return home. The large-scale calamity that had resulted had provided her a chance to do so but after a moment of temptation 'she made her brother release her arm, turned back to where Rashida was standing and clasped her son to her bosom' (Pritam 2015: 127).

Finally, it is through the language of the body that Amrita exposes the limits of conventional language in response to trauma. To turn to Das again, 'failure of the grammar of the ordinary' (Das 2007: 7) constitutes one of the ways in which trauma is folded into ordinary lives. Loss of a familiar world implies a consequential loss of familiar language. Individuals lose the framework within which abstract qualities of love and grief could be understood. Necessity arises for a new, shared language; but precisely because the secure foundations on which this language could be built is lost, it might result in the subject becoming voiceless. This does not imply that individuals lose their ability of speech. They might produce utterances but the utterances may either have a spectral quality about them or be possessed by another voice. Alternatively, an individual might choose to remain silent. This gap between what is spoken but not voiced and what is voiced in an absence of speech constitutes a significant way in which we can understand the response to trauma. Body and language are crucially linked in such a traumatic response where the body 'form[s] its own speech' (Das 1991: 72). In *Pinjar*, Taro enacts the trauma she faces in her husband's house through a fit she has. The mad woman does so through her animal-like mannerisms, hysterical laughter and shrieks. Significantly, the intertextual trope of madness also enables Amrita to echo the defiance of much of Partition literature to socio-political and rational dictums. Just like Manto's eponymous madman's gibberish in 'Toba Tek Singh' and the bizarre paintings drawn on her body by the protagonist in Manto's 'Fundanein' ('Pompoms'), the mad woman's fiendish laughter and Taro's fit is at once a reflection of trauma and a resistance to an imposed order.

Conclusion

The 'cursed daughter of Punjab' asks, 'How can I speak?' and, in so asking, performs an ambiguity central to trauma: the necessity of articulating trauma and the failure to do so in speech. *Pinjar* provides a testimony to the trauma of women within the culture of *izzat* wherein their being is significant merely as bodies and their lives are structured in accordance to patriarchal gender roles. Exploring the theme primarily through Pooro's trauma of abduction, Amrita gives insights into her fragmented self and the manner in which it is reflected in her daily activities and dreams. Pooro's dreams in particular highlight the split between her body and being as indicative of her liminal position with respect to the worlds of lost and avenged honour. By framing women's experiences in a single narrative beyond the legitimacy of acts – of marriage, abduction or rape – and the temporal marker of Partition, she argues that the very condition of women in the established moral code is traumatic. However, even while remaining sensitive to the disruptive consequences of traumatic experience, the novel resists the identification of women as mere victims without any possibility of escape. In choosing to stay in 'the very place of destruction' (Das 2007: 6), Pooro transcends the subject position of a victim and is invested with agency. *Pinjar* does not end on a note of a conventional 'happy-ending' but it is precisely in not reconciling the two strands, in allowing the tension between trauma and agency to persist, that the novel becomes a faithful representation of trauma.

Notes

1 Though loosely translated as honour, *izzat* also includes related notions of reputation and prestige, and invites gendered responsibilities for its preservation.
2 The reference is to Amrita's poem 'I am the Cursed Daughter of Punjab from History.' Nonica Datta, 'Transcending Religious Identities: Amrita Pritam and Partition' in *Partitioned Lives: Narratives of Home, Displacement and Resettlement*, ed. Anjali Gera Roy and Nandi Bhatia (New Delhi: Pearson Longman, 2008), p. 10.

3 Urvashi Butalia in *The Other Side of Silence* documents that male Punjabi survivors of Partition refer to the women who were either killed by their male relatives or chose to give up their lives, as martyrs. It is popularly held that true to the spirit of the Sikh race, these women did not fear death; but rather dishonour at the hands of Muslims. Significantly, their sacrifices had elevated the honour of their families and communities as she notes the relative awe and respect for survivors of Thoa Khalsa which had become a site of mass suicide of women. 194-196.

4 Following from Freudian psychoanalysis, the classical trauma theory of Caruth (1996) and others (Shoshana Felman and Dori Laub 1992; Dominick LaCapra 2014) conceptualises trauma as an aporetic event, known only as an absence. It is the belatedness characteristic of trauma that lends it a paradoxical quality – an incessant return to the traumatic event which evades the survivor's comprehensibility. Trauma, thus, lies not only in the original, sudden encounter with the event but also in the repeated return to the event.

5 While the Caruthian approach helps unravel trauma's dissociative consequence on the self's understanding of itself and its world, it has come under sharp criticism from cultural studies and postcolonial theorists (Craps 2013; Leys 2000; Rothberg 2008) for the model's perception of trauma as essentially unknowable, stemming from a sudden and violent encounter. As such, the Caruthian approach fails to account for every day, insidious forms of trauma such as slavery, racism and colonialism.

6 Rajinder Singh Bedi's short story 'Lajwanti' meditates upon the subtle erasure of selfhood of an abducted woman. Lajwanti is brought back into the fold of the legitimate – the legitimate nation, the legitimate religion and the legitimate family – but the trauma she endured, due to abduction and continues to endure in the form of a mere metaphoric acceptance in her husband's life, is forever silenced. This can simultaneously also be read to mean that with the body's obliteration, the medium through which trauma could be articulated remains unavailable.

References

Butalia, Urvashi. 1998, 2017. *The Other Side of Silence: Voices from the Partition of India*. Gurgaon: Penguin Random House.

Caruth, Cathy. 1996. *Unclaimed Experience: Trauma, Narrative and History*. Baltimore: John Hopkins University Press.

Craps, Stef. 2013. *Postcolonial Witnessing: Trauma Out of Bounds*. London: Palgrave Macmillan.

Das, Veena. 1991. "Composition of the Personal Voice: Violence and Migration", *Studies in History* 7.1: 65–77.

———. 1996. "Dislocation and Rehabilitation: Defining a Field", *Economic and Political Weekly* 31.24: 1509–14.

———. 2007. *Life and Words: Violence and the Descent into the Ordinary*. London: University of California Press.

Datta, Nonica. 2008. "Transcending Religious Identities: Amrita Pritam and Partition", in Anjali Gera Roy and Nandi Bhatia (eds.), *Partitioned Lives: Narratives of Home, Displacement and Resettlement*, pp. 1–25. New Delhi: Pearson Longman.

Didur, Jill. 2006. *Unsettling Partition: Literature, Gender, Memory*. Toronto: University of Toronto Press.

Felman, Shoshana and Dori Laub. 1992. *Testimony: Crises of Witnessing in Literature, Psychoanalysis and History*. London: Routledge.

Freud, Sigmund. 1990. *Beyond the Pleasure Principle*, trans. & ed. James Strachey. New York: Norton.

Kakar, Sudhir. 1995. *The Colours of Violence*. New Delhi: Penguin.

Kidwai, Anis. 2004. "In the Shadow of Freedom", in Mushirul Hasan (trans. & ed.), *India Partitioned: The Other Face of Freedom* 2, pp. 167–80. Delhi: Roli Books.

LaCapra, Dominick. 2014. *Writing History, Writing Trauma*. Baltimore: John Hopkins University Press.

Leys, Ruth. 2000. *Trauma: A Genealogy*. Chicago: The University of Chicago Press.

Menon, Ritu and Kamla Bhasin. 1998, 2018. *Borders and Boundaries: Women in India's Partition*. New Delhi: Women Unlimited.

Mucina, Mandeep Kaur. 2018. "Exploring the Role of Honour in Son Preference and Daughter Deficit within the Punjabi Diaspora in Canada", *Canadian Journal of Development Studies* 39.3: 426–42.

Nehru, Rameshwari. 1949. "Memorandum on Recovery", in *Rameshwari Nehru Papers*. New Delhi: Nehru Memorial Museum and Library.

Pritam, Amrita. 1950. *Pinjar*. 2015. *The Skeleton* trans. Khushwant Singh, 2nd ed. New Delhi: Tara.

Rothberg, Michael. 2008. "Decolonizing Trauma Studies: A Response", *Studies in the Novel* 40.1/2: 224–34, https://www.jstor.org/stable/29533869 (accessed on 21.12.2021).

Whitehead, Anne. 2004. *Trauma Fiction*. Edinburgh: Edinburgh University Press.

12

MULTIPLE PATRIARCHIES AND THE SYNCRETIC, GENDERED VOICE OF AMRITA PRITAM

Tanvir Sachdev

In a post-feminist world where the woman question is seen as redundant, developing nations like India still grapple with issues of gender, sexuality and the taboos imposed by national, regional and communal patriarchies. In partitioned India, as 'Punjab is carved up, the venomous serpent of patriarchal ideology grows into a ferocious Hydra; its many-headed form signifying the convergence of the "multiple patriarchies [national, colonial and communal] at work in women's lives"' (Kazmi 2019: 9). Patriarchies encode women with various scripts and interpellate them with ideologies – providing them with models of who they are or should be. Apart from the prescriptive roles for women, the regional reformist patriarchy of Punjab overshadowed the syncretic culture and pluralist traditions that had allowed fluid identities and alternative spiritual practices to exist as a parallel subtext in Punjab for generations. This chapter explores the voice of Amrita Pritam, the postcolonial woman intellectual who subverted national, communal and religious identities and hegemonies of social respectability both in her writing and life and 'dare[d] to live the life she imagine[d]' (Tharu et al. 1993: 161). This transgressive voice can be located within the discourse of resistance already present in the literary tradition of Punjab, as in Waris Shah's popular *qissa*, *Hir* and the syncretism of Punjabi culture rather than western feminism. The texts chosen for this reading are Amrita's poems, 'To Waris Shah' ('Ajj Aakhaan Waris Shah nu'), 'Scar of a Wound' ('Majboor') and 'Nine Dreams and Annunciation' ('Nau Supne') wherein the poet gives voice to and empowers voiceless women.

Multiple Patriarchies

The rediscovery of India's past and the reconstitution of the golden age of Indian civilisation aided by the work of European scholars and Orientalists

DOI: 10.4324/9781003214656-20

was taken over by 19th century Indian reformers and writers to construct two identities simultaneously – the national identity and that of Indian women. The identity of women was reformulated in two oppositional ways, one, by the traditionalists/revivalists/conservatives who attempted to resurrect pre-colonial feudal scripts for women by protesting against British intervention (the Abolition of Sati 1829, the Age of Consent Bill 1891), and two, by the reformers who pressed for change. In fact, it was not just feminine identity but patriarchies themselves that were recast along with the extended thresholds that gave more space to women. Patriarchies defined themselves in accordance with liberal or conservative strains in the nationalist discourse, later crystallising into paradigms demarcated by class, caste, community and religion. Tending to fix women within the private space, these defined not only the space they inhabited, but more importantly, provided them with images and ideologies to live by, and dictated their subjectivity and identity. The woman's question was being hotly debated at the beginning of the 19th century but by the middle of the century, it was resolved and reformulated; as Partha Chatterjee has pointed out, the identity of women was recast and expressed in Brahmo terms as *sakhi, sumata* and *sugrihini* – one that would make women better 'companions' to their husbands, better 'mothers' to their children and better 'homemakers'.

In line with national restructuring, the Sikh renaissance in Punjab in the early 20th century too recast women in the crucible of *sakhi-sumata-sugrihini* model as part of the anti-colonial discourse, but for a different purpose – to align their interests with the British. The Amritsar Dharam Sabha was formed as a joint effort of the Hindus and Sikhs to expunge or 'eradicate evil practices and rituals amongst women' like *Kanagats* and *Sada Talla*,[1] singing love songs, or uttering obscene words at the time of marriages or in public spaces or visiting miracle shrines. Such practices that had hitherto been outside the purview of male supervision were erased to create a new purified image of the 'Punjabi' that patriarchies wished to project to imperial rulers (Jakobsh 2000: 155). Sikh patriarchies in Punjab were themselves reinvigorated by an infusion of the historical 'hyper-masculine militarist' (Jakobsh 1999: ii) construct of bravery, piety, purity and the defender of all women, as Christine Fair points out, by Singh Sabha – the major reformist agency in Punjab and its prominent exponent, Bhai Vir Singh. Consequently, the image of its women was also cast along community lines. In addition, Bhai Vir Singh added the concept of courage analogous to the Sikh faith, to the image of the ideal Sikh woman who defended her honour from Muslim men. Novels like *Sundari* portrayed Sikh woman as 'true to the faith, devout and pure, active in battle and elevated at times to the status of a goddess' (Jakobsh 2000: 275). The reconstitution of the ideal image of the Sikh woman was an attempt not merely to glorify the status of Sikh women but also 'to show the complete separation of Sikhism from the dominant Hindu tradition' (2000: 275). Despite this re-inscription of Sikh women, the injunction of being carriers of tradition fell on women, much like in national patriarchies where tradition is interpreted as upholding the '*dharam*'/religion. However, the images of Bhai Vir Singh's fictional representatives like Sundari and Sheel also serve to reiterate the role of woman as householder. Any transgression from the private to the public forbids re-entry for women in the domestic fold. '[H]aving left the realm of "patriarchal civilisation" for the liminality of the "uncultivated world" of the forest, they can never return. Their options are death/martyrdom or to become sewa-performing ascetics' (Fair: 120). This inherent contradiction in the projection of Sikh women as brave upholders of faith and honour and the underlying script of their expulsion from the private domestic sphere posits the hypocrisy of the Sikh patriarchies.

The process which started in the late 19th century was completed with the hardening of communal identities by focussing on the 'great' tradition and 'abjure heterodox Sikh religious practice' in its 'little' traditions like visiting shrines, believing in charms, the element of miracle, the practice of Hindu rituals, etc. (Fair 15). Many of these 'unwanted' aspects had been syncretic, resulting in porosity with Hindu and Sufi traditions.

This syncretism existed in Punjab as 'an under specified "mystical", for example as a common religious core, regardless of historical difference' (Murphy 2019: 308). Murphy, while warning about the dangers of over-simplification, locates this commonality in the historical specificity of the Sufi and Yogi tradition, while Farina Mir traces this regional tradition of shared piety, 'one that incorporated local aesthetic principles and responded to the religious plurality and social organisation of the Punjab' to the 'Perso-Islamic literary aesthetic' of the *qissa* (2006: 728). According to Oberoi, 'most Sikhs moved in and out of multiple identities grounded in local, regional, religious, and secular realities. Consequently, the boundaries between what could be seen as Sikh "great" and "little" traditions were highly blurred: several competing definitions of who constituted a Sikh were possible' (qtd. in Murphy 2019: 293). However, by the beginning of the 20th century, communal and regional patriarchies like Singh Sabha, Tat Khalsa and the *shuddhi* practices of the Arya Samaj hardened the erstwhile fluid and porous communal identities and intercommunity solidarities, thereby eroding Punjab's syncretic commonality.

According to Foucault, it is not power alone, but resistance to power that is embedded in each discourse. Through the ages, several women have crossed the boundaries set by multiple patriarchies, broken out of their confining barriers and created a rich heritage of women's protest, even if at a subliminal level. Female voices of dissent existed both in precolonial and postcolonial times – of women Bhakti saints and later, of early women writers like Tarabai Shinde, Rokeya Sakhawat Hossain and many more. The voices of these women have been only selectively incorporated into history. Postcolonial women intellectuals and writers in India like Amrita Pritam,

124

Kamal Desai, Ismat Chughtai, Qurratulain Hyder, Kamala Das, etc. have often subverted the injunction of silence imposed by multiple patriarchies and interpreted it as a symbol of their oppression, protest and resistance; thereby creating an alternative literary tradition of women's writing. The voice of postcolonial women enshrined in their 'stories and poems that might ... appear to be concerned only with existentialist agony or with spiritual endurance lay bare their politics.... [They] ... are engaged in negotiation, debate, and protest ... or are closely related to *what it means to be a woman in each historical moment*' (Tharu and Lalitha vol 2 1993: 70, emphasis added)

Amrita rebelled against regulatory moulds prescribed by national and regional patriarchies – both of gender and community. She herself was steeped in the syncretic, pluralistic and composite cultural and literary traditions of Punjab through the influence of her father who was well versed in alternative parallel religious traditions, having spent many years in Sant Dayal's ashram. She grew into adulthood reading the *kalaam* of Sufi poets like Shah Husain, Sultan Bahu and Bulle Shah that was not only part of her cultural inheritance and education, but also of everyday language:

Bulla [says], what do I know who I am?
I am neither a believer in mosques nor do I believe in the rites of nonbelievers
I am not a Hindu, not a Muslim.
(qtd. in Murphy 2018: 246)

In *Shadows of Words*, Amrita voices a self that subverts caste, community and religion demarcations established by multiple patriarchies when she affirms that 'writers are the *zamir* (conscience) of our own people. And can *zamir* be Hindu, Sikh, or Mussalman.... Is the light of the sun also Hindu, Sikh, or Mussalman?' (qtd. in Datta 2008: 5).

Destabilising the tropes of organised religion, Amrita nonetheless adheres to the 'underspecified mystical' or what Murphy calls 'a shared mystical imaginary' (qtd. in Murphy 2018: 247) and syncretic Sufi traditions that were a hallmark of the shared cultural traditions or Punjabiyat as a lived experience; 'Main apne hujre ki mitti hun, main khuda ke shajre ki lakeer hun' ('I am the soil of meditation, I am the line of divine hierarchy') (qtd in Datta 2008: 1). Amrita created an alternative syncretic universe transcending the divisive formulations of class, community and nation. Even in her childhood, Amrita had rebelled against divisive identities that had found a way into their home in the rites of purity and pollution practised by her grandmother who kept separate tumblers for her father's Muslim friends. 'Deep down in the layers of my mind, was the first impact of a religion against which I had risen as a child, when I had seen that glass tumbler touched by someone with a different faith became impure' (Pritam 1994:

125

15). Amrita had even found a way to circumvent the 'great' Sikh tradition by letting in forbidden dreams of Rajan before the recitation of the fortifying prayer of the Sikhs, the *Kirtan Sohila*:

> Around me forts have been raised and demolished but the reality of the One, has in one form or the other, always been with me. At one time in the features and forms of a man's face; at another ... some sort of divinity has arisen from the leaves of a book.... It pervades all my thoughts and dreams to such a degree that even fleeting goodness seems to be a manifestation of that One.
>
> (7)

Thus, Amrita can be located in a contested space vis-a-vis national, regional or communal patriarchies that her subversive voice endangered. She evoked a commonality of humanity that is situated both in the individualisation of the mystical and in the pre-colonial syncretic traditions of Punjab, ever-present as a subtext to mainstream religions. Her subversion of oppressive patriarchies can be located in Waris Shah's Hir's 'resistance to ... religious and legal authority in the narrative' (Mann 2018: 28). Amrita, much like Hir, was acceptable as long as she obeyed the norms of society; once she crossed the prescribed threshold, 'society castigated her' (23). Her challenge to the authoritarian male prescription of women's silence and conformity to contemporary social mores can be traced to Hir's hermeneutical challenge to the Qazi who is called to intercede on behalf of Hir's parents so that she may be amenable to leaving Ranjha and agree to a match of her parents' making. The Qazi as the patriarchal voice of religious authority enmeshes the social and religious in his argument and invokes the *Shariah* for adherence to social convention. He commands Hir to leave her transgressions and have some shame. Hir subverts the Qazi's argument through a counter reference to the *Shariah* and a 'reinterpretation of "faith" as love.... She hints at this through the Quranic verse she cites in the original Arabic, "we have created everything in pairs"' (Kazmi 2019: 5). His injunction to Hir to have faith is reinterpreted by her as love. According to Kazmi, Hir's 'reinterpretation of tradition ultimately subverts the Qazi's discourse, and forces her way into domains of discourse traditionally denied to women' (4). According to Kazmi, in the politics of voicing, Amrita appropriates the voice of Waris Shah in a reflexive engagement with *Hir*. She raises issues of gender, nation and the role of 'nefarious' and 'toxic' patriarchies in the traumatic experiences of women during Partition.

To Waris Shah

The patriarchal narrative of Partition history is silent about the innumerable women who were raped, mutilated, abducted, forcibly impregnated or shamefully traded for freedom – whose disappearance was designated as 'honourably dead'. The polarisation of the country on religious lines resulting in the Partition had a profound impact on Amrita and, as Nonica Datta points out, 'is the most crucial moment in defining her worldview; it enables her to forge a *kainaati rishta* (fraternal relationship) with the universe, to create her world in accordance with Punjab's language, culture, and social history' (Datta 2008: 1). The invocation to Waris Shah and *Hir* in her poem 'To Waris Shah,' with which the poem opens, locates the etymology of voicing within the syncretic tradition of Punjab and not in any western concept of feminism. Exhorting him to rise from his grave, she not only constructs a 'feminist poetics of the vernacular that remains equally critical of national, regional, and communal patriarchies' but also expresses the voiceless anguish of women (Kazmi 2019: 2); unearthing 'so many layers of silence encoded into these histories' (Butalia 1998: 127). In doing so she not only fixes responsibility and indicts 'poisonous patriarchies' for the brutal violation of its women but also condemns these for the destruction of Punjab's syncretic culture. The poem 'underlies the destructive and interrelated role of colonial complicity, nationalist ideology, regional patriarchy, and religious identity in creating the situation in which ordinary people turned to killing their own neighbours' (Kazmi 2019: 9).

> When one daughter of the Punjab did cry
> You filled pages with songs of lamentation,
> Today a hundred daughters do cry
> O Waris Shah to speak to you.
>
> (Pritam, Singh 1982: 93)

According to Anne Murphy, Waris Shah's *Hir* 'articulates a shared sense of "Punjabiyat" or Punjabiness.... [that] continues to be a valued cultural resource on both sides of the Indo-Pakistan border' (Murphy 2019: 291). The text presents 'a vision of late nineteenth-century sociality and religiosity in which religious community, be it Hindu, Muslim, Sikh was not of paramount importance' (Mir 2006: 151). In the poem, to speak up from the other side of the grave is suggestive not only of the resurrection of Waris Shah (on whose opus *Hir*, Udham Singh the anti-colonial revolutionary took oath on trial), but also of the dire need to resurrect the syncretic culture of Punjab that has been eroded by Partition. Waris Shah, a poet who is seen as the 'friend of the sorrowing' by giving them a voice, is also an epitome of valued humanity and shared cultural ethos that is desecrated in violence and bloodshed. Corpses are strewn in the pastures of Punjab, and the river Chenab, once associated with the soulful love of Hir and Ranjha, is inundated with blood. The waters of the river that once irrigated the fertile fields of Punjab have been infused with poison and now sprout 'venomous weeds'. According to Mir, Amrita 'reworks this play on "dissolving poison" to analyse the carnage and social devastation wrecked during Partition.... This idea of venom or poison is generalised into [an] ideology ... which takes the form of a masculine nationalism informed by communal consciousness' (Kazmi 2019: 9). The air itself becomes heavy with the poison of communal hatred in the body politic which turns the limbs of Punjab blue. She deploys the motif of the serpent 'as a symbol of patriarchal control and toxic masculinity, lurking menacingly in the domestic and public sphere' (8–9). She deploys images from the shared cultural repertoire of Punjab with its flutes, swings, spinning wheels, snake charmers and Hir. The loss of syncretic culture and humanity is bemoaned with the most monstrous transformation of the flute into a snake and the loss of the song itself:

> Where the wind pipe trilled songs of love
> That flute has been lost
> Ranjha and his brothers have lost their art.
>
> (Pritam, Singh 1982: 95)

The loss of syncretism is suggested by the loss of the song itself 'that was crushed in every heart'. The violation of women is painted in delicate and evocative imagery – in threads being snapped from spindles and the normal everyday activities of women with the attendant hum of the spinning wheel being silenced. Women are snatched and severed from their gatherings. Not only are the swings empty, but the very branches of the peepul tree which supported them are broken. The quintessential figure of the romantic hero embodied in the figure of the Ranjhas of Punjab has become 'despoilers of love and beauty'.

The plea for articulation is couched not in the selfhood of women but in Punjab's terminology of 'dhee'/daughter. A 'million daughters' now weep as opposed to only one Hir who bewailed a lost love in Waris Shah's qissa; she is a loaded cultural symbol well-known in legend and folklore who subverts parental, familial, social, religious boundaries in her love for Ranjha. Although the story ends in tragedy as the lovers are separated yet Hir's subversion of the Qazi's religio-temporal authority is a tradition followed by Peero, the precolonial Punjabi woman poet (the only one known before Amrita), who transcends religious boundaries to locate woman's identity in an essentialist 'universality', to use Bal's term. In her discourse with the Qazi, Peero says, 'Oh Qazi listen to me. I am neither a Hindu nor Muslim. How can you know what I am? Why are you involved only in the material world?' (qtd. in Bal 2006: 92) While Hir's voice is accorded to her by the authoritarian male voice of Waris Shah, Peero's is a distinctly self-authenticated voice of a woman.

Amrita taps into this syncretic literary tradition of the qissa as well as the latent precursor of woman's dissent and evokes the image of Hir's uncle,

Kaidoo, who exposed her liaison with Ranjha and stirred poison in her life, to indict both national and Punjabi patriarchy:

> It seems all people have become Kaidoos,
> thieves of beauty and love –
> where should I search out
> another Waris Shah.

(Pritam, Singh 1982: 95)

Nothing less than the resurrection of Waris Shah is needed, not just to voice the trauma of millions of hapless women but to fashion 'an emancipatory cultural identity in a society ... [where] the burden of nation formation will fall so heavily and so literally on the body of the woman' (Kazmi 2019: 10). According to Kazmi, the 'macabre' resurrection of the poet:

> is not merely an act of nostalgia stemming from a romantic sense of cultural loss – it is also Pritam's attempt to prise away male autho-rial privilege to fashion a feminist reworking of cultural identity and nationalist critique that became imperative to the nascent pro-cess of nation building.... Much like Hir's hermeneutical challenge to the Qazi at the height of crisis in the narrative, a woman must rise to the task of reinterpreting tradition.

(10)

Thus, Amrita appropriates 'Waris Shah's authorial privilege' in a reflexive tradition of intertextuality to give voice to anguish of millions of daughters of Punjab.

The Scar of a Wound

In 'The Scar of a Wound' that appears to be a logical corollary to the Waris Shah poem, Amrita voices her dissent against the metanarrative of the birth of the nation as a euphoric event constructed by nationalist patriarchies. The first Indian Prime Minister, Pandit Jawaharlal Nehru's famous 'tryst with destiny' speech refers to independence as an epoch-making event mark-ing the victorious culmination of the freedom struggle. Partition is referred to in passing as 'the pain and labour' and 'memory of sorrow' (Nehru 1958: 25). While 'the official nationalist hagiographers were celebrating the birth of the nation', the voice of the postcolonial woman poet subverted this nar-rative re-writing of the 'birth-related imagery to undermine the triumphant nationalism which was ... entirely inappropriate to the trauma of Partition' (Raychaudhuri 2018: 126). Raychaudhuri argues that in the poem Amrita powerfully 'rewrites the mythology of the birth of the nation' and rein-scribes it as 'a violent and horrific act of the child being forced from the mother's womb' (126). However, from the subject position of a middle-class woman from Punjab associated with indigenous academia sensitised to the trauma of women during partition, the poem can be seen from another perspective too. Apart from the dominant interpretation of the metaphoric birth of the nation, the child in the poem can refer literally to the numerous post-abduction illegitimate children that Partition and the independence of the country spawned. In the poem, Amrita assumes the persona of the child of the abducted, violated woman, thus foregrounding not only the body of the woman but also the contested space that these children inhabited:

> When they forced my mother's womb
> I came as every child must come;
> I'm the mark of that blow....
> They seared my mother's brow with me
> When they forced my mother's womb.
>
> (Pritam, Singh 1982: 97)

The poem acknowledges the abduction and rape and forced impregnation of thousands of women and their illegitimate children that befuddled neat religious and communal identities inscribed by multiple patriarchies. The forcing open of the mother's womb highlighted the traumatic images of violence – 'violation', 'mark of the blow', and the twice repeated 'forced my mother's womb' along with the attendant humiliation and shame that 'seared my mother's brow with me', suggesting an ironic contrast both to the representation of the nation as woman/mother as well as the nation as protector of its women and children.

Characteristic of Amrita's imagery, the very natural order of the universe is disturbed as violence is unleashed upon the women who bore the weight of independence in 'a wound of time':

> Sun and Moon hid their light
> And stars fell dead in thick night
>
> (Pritam, Singh 1982: 97)

So, while the country awakes to a new dawn of independence, the world of the abducted women and their illegitimate children is darkened by the violence and atrocities of the history of the nation-in-the-making. Amrita subverts the euphoria attendant upon Partition, focussing instead on 'the strange fruit ripened on the tree of independence' – the marginalised and excluded children:

> I am the shame she nursed within
> The stench and loathsomeness of man,
> The sign of torment she must bear.
>
> (Pritam, Singh 1982: 97–99)

The fate of thousands of such children was pushed into what Butalia calls 'the troubled space of ... illegitimacy' (1998: 270). As the offspring of independence, they stood excluded on the margins of the nascent nation-state ignored by the state's self-proclaimed role as 'parent protector benevolent patriarch' (276). These children of 'mixed' blood occupy 'an ambivalent space wherein they belonged to both communities, which therefore complicated the matter of their citizenship, but ... the lesser space occupied by their mothers as citizens, also devolved on them' (Butalia 277). The existence of these children with their brutally mixed parentage threatened the separation of religious boundaries newly inscribed by the very borders of the nation-state. As no clear lines could be drawn about their identities and space they were to inhabit, the state responded by forgetting about them and pretending 'that they did not exist' (282). Amrita's focus on this ancillary minor-citizen-subject is heightened by an agonised call to attention both to itself and its mother, in the dramatic 'Look and see!':

> Strange fruit ripened on the tree
> Of independence – look and see!
>
> (Pritam, Singh 1982: 99)

At another level, the poem also problematises the traditional concept of motherhood constructed by patriarchies for 'the mothers of illegitimate children had somehow forsaken their claim to legitimate motherhood. The "purity" of the mother, the sanctity and suppression of sexuality was thrown into question by the presence of such children' (Butalia 1998: 278). Amrita, through the voice of the illegitimate child, attempts to re-inscribe the contested body of the violated woman as mother by a repetition of the word 'mother' six times in a short poem of twenty-one lines. While the partitioned nation has metaphorically both been torn *from* the womb of the nation-as-mother, real women have been ravaged, their wombs forced *into* impregnations, while simultaneously robbed of the status of the venerated mother.

The Annunciation

In the poem 'Annunciation' Amrita topples the established religious hermeneutics that had established Nanak as the fountainhead of the Sikh faith by demystifying him as the son of his mother, Tripta. Unlike Christianity which venerates Mother Mary as the mother of Christ, Sikhism does not deify mother Tripta. In fact, Sikh tradition and history merely identify her as the mother who recognised the divinity of her son, but her voice, like that of the Guru Mahals (the wives of the Gurus), is relegated to silence. Beyond this limited portrayal, her voice as a real woman, lost in oblivion, is recovered by Amrita. In the Sikh tradition, the gurus themselves had accorded egalitarian space to women and incorporated syncretism through the inclusion of Muslim Sufi saints in the *Adi Granth*. However, there is a contradiction inherent in the oft-quoted verse of the *Adi Granth* that calls for a relocation of women from the space of evil where she was fixed to the realm of respect on the grounds that she had given birth to kings and prophets. The argument for an honoured space for women rested not on the premise of *woman as a person* but on account of her stereotypical role as a mother.

Amrita's reinterpretation of a discourse that intertwines issues both of religion and gender resulted in an ugly controversy, particularly as it was supposed to commemorate the 500th birth anniversary of Nanak. Although Bhakti and Sikh traditions appropriated the female voice in devotional poetry, 'the female as object within a spiritual journey is still yet an object: to speak *as* woman is not to give woman a voice' (Murphy 2019: 249–250). But in this poem, Amrita speaks *as* woman reinterpreting traditions of religion, writing the poem in the throes of intense maternal love that welled up in her as she chatted on the phone with her son living in a hostel. She subverts the devotional veneration expected in such a poem by not only foregrounding Tripta the mother instead of Nanak the son, but also by demystifying the religious, patriarchal codes by presenting her as a real woman having a sexed and gestating body. The nine stanzas delineating rich imagery of the milk and the body of women in nine months of pregnancy blur the boundaries of the sacred and the profane. The poem begins with the morning after copulation and conception with a dream that mother Tripta has. It opens with a suggestive sex act, when she awakes 'all a-tremble' smoothening 'the creased coverlet' blushing and covering her 'bare shoulders' with the crimson veil of the married woman, gazing timidly at the man lying beside her – Guru Nanak's father ('Annunciation'). The sensual, sexualised portrayal of Tripta was seen as a vulgar blasphemy; a culture of misogyny in Punjab had earlier found even the sexualisation of Hir unacceptable and the depiction of Nanak's mother as a sexual being was seen as downright obnoxious.

Although the respect that accompanies the ideology of motherhood is pervasive in Indian culture, the woman's experience of pre- and post-natal pregnancy is shrouded in silence and seclusion, and seen exclusively as a woman's preserve. Her experiences of gestation, childbirth, mothering and breast feeding during the puerperium period are considered taboos that belie the sacrosanct image of motherhood. National patriarchies had recast the mother as a de-sexed, caring-nurturing being. According to Jakobsh, focussing on the hopes, dreams and bodily experiences of the pregnant Tripta was not typical devotional poetry written for this quincentenary (2000: 280). Amrita subverts not only the idea of the de-sexed mother but also the cultural construct of silence around pregnancy to centralise the sexualised, impregnated body of the woman. Further references to the 'cravings of pregnancy / Restless palpitation of the heart', the 'flutter of its wing / within my womb' subverted the ideology of Sikh orthodoxy that had newly been fortified with the 'great' tradition (280).

The matri-centric perspective of lactation and birthing, complete with a reference to the midwife, is juxtaposed with the ethereal nature of the divine dream, thus combining the sacred and the profane:

> I touched my breasts and the juice of the coconut
> Oozed out.
> ....
> Send for Earth, the midwife,
> I am having my first birth-pangs.
>
> (Pritam, Singh 1982: 153–155)

Although in a colossal overturning of the patriarchal religious tradition Amrita reduces the founder of the Sikh faith to a foetus growing in the womb of Tripta, she touches upon the mystical in a recognition of the godly nature of the baby. The idea of the transcendent is introduced in the dream that Tripta narrates to her husband where, in the extremity of winter, she touches the surprisingly warm water in a stream that miraculously turns to milk. In an ablutionary gesture:

> I put the moon on my palm, took a sip....
>   And the same moonlight quivers in my womb.
>
> (149)

In a juxtaposition of the ethereal and terrestrial, she becomes instinctively aware not only of the pregnancy but the divine and prophetic nature of the infant, 'Do mothers see their gods in their wombs?' (149) In her characteristic style, Amrita touches upon the mystical with delicate, evocative images interspersed in the poem, as 'the hymn of divine creation' and the divine status of Nanak is referred to as 'the odour rising from my navel' (149).

Conclusion

In 'To Waris Shah', Amrita confronted both national and regional patriarchies, in 'The Scar' challenged the nation-state and in 'Annunciation' defied regional patriarchies. Critics believed that 'To Waris Shah' ought not to have been addressed to Waris Shah seen as a symbol of Muslim cultural production. They felt that as a daughter of the soil, she should have addressed the poem to Guru Nanak; while communists felt that the poem ought to have been dedicated to Lenin. However, the attack on 'Annunciation' was far more virulent; by underscoring the hypocrisy of religion, she came in conflict with Sikh orthodoxy for questioning what they said was the paternity of Nanak and declaring that 'the child is neither thine nor anyone else's/it is a timeless yogi'. According to Jakobsh,

> The outcry that followed the publication of the poem was ruthless, demanding that the poem be banned by the government and questioning how a lowly 'love's worm' could write on so elevated a theme.... It would appear that history, understood and presented from the perspective of the feminine, can only be vilified and postulated as incompatible to real history, that of the male perspective.
>
> (2000: b 280)

In all these poems, Amrita reinterpreted tradition – in 'To Waris Shah' she appropriates the tradition of the male poet to speak of the sorrowing, thus seizing 'the intellectual tools of the male'; in 'The Scar' she reinterprets the idea of the nation-state as protector; and in 'Annunciation' she reinterprets tradition by foregrounding Nanak's mother as a real woman who looks forward to the birth not of a spiritual luminary but a physical baby. She critiques divisive religious and toxic multiple patriarchies to reaffirm individual humanity and challenges prescriptive roles imposed upon women.

The way she chose to live her life – the fact that she smoked, cut her hair, wore trousers or 'loved a drop of whiskey occasionally', her unabashed declaration of love for Sahir Ludhianvi, separation from her husband, live-in relationship with Imroz – in violation of the prescriptive codes brought her in conflict with multiple patriarchies. She said, 'Society attacks anyone who dares to say its coins are counterfeit, but when it is a woman who says this, society ... picks up the weapons of filth to fling at her' (Tharu et al. 1993: 60). When she wrote her autobiography, protesters lobbied for a ban in Punjab. Her periodical, *Nagmani* was denounced as vulgar and pornographic. When she planned to pen her autobiography, fellow intellectual Khushwant Singh demanded to know, 'What is there to your life...? Just an incident or two.... You could use the back of a revenue stamp to write it' (qtd. in Sunwani). The very act of writing is subversive and Amrita, a born rebel, expressed her transgressive voice through her writings, saying, 'Why not talent? They can admire a beautiful woman, but not a talented one' (qtd. in Sharma 2020).

According to Tharu, the enterprise of women's writing in India raises fundamental questions that include

> changing ideologies of class, gender, empire in which women wrote ...; questions about the politics, sexual, and critical that determined the reception and impact of their work; questions about the restraints and subversions ... that characterised the subtlest and most radical woman's writing.
>
> (1993 vol 1: 15)

Multiple patriarchies attempted to belittle Amrita's writings in line with the inherent contradictions espoused by 'a Sikh narrative of gender equality' and the individual 'ontological narratives that give rise to gender-based discriminatory practices' (Behl 2010). This ontological narrative becomes even more stringent in the case of a woman who writes. Amrita, through her gendered syncretic voice, seeks to recover and reconstruct the anguish of women silenced by history and society by transcending the barricades of religion and gender in an individuality unique to her.

Note

1 According to Jakobsh, during *Kanagats* women hurled abuses at women from another locality and sometimes, there were physical fights between women that were a source of amusement to the spectators while *Sada Talla* was a fertility rite whereby women bared their bodies up to their bodices and rolled in the mud in hope of conceiving children. During the rite, they would be almost entirely naked (2000, p. 151–152).

References

Bal, Gurpreet. 2006. "Construction of Gender and Religious Identities in the First Punjabi Novel *Sundari*", *Economic and Political Weekly* Vol. 41, Issue No. 32, 12 August. https://www.epw.in/journal/2006/32/special-articles/construction -gender-and-religious-identities-first-punjabi-novel?0=ip_login_no_cache%3D9 7087414c4fb6864f5ec8a804e4a13ee (accessed on 21.12.2021).

———. 2008. "Religion and Gender in Identity in the Writings of a Nineteenth Century Woman Poet Peero", in Paramjit S. Judge and Gurpreet Judge (eds.), *Reconstructing Identities: Society through Literature*, pp. 82–100. New Delhi: Rawat Publications.

Behl, Natasha. 2010. "Sikh Politics, Gender, and Narrative Identity", Annual Meeting Paper of University of California Los Angeles. Western Political Science Association. https://poseidon01.ssrn.com/delivery.php?ID=8700670881140 (accessed on 04.02.2021).

Butalia, Urvashi. 1998. *The Other Side of Silence: Voices from the Partition of India*. New Delhi: Penguin.

Datta, Nonica. 2008. "Transcending Religious Identities: Amrita Pritam and Partition", in Anjali Gera Roy and Nandi Bhatia (eds.), *Partitioned Lives: Narratives of Home, Displacement, and Resettlement*, pp. 1–25. New Delhi: Pearson Longman.

Fair, Christine C. "The Novels of Bhai Vir Singh and the Imagination of Sikh Identity, Community, and Nation". https://www.researchgate.net/profile/Carol _Fair/publication/265427366 (accessed on 14.02.2021).

Jakobsh, Doris R. 1999. "Relocating Gender in Sikh History: Transformation, Meaning and Identity", Unpublished Ph.D. dissertation, University of British Columbia. https://open.library.ubc.ca/cIRcle/collections/ubctheses/831/items/1 .0089814 (accessed on 10.01.2021).

———. 2000. "The Construction of Gender in History and Religion: The Sikh Case", in Mandakranta Bose (ed.), *Faces of the Feminine in Ancient, Medieval, and Modern India*, pp. 270–285. New York: OUP. https://books.google.co.in/books?hl=en&lr=&id=lNOUSo6Eb-oC&oi=fnd&pg=PA270&dq=amrita+pritam (accessed on 10.01.2021).

Kazmi, Sara. 2019. "Radical Re-tellings of Hir: Gender and the Politics of Voice in Postcolonial Punjabi Poetry", *South Asia Multidisciplinary Academic Journal.* https://doi.org/10.4000/samaj.5294.

Mann, Gurinderpal. 2018. "Jat Masculinity and Deviant Femininity in a Punjabi Romantic Epic: Exploring Gender through Waris Shah's *Hir*", Unpublished M.A dissertation, University of British Columbia. https://open.library.ubc.ca/cIRcle/collections/ubctheses/24/items/1.0365972 (accessed on 12.01.2021).

Mir, Farina. 2006. "Genre and Devotion in Punjabi Popular Narratives: Rethinking Cultural and Religious Syncretism", *Comparative Studies in Society and History*, 48(3): 727–758.

Murphy, Anne. 2018. "At a Sufi-Bhakti Crossroads: Gender and the Politics of Satire in Early Modern Punjabi Literature", *Open Collections*, https://open.library.ubc.ca/cIRcle/collections/facultyresearchandpublications/52383/items/1.0391029 (accessed on 10.01.2021).

———. 2019. "Sufis, Jogis and the Question of Religious Difference: Individualisation in Early Modern Punjab", https://open.library.ubc.ca/soa/cIRcle/collections/facultyresearchandpublications/52383/items/1.0391027 (accessed on 21.12.2021).

Nehru, Jawaharlal. 1958. *Jawaharlal Nehru's Speeches Vol I. Sept 1946–May 1949.* New Delhi: Ministry of Information and Broadcasting, Govt. of India.

Pritam, Amrita. 1982. *Amrita Pritam: Selected Poems.* Ed. Khushwant Singh. Delhi: Bhartiya Jnanpith.

———. 1976, rpt. 1994. *The Revenue Stamp.* Trans. Krishna Gorowara. Delhi: Vikas Publishing House.

———. 1999. *Aksharon ke Saaye: Atamkatha.* Delhi: Rajpal.

———. 2001. *Shadows of Words.* New Delhi: Macmillan.

Raychaudhuri, Anindya. 2018. "Friends from an Earlier Life: Radical Possibilities of Nostalgic Melancholy in Poems of the 1947 Indian Partition". https://riull.ull.es/xmlui/bitstream/handle/915/7561/RCEI_76_ (accessed on 14.01.2021).

Sharma, Ishita. 2020. "Reading Amrita Pritam as a Feminist In 2020", *Intersectional Feminism Desi Style.* August 31, 2020. https://feminisminindia.com/section/intersectionality/ (accessed on 29.09.2020).

Sunwani, Vijay Kumar. 2005. "Amrita Pritam: The Black Rose", *Language in India.* http://www.languageinindia.com/dec2005/amritapritamsunwani1.html. (accessed on 20.09.2020).

Tharu, Susie and K. Lalitha (eds.). 1993. *Women Writing in India: 600 BC to the Present.* Vol. 1 & 2. New Delhi: Oxford University Press.

13

NEGOTIATING GENDERED CONTEXTS OF THE NATION-STATE

A Reading of Amrita Pritam's Select Fiction

Bharti Arora

> Our country's civilisation does not teach men to take consent (*ijaazat*) from women...
>
> – *Dilli ki Galiyan* 125

> Anita recalled how she would get up early and prepare tea for her husband, send his lunch to office, sew her mother-in-law's and sister in law's clothes, and listen to her husband's woes about rising prices at dinner table.... Even as she did that, a certain dampness of soul entrapped her [...] She would not speak much and had nearly stopped listening.
>
> – *Anita* 175

> Mukta's parents thought that her college education was necessary in so far it comprised the mandatory ritual of dowry.
>
> – *Ek Khali Jagah* 120

The patriarchal, virilocal, patrilineal structures of family disregard women's claim to equality in marriage, according to them a secondary place within it. This affects an alternative conceptualisation of subjectivities within and outside marriage. It is imperative to challenge the patriarchal underpinnings of institutions that throw women at the mercy of disparate gendered contexts of families and society. In fact, women must become, to use Rashmi Varma's phrase, 'unhomely' (2012: 26); to not simply break such spatial divisions but also renegotiate their claims to citizenship. Reading Amrita Pritam's *Dilli ki Galiyan* (*Streets of Delhi* 1968), *Ek Khali Jagah* (*An Empty Space* 1977) and *Ek thi Anita* (*Anita* 1964), the essay proposes to explore the (re)production of upper-/middle-class women's sexualit(ies) at the interstices between patriarchal, virilocal and patrilineal structures on the one hand and the legislative adjudicatory framework on the other. While *Dilli ki Galiyan* is a bold proclamation of women's right to cultivating their identity as individuals, the other two novels

DOI: 10.4324/9781003214656-21

highlight women's negotiation with the structural inequities of marriage. They also explore how women's bodies, desires and sexuality are mapped, scrutinised and negated in the context of marriage, impelling them to lead a constrained existence. The novels interrogate patriarchal biases inherent in epistemological and institutional structures of the nation-state, illustrating ways in which familial, communal and gendered violence is structurally propounded against women.

Highlighting these aspects of Amrita's literary oeuvre, the essay argues that the aesthetic vision of women performs a concomitant role with the actual feminist endeavours of the time to challenge and redefine the dominant discourses around women sexualities. The selected novels significantly challenge the euphoric institutionalisation of the Hindu Code Bill (1950s) and its supposed endorsement of Hindu women's claims to gender equality by declaring bigamy punishable by law, giving women rights to institute divorce proceedings and inherit paternal property. However, even as the Bill upheld a liberal outlook in facilitating women's access to legal privileges, religious orthodoxy, present both inside and outside Parliament, contested it by emphasising women's confinement within the customary rituals of Hindu community. The reading is relevant as it critiques the dominant perceptions of marriage and family as sanctimonious, normative and essential to nurturing the legitimate progeny.

The chapter is divided into three sections. The first section titled 'Victimised by Partition, Building the Nation: Being Pooro and Becoming Kamini' takes up Amrita's novels *Pinjar* and *Dilli ki Galiyan*, highlighting that even while the emergent state defined the category of women citizens and marked their legal rights, it continued to perceive them through the prism of familial and cultural contexts. The second section titled 'Women's Negotiations with Gendered Biases and Legal Discourses of the State' highlights Kamini's (*Dilli ki Galiyan*) struggle to build her identity as a professional woman. It further explores how women negotiate gendered biases and sexist attitudes of society and the legal formations of the state. Amrita refrains from endorsing homogeneous perspectives on both masculinity and femininity, proposing ways to alter and re-forge them. The final section titled 'Illusions of Love and Disillusionments of Marriage: The Case of Anita and Mukta' challenges the structural hierarchies embedded in the discourses of love, romance, intimacy and marriage, showcasing how they affect women's rights as citizens and individuals. Both Anita (*Anita*) and Mukta (*Ek Khali Jagah*) settle into marriages of convenience, which severely affect their engagement with the hierarchical matrix of gender relations.

Victimised by Partition, Building the Nation: Being Pooro and Becoming Kamini

Amrita writes about the trauma suffered by women in the wake of Partition, 'Partition of India continued to become a festered wound in the bosom of history. Nobody would ever know – that the dreams of how many girls of this country were slaughtered' (qtd. in Datta 2008: 10). At the stroke of midnight, when the nation awoke to 'life and freedom', women were abducted by enemy communities and condemned to suffer trauma for years to come. Their status as citizens was further compromised when the patriarchal nation-state deliberated on ways to exchange them on the basis of their religious identities.

Pinjar exposes how the shadow of women's 'abducted/polluted bodies' in the wake of Partition looms large over their legitimate demands to claim equal rights. Amrita delineates her disenchantment with the nascent state and the allied terror of communalism by comparing them to an unwanted child that grows in the belly of the abducted woman, signifying her trauma,

> Pooro would hate each and every part of her body. How she wished to throw away the worm infesting her body, to not have anything to do with it, as if one extracts a thorn stuck in the body by pressing it between the nails.
>
> (Pritam 2003: 8)

By so doing, Amrita underscores the hollowness inherent in words like 'honour' and 'rescue' propagated by the state in order to demarcate women's identity and existence.

The asymmetrical inter-communal relations are inscribed on gendered terrains, impelling women to preserve the deep-seated prejudices and taboos of their respective communities. When Pooro returns to her house after escaping Rashida's confinement, her parents don't want to maintain filial ties with her; the emotional violence inflicted by her parents' rejection merges with Pooro's sexual violation by Rashida which takes place later in the narrative. Pooro is perceived as property and a pawn in the brutal logic of violent transactions that take place in the name of religious/gender identity.

Later in the novel, Pooro's refusal to go back to her 'original home' marks her defiance against the patriarchal injunctions of communities and the state that framed women as victims of Partition. It is noteworthy that the Abducted Persons (Recovery and Restoration) Bill, tabled in the Lok Sabha on 31 December 1949 denied any provision of choice to women. Their unwillingness, if any, to return to their family was ignored; nor did they have any recourse to legal rights and justice. Many women were recovered against their wishes and later branded 'impure' or disowned by their families. The state's descriptions of women as Hindu women and Muslim women during the Constituent Assembly debates about the procedures of exchanging and restoring them to their 'legitimate' families further illustrated a reneging on the state's provisions for women as citizens.

In fact, the Abducted Persons Act was remarkable in the way it violated the suggestions of both the Karachi Resolution of the Congress[1] (1931) and the Sub-Committee on 'Women's Role in Planned Economy' (1939). They inscribed the category of women workers, emphasising their equal right to develop themselves and to not be discriminated against in any employment or profession on the ground of religion, caste or sex. In reality, the state was no less than a conglomeration of multiple patriarchies at work. *Pinjar* foregrounds the partitioned state's betrayal of its welfarism by treating women as symbolic markers of national honour. Thus, Pooro's refusal to return to her 'original family' not only problematises the patriarchal family and its sense of ownership and control over women but also interrogates the protectionism offered by the *parens patriae* state.

Dilli ki Galiyan takes this argument further as it probes how the nation-state continued to treat women as appendages to their families and communities. It relates Kamini's struggles as a woman and journalist and ways in which she perceives the inextricable links between the unequal class/caste systems and gender relations on the one hand and oppressive state structures on the other. By doing so, Amrita exposes the gap between women's roles as perceived and recognised by society and those that they were actually capable of performing. Simultaneously, she defamiliarises women's silent protests, grievances and their submissions to societal and state structures.

Kamini's unconventional upbringing as a child plays a significant role in shaping her career as a working woman. The death of Kamini's mother soon after her birth teaches her quite early in life how a mother need not be the only caregiver and a father may also perform domestic responsibilities with equal rigour and intensity. In his youth, Kamini's father had challenged the patriarchal code of sexual purity by marrying Kamini's mother who was a widow; thereby redefining the dominant ways in which marital and emotional subjectivities are conceived by society.[2] Here, Amrita provides a glimpse into an alternative approach to masculinities, suggesting how it neither has an inner essence, nor is it static. It is, as Lynne Segal calls 'a set of fictions' (1993: 630) which acquires a palpable quality with a series of investments in it.

Her father encourages Kamini to read books and cognitively engage with the world on her own terms. This facilitates her tryst with higher education and a career as an independent woman. He neither imposes the traditional gendered codes on her nor forces her to get married unless she is ready. Radha Kumar states how the feminist negotiation of the woman question in post-independence India replaced the symbol of mother and/or wife with 'two self-images ... the woman as daughter and the working woman' (1993: 2). She further asserts, 'The former focussed on the formation of a woman rather than her role; the latter looked at her productive rather than reproductive capacities. This marked a sharp turn from the pre-independence movement, which was almost exclusively concerned with women in relation to men' (1993: 2).

The upper middle-class women were the immediate beneficiaries of the increasing rate of development. The expansion of employment opportunities in tertiary sectors further enabled these women to become productive citizens of the new nation. As the *Towards Equality* (1974) report on the status of women in India informs, 'The possibility of employment under Government provided the stimulus that women's education had lacked so far, particularly in the field of higher education' (Sharma and Sujaya 2012: 155). It is noteworthy that Kamini's engagement with her career is not driven by any specific need to support her family but to build her identity as a career-oriented woman.

> Kamini had numerous career options to choose from. However, when she learnt that she may get the job of a columnist in the office of *Delhi Times* if she works hard for it, she started pursuing it with single minded attention.
>
> (Pritam 2019 b: 90)

Kamini negotiates her identity as a working woman to interrogate the oppressive analogy of home, women and sexuality. Such a dialectical engagement with the woman question after independence significantly intervened in the dominant cultural attitudes pertaining to women.

As the *Towards Equality* report affirms, women's status within their family and socio-cultural milieu hardly underwent any radical transformation from the pre-independence to post-independence period. The First Five Year Plan particularly emphasised that there was a need to promote 'adequate services in order to fulfill women's legitimate role in the family and the community' (Sharma and Sujaya 2012: 224). Thus, women's development was confined to family-centric strategies like reproductive health, children's education and family planning. Alternatively, in the novel, Kamini's feminist lens negotiates the gendered contexts and biases around her. She critically analyses Nasir's paintings and, while appreciating his skill as an artist, highlights how Nasir's art is sexist and lacks creativity. The only way he could represent women in his paintings is by objectifying them, 'We can make a few inferences from the kind of paintings drawn by this artist. They are as follows: a woman with a flower, a woman with a comb, a woman with a bangle ... and we shall wait for the day when we witness this artist painting a woman with a mind' (Pritam 2019 b: 101).

Nasir is embarrassed when he realises that his paintings have violated women's status as individuals because he has perceived women through the constricted lens of cultural and sexual assumptions.

His encounter with Kamini makes him realise the importance of perceiving women as independent beings. He likes Kamini but does not force her into loving him back. Instead, he reads Kamini's newspaper columns to learn more about her personality and perspective on art and social issues. Gradually, he unlearns the masculine gaze that perceives women as sexualised objects meant to amuse men. He also realises the epistemological harm caused by the masculinist gaze of art which objectifies women as either beloved or wailing wives and mothers. 'This art is comparable to a letter of eternal silence, impelling women to discover their life's meanings on their own' (Pritam 2019 b: 108). Nasir's accommodative and sensitive personality stands out in the novel; he is neither like Sunil, Kamini's former boyfriend who perceives her as an antidote to his loneliness, nor like Jagir Singh who wants to harass Kamini into sexual submission. The novel highlights the futility of perceiving femininity as a cultural marker of women's vulnerability or approaching masculinity as always already a violent phenomenon. These categories are contingent on a variety of parameters like age, employment patterns, caste-class, community contexts, level of education and/or its absence and so on. In the words of Lynne Segal:

> We need to pay attention to the variety of masculinities that jostle uneasily within our culture. This does not mean ignoring the prevalence and variety of exploitative, abusive, and coercive actions from men, quite the contrary, but rather attempting to situate them within the social and discursive conditions and frameworks that either foster or discourage such behaviour.
>
> (1993: 638)

By so doing, one can challenge the unequal distribution of resources among genders, highlighting systemic ways in which patriarchal biases make way into the structures and institutions of the state.

More to the point, the division between the private and public spheres is so prevalent that it affects women's engagement with the state outside these spheres. Rajeswari Sunder Rajan states that it is pertinent to explore the relation between the words 'women' and 'citizens', 'How does citizenship function as identity and existential reality for women ... how does the state identify women's issues? What kinds of commitments or pressures operate in determining its address to women as citizens, to women's issues and to gender equality?' (2003: 4).

Kamini learns how women's concerns have been consistently relegated to the private sphere when she attends a meeting of the All India Women's Conference as a journalist. The conference raises issues of price rise of essential commodities, black marketing and corruption in public life. It further advocates improvement in working conditions for women so that they contribute productively to society without any fear of harassment at workplace. As Kamini writes in her newspaper report, 'None of these women present at the conference, who had either foregrounded these demands and/or supported them, could figure out who their addressee was [...] who could rightfully address these concerns' (Pritam 2019: 127). Here, Amrita represents the concerns, achievements and challenges of contemporary Indian women's movement and the ways in which it resisted the tyranny of the state. By doing so, one could also interrogate one's privileges with respect to the caste/class, communal and gendered oppression faced by women and other marginalised sections of society. Kamini realises that feminism culled solely from her own privileged experience would never be politically effective unless it recognises the deprivations operating within society. She reflects how the post-independence government conveniently settled itself into the violent institutions and epistemological structures left behind by the colonial government. She suggests that the politics of the 'welfare state' has not sufficiently addressed the concerns of women and vulnerable sections of society. Thus, the novel defamiliarises women's identities as citizens, foregrounding ways in which their perception of the oppressive structures and value systems of the nation could betray inequitable class, caste systems, and asymmetrical gender relations.

Women's Negotiations with Gendered Biases and Legal Discourses of the State

Dilli ki Galiyan problematises the so-called politics of the state which not only overlooks the cultural and patriarchal contexts of its legal institutions but also fails to acknowledge their violent implications for women. For instance, Nasir's cartoon strip for a newspaper illustrates how gender inequality vis-à-vis control of resources and power structures comprises a systemic phenomenon.

> A teacher asked his students which the most popular word of their times was. To this, a student replies, 'These days, the most frequently used word is "anti" – because people are becoming anti-women, anti-mind, and anti-life in their day-to-day affairs'.
>
> (Pritam 2019 b: 123)

The message of the cartoon strip, as this section illustrates, sums up the experience of being a woman for Kamini in ways more than one.

During one of her assignments, Kamini strikes a unique bond with an English woman, Alice Tanveer, who narrates her disappointments pertaining to the institution of marriage and allied juridical contexts. The novel illustrates how the dominant constructions of women's sexuality systemically marginalise them across socio-cultural contexts. Kamini and Alice, despite differences of age, status, education and class/community/national contexts share a peculiar predicament. As Madhu Kishwar asserts in the first editorial essay of *Manushi*:

> Is it possible to talk of women as an undifferential mass?... There are a lot of factors dividing women from each other – class, caste, religion, race, education (or the lack of it) and many other complex historical forces. Yet if we look at the nature and basis of women's

oppression, we discover that our sex determines our common predicament in a very fundamental way.

(1979)

Alice confides in Kamini that Tanveer, her Indian husband, a navy officer,
has murdered Mr. Lal, his accomplice in smuggling contraband across international waters, because he refused to pay him commission. Taking advantage of the institutional immunity offered to the armed forces, Tanveer seeks
to defend himself in court by implicating Alice in the case; he accuses Alice
of having an illicit relationship with Lal, thus converting his crime into a
righteous act of avenging his honour as a husband. Alice informs Kamini,
'This was the only way of saving Mr. Tanveer and I saved him. Not only
him, I managed to save the "name" [the honour] of the nation' (Pritam
2019 b: 148). Amrita obliquely exposes the double standards of both civil
and military laws pertaining to adultery.

The contradictory familial ideology endorsed by the judicial structure of
the country affects women's negotiations of these legal provisions. While
in matters of civil law, Section 497 of the Indian Penal Code (IPC) holds
men guilty of adultery when they have sexual intercourse (not amounting
to the offence of rape) with a woman without the consent of the husband,[3]
the armed forces interpret the said act as a crime (in case an armed person-
nel has sexual intercourse with the wife of a fellow officer) leading to court
martial.[4] Tanveer takes advantage of the legal discrepancy by accusing his
wife of adultery and thereby justifying his act of murder. The incident shows
how women's bodies are sexualised to the extent of erasing their individuality and identity as a citizen subject. Lynne Segal rightly asserts, 'The concept of "masculinity" condenses, above all, the cultural reality of women's
subordination. This reality is embodied [...] in the daily functioning – the
routines and rituals – of the state, industry, and every other institution of
social, economic, and political power' (1993: 629).

Desiring to live life on her own terms, Kamini constantly challenges the
gendered contexts of society, renegotiating her relationships with the men
around her, but things get difficult when she is harassed by a poet called
Jagir Singh. Kamini's work profile demands that she meet poets and artists,
observe their creative skills and write about them. Mistaking this professional meeting with Kamini for a personal one, Jagir Singh assumes that
she must like him. He starts to stalk her, disregarding the fact that she is
not interested in his overtures. He even pretends to seek forgiveness when
Kamini gets offended, 'Maharani! Tum mujhe maaf nahi karogi?'/'Princess!
Won't you forgive me?' (Pritam 2019 b: 121). The use of words like 'maharani' and 'tum' smacks sexist assumptions whereby women could be simultaneously raised to a pedestal as well as held guilty for exercising their
choices and consent vis-à-vis men. Also, Jagir Singh's diplomatic usage of
words delegitimises Kamini's experience of sexual harassment.

What makes the situation worse is that these same assumptions percolate the debates/discourses on and around women's legal rights against sexual harassment for which there was no specific law in India until 1991. *The Crime in India* (1992) report reveals that no specific crimes against women except rape and kidnapping were recorded. Pratiksha Baxi (*India-Seminar* website) informs that sexual harassment was not considered a serious crime; instead, it was euphemistically called eve-teasing, which tended to normalise it as an unavoidable, everyday reality for women.

Thus even as Kamini has an aversion to Jagir Singh and his sexual overtures, she can only deploy indifference to cope with it. In fact, women are culturally trained to cultivate indifference as a defence mechanism against sexual harassment, which jeopardises their right to freedom of expression and right to gender equality. Veena Das quotes Mac Kinnon in this regard:

> The everyday heterosexual practices and the practice of rape participate in the same structure of relations defined by patriarchal ideologies .... Sexuality is a set of practices that inscribes gender as unequal in social life. On this level, sexual abuse and its frequency reveal and participate in a common structural reality with everyday sexual practice.
>
> (1996: 2411)

Even as Amrita foregrounds Kamini's dilemma and struggles vis-à-vis dominant sexual and gendered asymmetries, she interrogates men's sexist bias against women and emphasises that they must reform – exemplified in representations of Kamini's father and Nasir. Another young man called Hardev, a minor but significant character, supports Kamini when he learns of Jagir's plan to defame her even though he is his friend. Hardev seems sensitively inclined to assess the implications of 'hegemonic masculinity' (Connell, qtd. in Srivastava: 1) for both women and men. He respects Kamini as an individual who has equal rights to pursue her profession without any fear of sexual assault or loss of reputation, 'It is extremely easy to write against women ... there is not enough mud that is slung on one's clothes due to wind, so much so as there are accusations flung at women' (Pritam 2019 b: 143). Herein lies the radical dynamics of the recast gender relations forged by a woman author, wherein men must confront the language of domination that they have hitherto taken for granted. It enables them to critique the dominant conceptions of masculinity and the licence that accompanies it.

Illusions of Love and Disillusionments of Marriage: The Case of *Anita* and *Mukta*

Marital relationships are construed as the cultural foundation of patriarchal societies and women are expected to prescribe to their normative structures of monogamy, heterosexuality and patrilineality. Amrita's *Anita* and *Ek Khali Jagah* critique these structures, probing the institution of marriage and sexuality within/without it.

The eponymous protagonist of *Anita* feels trapped in her 'normal' marriage and aspires to escape its drudgery by losing herself in a lyrical-romanticised world of dream sequences. The dramatic entry of Sagar in her life hastens Anita's realisation of the invisible, emotional violence embedded in her marriage with Rampal, but she is unable to break the 'sanctimonious' marital tie despite being extremely attracted to Sagar. Her hesitation in reciprocating his sexual advances antagonises him and he moves to another town to start afresh. Anita fails to question the dominant perception of marriage as an institution that offers protection and financial stability to women. Her relationship with Iqbal is equally disturbing when, despite their best efforts, they fail to forge bonds of empathy and love. She dies a painful death as Iqbal loses interest in her, leaving her in a vulnerable position.

On a similar note, Mukta of *Ek Khali Jagah* is shown musing over the (im)possibilities of becoming a second wife to a rich man Dilip Rai, whose first wife and child have died. The novella describes how petty coercions work in a familial and marital setup, expecting women to sacrifice their ambitions and aspirations at the altar of domesticity. It also deconstructs the romanticisation of natal family vis-à-vis the affinal family, whereby most young women are conditioned to feel obligated for the comfort and privileges of their parents' home; revealing how women's life in natal families could be equally constrained and exploited. The pressure to get married makes young women abandon their aspirations and familial biases against women's education often reflect institutional biases that view women's education as secondary to their roles as wives and mothers. The *Towards Equality* report quotes the *Report of the University Education Commission* (1949) in this regard, highlighting conservative attitudes towards women's education:

> Women's and men's education should not be in general [...] identical in all respects, as is usually the case today. Her education should make her familiar with problems of home management and skilled in meeting them so that she may take her place in a home with the same interest [...] that a well-trained man has in working at his calling.
>
> (235)

In fact, both *Anita* and *Ek Khali Jagah* highlight that women within marriage or those who remain single are, at times, so ideologically trained that their attempts to carve out an independent identity fail. Anita inhabits a precarious zone between fantasy and reality where all her desires lead to Sagar.

146

As she confesses, he was no less than 'Aladdin's jinn' (Pritam 2019 a: 183), whose only task was to appear before her every time she beckoned him. Even as these fantastical rendezvous with Sagar represent her as a desiring subject, they do not empower her in any real sense of the term. Loving Sagar becomes a means to escape the deprivations of matrimony. Alternatively, even as she experiences boredom in marriage, Anita does not necessarily want to sacrifice the material comforts provided by her marital context, nor does she aspire to becoming financially independent.

Similarly, even as Mukta in *Ek Khali Jagah* marries Dilip after the death of his first wife, she is unable to come to terms with the absent presence of the woman in the marriage. Perceived largely as a replacement whose role is limited to becoming the second wife and mother to Dilip's child from his first marriage, 'Mukta tried envisioning him as someone who completely belonged to her, based on love and legal processes as well. However, Dilip remained a stranger, on whom she had no rights whatsoever' (Pritam 2003: 126). She rues that she is not Dilip's first choice. The novel shows how middle-class women like Mukta have limited choices in life; though she is equally troubled by the structural asymmetry of their socio-economic status. In fact, her response to Dilip's marriage proposal is similar to how she has toyed with the possibility of participating in a city-based beauty contest in the past. Both instances offer her possibilities of liberating herself from the poverty-ridden context of the natal home.

It is noteworthy that there was a significant rise in female-headed households around the 1970s–1980s, when women and children lived apart from the husband and father due to broken marriages, widowhood, desertion, or abandonment.[5] Even as a few upper class, educated women were euphoric about the legislative achievements pertaining to the passage of the Hindu Code Bill, more and more women from lower income strata continued their struggle to secure jobs and economic stability in the face of inegalitarian access to resources. As Nirmala Banerjee (1998) asserts, 'The official policies vis-à-vis women in India's plan for development continued to regard them merely as targets for household and motherhood-oriented welfare services' (WS-2).

Given the extent of socio-political and economic vulnerability experienced by women, one can presume why Anita and Mukta feel discouraged to move out of their marriage. Talking about middle-class women and their marital adjustments, Promilla Kapur says, 'Wherever there are disagreements between husband and wife, the wife gave in two and a half times more frequently... a wife's being too individualised proves particularly detrimental to marital harmony because men still like to marry less individualised women' (1970: 419). Women 'bargain with patriarchy' (Kandiyoti 1998: 283), assuming subordinate, traditional roles imposed on them by their respective familial/ marital contexts. Anita and Mukta negotiate their marriages by submitting to the altar of obligatory sexual relations and

147

domestic responsibilities, thereby upholding the dominant cultural prescriptions on women.

In *Anita*, Rampal, Anita's husband, is neither abusive nor violent towards her but the two are unable to perceive and connect with the world at a similar wavelength. While Rampal has a matter-of-fact approach towards life, he would 'meticulously approach his circumstances vis-à-vis the realities of life, Anita strives for connecting the innumerous nodes of her life's dreams' (Pritam 2019 a: 203). Mental incompatibility amounts to cruelty in marital contexts (Section 498 A 1983 of the IPC). Amrita's engagement with violence within a domestic situation and otherwise aptly brings out the asymmetrical gender relations extant in society.

Nevertheless, Amrita steers clear of distinguishing arranged from love relationships, highlighting how the ideology of romance is embedded in emotional/physical violence. The novel raises questions like: Is it a viable idea to locate one's completeness in someone else? Is romance not inspired by a heterosexual ideal, whereby desire and pursuit dominate the overall structure of relationships?

There are instances in *Anita*, wherein the charm of relationship (either with Sagar or Iqbal) for Anita lies in masochistically pining for the absent lover. She regrets refusing Sagar's sexual overtures, wondering why he did not assault her, 'He should have understood that saying "no" is a part of a woman's cultural context. Why did he not assault me – he has a right to do so – he owns me' (Pritam 2019 a: 201). Anita is so used to the asymmetry, violence and paternalism embedded in marriage that she ends up succumbing to them. Her wanting to get assaulted and being owned by Sagar is extremely disturbing as these desires not only condone marital/gendered violence in society but also reveal how women are systemically trained to participate in and accept it. This further betrays the self-annihilating nature of Anita's desires which is manifested in terms of brain haemorrhage, followed by her death towards the end of the novel.

The institution of marriage draws its legitimacy from specific juridico-legal parameters pertaining to the age of marriage, monogamy, legitimate progeny and property ownership. In absence of any of these conditions, either spouse can file for separation and divorce. However, how does one qualify the breaking up of relations outside the marital tie? Amrita is much ahead of her times in raising these pertinent questions. When Iqbal, Anita's other love-interest, falls out of love with her, she has nowhere to go. Since legal discourses do not accommodate provisional (live-in) relationships in their ambit, Anita is unable to hold Iqbal accountable in any way.

Interestingly, even as the juridico-legal discourses of the country have made provisions to facilitate divorce proceedings in case of completely failed, unworkable and emotionally dead marriages, there are no provisions to hold a live-in partner responsible for aggravating mental cruelty.[6] In *Anita*, Anita's relationship with Sagar and Iqbal pushes her towards emotional and mental breakdown more aggressively than her failed marriage does. This problematises the hierarchical structuring of relations in society and the state, whereby the legitimacy, commitment and cultural sanctity of marriage are deemed far more important than the 'trifling' disappointments and 'illegitimate' consequences of simply romantic engagements. An additional complication is that Anita constantly lives under the shadow of this fear that Rampal might initiate legal proceedings against her for committing adultery.[7]

Thus, Amrita interrogates the patriarchal discourse of the nation-state that cultivated such gendered contexts post-independence. She asserts how asymmetrical power relations between men and women within the family are a product of, and in turn, influence the patriarchal and homogenous nexus of the family, caste, community and nation. By foregrounding issues concerning love/marriage, divorce, women's desertion and sexual harassment, the essay not only highlights their implications for women but also the patriarchal biases embedded in the discursive formations and legislative-juridical contexts of the nation-state. It draws attention to the inherent contradictions that exist between the ideas of equal citizenship offered by the modern nation-state and the ossified social practices of patriarchal control and possession of women as properties. By doing so, the essay has shown how women contest and are also determined by the dominant schema of the nation-state manifested in terms of tradition and modernity; cultural assimilation on the one hand and state control and/or social welfarist drives on the other.

Notes

1 The Karachi Congress Resolution prepared a draft of fundamental rights, defining the role of the Swaraj government.

2 The novel has autobiographical references here. Amrita's father had been a sadhu (monk) in his youth but when he met her mother, who was a widow, he left his saffron robes and married her.

3 This provision was abolished in a landmark judgement delivered by the Supreme Court of India in September 2018. A five-judge Constitution bench upheld gender justice, declaring that 'Adultery cannot and should not be a crime' (*NDTV* 27 September 2018). https://www.ndtv.com/india-news/adultery-law-is-arbitrary-says-chief-justice-dents-the-individuality-of-women-1922922 (accessed on 22.05.2022).

4 Even as the apex court decriminalised adultery within the ambit of civil laws, the armed forces continue to interpret the said act as a criminal offence owing to the special working conditions of the forces.

5 The *Towards Equality* report notes, while the number of widowed women was 2772 per 1000 males, divorced or separated women constituted 1630 per 1000 males, exposing how kinship norms oppressed women.

6 As per the Domestic Violence Act 2005, women in live-in relationships are eligible to get the benefit of this legal provision provided they live with their partner in a relationship that is in the nature of marriage.

7 The Hindu Marriage Act, 1955 provides a provision for divorce when either the husband or wife are 'living in adultery (or) if the husband has more than one wife living' (Sharma and Sujaya 2012: 89). As Kapur and Crossman (1996) inform, Section 10 of the Indian Divorce Act, 1869 provides that a husband may petition for divorce on the basis of his wife's adultery alone, but that a wife may only petition for divorce on the basis of her husband's adultery coupled with desertion, cruelty, rape, incest or bigamy. The judicial interpretation of this law reeks of its patriarchal bias and moral regulation of women's sexuality (187).

References

Banerjee, Nirmala. 1998. "Whatever Happened to the Dreams of Modernity?: The Nehruvian Era and Woman's Position", *Economic and Political Weekly* 33(17): WS2–WS7.

Baxi, Pratiksha. 2001. "Sexual Harassment", *India-Seminar*. https://www.india-seminar.com/2001/505/505%20pratiksha%20baxi.htm (accessed on 20.03.2021).

Das, Veena. 1996. "Sexual Violence, Discursive Formations, and the State", *Economic and Political Weekly* 31(35-36-37): 2411–2424.

Datta, Nonica. 2008. "Transcending Religious Identities: Amrita Pritam and Partition", in Anjali Gera Roy and Nandi Bhatia (eds.), *Partitioned Lives: Narratives of Home, Displacement, and Resettlement*, pp. 1–25. Delhi: Pearson Longman.

Kandiyoti, Deniz. 1998. "Bargaining with Patriarchy", *Gender and Society* 2(3): 274–290.

Kapur, Ratna and Brenda Crossman. 1996. *Subversive Sites: Feminist Engagements with Law in India*. Delhi: Sage Publications.

Kishwar, Madhu. 1979. "Towards Redefining Ourselves and the Society we Live in", *Manushi* 1. *manushi-india.org* (accessed on 23.05.2012).

Kumar, Radha. 1993. *The History of Doing*. Delhi: Kali for Women.

Pritam, Amrita. 1950, rpt. 2003. *Pinjar*. Delhi: Hindi Pocket Books.

———. 1964, rpt. 2019 a *Anita*. Delhi: Rajpal Publishing.

———. 1968, rpt. 2019 b *Kamini* [*Dilli ki Galiyan*]. Delhi: Rajpal Publishing.

———. 1977, rpt. 2003. *Ek Khali Jagah*. Delhi: Hindi Pocket Books.

Segal, Lynne. 1993. "Changing Men: Masculinities in Context", *Theory and Society*. Special Issue of *Masculinities* 22(5): 625–641.

Sharma, Kumud and C. P. Sujaya (eds.). 2012. *Towards Equality: Report of the Committee on the Status of Women in India*. Delhi: Pearson.

Srivastava, Sanjay. 2010. "Masculinity and its Role in Gender-Based Violence in Public Spaces", Centre for Equality and Inclusion. www.cequinindia.org (accessed on 11.07.2016).

Sunder Rajan, Rajeswari. 2003. *The Scandal of the State: Women, Law, and Citizenship in Postcolonial India*. Durham: Duke University Press.

Varma, Rashmi. 2012. *The Postcolonial City and its Subjects*. Delhi: Routledge.

Part IV

EMPOWERING THE 'I'

Figure 13 Empowering the 'I': Amrita at Her Writing Table

Figure 14 Lamp painted by Imroz with lines from Amrita's poem

14

AMRITA PRITAM'S LEGACY
Envisioning a Brave New World

Paul Kaur
translated by Hina Nandrajog

> If whatever I had is today buried under snow, then when the snow melts, its rivers-streams will be those who shall, with all honesty, hold new pens in their hands; and in the power of their pens will mingle all what is mine lying buried in the snow of silence today.
> – (*Rasidi Ticket* 100)

The insights and messages that a writer leaves behind for her readers and later generations is the legacy that is drawn from the totality of her life experiences. Amrita Pritam had a long and difficult journey both as a woman and a writer and the torment meted out by society on both accounts was embedded deep inside her. She often felt that her writing had not been understood adequately; as if it were buried under snow. But she did not despair and had a hope from the next generation. When one analyses the entire oeuvre of her writing, one can see the rich treasure that she bequeaths as her heritage to future writers and society. Amrita was a woman, writer, poet, who felt the pain of the women of the entire world and wove some dreams for the women of the next generations. Her lasting legacy is the envisioning of a new world order that is free from all discrimination and injustice; something that is not attainable till the time one-half of the population, that is women, do not learn to be independent and claim their rightful space in society. This essay looks at the image of a self-confident woman that Amrita leaves behind as her legacy in her writings – a woman brave enough to carve her own path in life. The chapter concludes with her own message to future writers.

'As I am now tied to you, all other relationships seemed dust'. This line sung during the Sikh rites of marriage is emblematic of the feudal, patriarchal Punjabi culture. When all relationships become merely an illusion in the face of a wife's duty, she is identified only as someone's wife, and later, as a mother. Her own identity as a woman is erased but even this total sacrifice does not bestow any respect, love or dignity upon her. Her being educated

DOI: 10.4324/9781003214656-23

153

and self-dependent is considered to be an affront to tradition. Articulating a desire to preserve her independent identity is met with frowns and knitted brows; nor is her attempt to articulate her angst taken kindly to. If at all she expresses her feelings and her hurt, she is not heard, and even if her voice is heard it is often misinterpreted.

Her journey to pick up a pen is difficult enough, but even more arduous is the journey after picking up the pen. If criticism of her writing does not sufficiently silence her, questions and accusations are raised about her personal life. Each of her creative endeavours is matched and assessed in relation to her life and found wanting; and she is accused of crying and complaining about personal experiences. More attention is paid to her physical attributes than to her compositions which prevents a balanced assessment of her work. However, Amrita is one such Punjabi woman writer who refused to succumb to the vitriol unleashed upon her life and writings and had the courage to outline the contours of a new woman and a world where one could be treated as an equal by men.

Right from her childhood, Amrita could not accept entrenched traditions of society unquestioningly and the inner voice in this young girl wanted to dialogue and debate these issues. The unwillingness of society to engage with any issue forced her to face stifling sadness time and again. She felt that she was not composed merely of her own revolt but also shaped by the revolt of her mother who had bowed to patriarchal duty and had gathered and kneaded all her resentment into a statue of Amrita; thus freeing herself but imbuing Amrita with all her anger (Pritam 2009: 66).

The poet in Amrita was born when at the age of eleven she addressed her first poem to a companion visualised in her dreams and whom she named 'Rajan'. Her father had encouraged her to develop religious ideas and write devotional poetry. But this poem was romantic and the piece of paper on which she had written it fell into his hands. Disowning the poem was rewarded with a slap and the tearing up of the poem. Amrita says, 'In this manner, I tried to pass off my first poem that I had addressed to you as someone else's poem, but the poem did not accept another name and clung to me with a slap' (Pritam 2016: 15-16).

Later Amrita describes how she began to string lines of poetry together to overcome and rise above the world of taboos. Initially, people did not accept her compositions as written by her; according to her, the disbelief was such an attack on her pride that it filled her spine with anger. This anger transformed the clinging creeper into a straight, strong tree. Then when her poetry was attributed to her, insult and abuse became the weapons of criticism because the sharpness in her songs did not suit society's traditional palate. Criticism was particularly virulent for a woman writer who was critical of society's norms, howsoever arbitrary and tyrannical, and she had to be punished and besmirched. When, despite all opposition, her courage and work began to carve a niche for itself in society, then the male world picked up yet another weapon to counteract it – the writer's youth, her face, and femininity were placed in the weighing scales to judge her verse. Amrita says, 'The hands of opposition have experimented with several weapons from time to time, but it has found the weapon of besmirching the reputation of a writer as the easiest, so now it has given up trying all other weapons and begun to use that exclusively' (Pritam 2009: 66–67).

In her book *Bure Siyalaan de Mamley* ('Enemies of Love'), Amrita briefly narrates the stories of 50 women writers, among whom are Greek writer, Sappho; English novelist, Virginia Woolf; feminist thinker, Mary Wollstonecraft; Russian poet, Marina Tasvetyeva; Swedish writer, Karin Boye; Italian writer, Antonia Pozzi; and Pakistani writer, Sara Shagufta – women who waged a war against society and patriarchal norms all their lives.

However, Amrita recognised the importance of being a woman. Asked by a journalist if she had committed any crime in this world that she would like to repeat in the next world, her answer was:

> I don't know about other births, but in this life it has often seemed that being a woman is a crime in itself; then this is the crime I would like to commit again, but on one condition that God would grant my wish to be given a pen in my next birth as well.
>
> (Pritam 1990: 214)

Amrita countered these critics by dazzling them with scintillating glimpses of a new woman and an ideal future for her. Right from her early writing, Amrita envisioned an ideal state of society and being for a woman – glimpses of an imaginary future in which both sexes are seen as equal partners. Noted Hindi writer, Kamleshwar presided over a programme organised on 31 August 1994 on Amrita and made two telling statements to point towards this quality in her writing. First, while other writers were writing about the physical attributes of a woman, her face and features, her complexion or her limbs, Amrita Pritam was writing about the whole woman. Secondly, while they were writing in Hindi, Bangla, Marathi, Urdu or Kannada, Amrita Pritam was writing poetry. In other words, Amrita did not remain confined to any boundary or ideology while writing her poetry. But the first statement is particularly significant because Amrita presents the inner world of emotions of a woman and her acceptance of her own bodily self. She writes of an individual that is whole and complete – with an integrated inner and outer self. She envisages a woman who is more than her mere physical self and heralds a time when a woman would be depicted with both her body and mind.

Amrita examines the ideal conditions for a woman in society and the obstacles in her path to find self-fulfilment. Punjabi folk songs testify to a woman being looked upon primarily as a child-bearing machine; she has no right even upon her own body. Amrita enunciates the struggle of a woman through a woman character writing in a letter that she married to ensure that the roof above her head remained secure – that is, built pillars under the roof.

Then children were born who became supports for the pillars; and then there was no danger of the roof collapsing, but it seemed that the entire space had been taken up by pillars and there was no place for her to even stand.... In her story 'Malka', she says that in the 'profession' of marriage, there is no promotion ever – one remains a husband or a wife forever. She visualises promotion in a husband becoming a lover, and then God; '... if a relationship that stands only on the basis of a rite, goes on to rest on the basis of the heart... on the basis of the soul...' (Pritam 2014: 91). If this cannot be, a rupture in the relationship in the form of a divorce is either further oppression for a woman, or as in Amrita's own case, a means of freedom and autonomy. In her diary, she records feeling light-hearted and liberated once the decree of her divorce was pronounced by the judge (Pritam 2018: 17).

She portrays the hopes that a woman nurtures for her life and living, her family, the state, society and from her companions and those around her. In a poem in *Patthar Geetey*, she says, 'a bit of the moon and a fistful of stars, have grabbed our sky' (Pritam 2019: 9). She appears to be commenting on the ironic fact that human beings become satisfied with very little, even though they have the ability, as well as the right, to win the entire sky. The poem is replete with similar nuances that not only does a woman have the right over the entire sky above her head but also has the capacity to achieve it. In a similar vein, the protagonist of her novel, *Ekta* says:

> Ekta felt her own self to be not a woman, but a road. A road that remains rooted to one spot, but is forever coming from somewhere, and going somewhere. The state of Ekta's mind was also at one point at the same spot, but this condition seemed to emanate from the history of mankind that had been written till date, and seemed to go towards that history that had not been written till date.
>
> (Pritam 2013: 6)

Women must write their own history, just as half a century ago, Amrita wrote a history from a feminist perspective through the heroines of her novels. Another incident in *Ekta* highlights Amrita's concern and visualisation of the future for women. One day, Ram Pyari, a maid who works for the protagonist, Ekta, brings her granddaughter, Kunti, to Ekta's house. Kunti rolls out a chapati from a ball of dough and gouges out the shape of a fish from it. She then proceeds to cook and eat it, considering it to be the fish that it was shaped into. She moulds the kneaded dough into other forms as well – a fish or a fowl, and cooks it and eats it. Watching her, Ekta gives her a sheet of paper and a pencil and tells her:

> 'All right, now you can make bananas or oranges with it, or whatever else you wish.'

'What's the use of that? I can't eat paper, can I?'

Whatever the little child thinks of, is in the shape of hunger – in the shape of a fundamental need. A little later in the text, Kunti goes out of the house and looks up at the sky. Ekta asks her why she was gazing at the eagle and the girl answers, 'I want to become an eagle.'

'You want to become an eagle, and maybe the eagle wants to become a girl, to become Kunti....' Ekta laughed.

'No, the eagle does not want to become a girl.' All the answers that the girl gave were simple, but they were delivered like a pronouncement. Ekta was surprised and asked, 'How do you know that the eagle does not want to become a girl; maybe it does.'

'That's not possible.'

'Why?'

'Because a girl does not have wings.'

(Pritam 1976: 24–25)

The conversation highlights the stifling air that women are expected to breathe in. Wings had been stolen from woman centuries ago, and Amrita is seeking to restore those wings to women to enable them to soar in the open skies.

Ekta is an example of a self-confident and self-reliant woman that Amrita envisions – someone who takes her own decisions, whether they ultimately turn out to be right or wrong. This woman does not want to be dependent on any other person and wants to live a life of dignity on the strength of her capability. This woman desires the freedom to think independently and be appreciated for her mind and not her body. For Amrita, financial independence for women is of prime importance and she takes up the issue in this novel. She is cognizant of the obstacles like sexual harassment and exploitation that a woman has to overcome at the workplace and is categorical that these must be eliminated so that a woman is able to contribute productively without hindrance. Amrita is also aware of the dangers of preening about superficial beauty because the consequence of that is the splintering of the inner self. One of Ekta's friends, Priya, talks about her daughter whose value system is of a new, different generation – an ultra-modern girl that Amrita crafted a long time ago. Priya talks about the increasing interest that modern girls take in enhancing their looks and Ekta comments that beauty should not come from the outside but from the inside.

But even then where will they reach or stand...? To reach somewhere one needs a path, to stand, some haven. It is not so difficult to break traditions, but to fashion new traditions in their place is very difficult. It is not she alone who has to create new customs.

The entire environment of society has to be part of that creation, and that environment does not exist at present....

(Pritam 1976: 45)

In another novel, *Annie*, the protagonist Annie leaves her husband, Anwar, and lives independently when she finds that he has been unfaithful to her. She also leaves her young son, Salaam behind. When he grows up, he makes regular visits to his mother who now lives abroad. Once, when Anwar asks him about this, he says, 'Papa I love her as she is' (Pritam 2014: 80).

For Amrita, loving someone 'as she is' is the crux of the matter. This is what her characters aspire to, especially women – to be understood and loved as they are, howsoever they choose to live; to be accepted as they are in all their relationships. A woman is always expected to be an epitome of affection, love and sacrifice. While both men and women need love, home and a family, it is only a woman who is forced to make a choice between these and her own being. A woman should be able to lead an independent life with her own personality and no weakness should chain her. For centuries woman had continued to be sacrificed; enduring all excesses because she was financially dependent on her husband and the shackles of tradition and love imprisoned her. But Amrita's heroines do not accept any such shackle.

The face of the woman in Amrita's works looks towards the future that she envisioned so many years ago, and this can also be recognised in two of her poems. One of them is titled 'Draupadi':

> The same body of five elements
> I am the same Draupadi
> Today I come to play dice...
> The Kauravas won the whole set
> And when the second round began
> Employed wiles and ploys
> I lost society with my right hand
> And politics with my left
> But the Kauravas exhorted
> That five elements equal my five Pandavas
> I got up in the crowded assembly
> And won all five back
> I am Draupadi in all lifetimes!

(Pritam 1990: 88)

This poem is a narration of the journey of a woman through the beautiful metaphor of Draupadi. In earlier birth cycles, Draupadi was an object to be staked in a game of dice, but in this birth she is the doer, the one with agency. Society and power are what the Pandavas lost the game for, and Draupadi loses society and power to win back the Pandavas. In the *Mahabharata*, when Draupadi is about to call a curse upon the Kauravas after the episode of her attempted undressing, Gandhari stops her and tells her to ask for three boons instead, and Draupadi asks for her husbands' slavery to end and for their kingdom to be returned to them. But what is revolutionary in the poem is the act of transformation – of becoming an active agent who plays and wins a game of dice instead of being merely an object staked in the game. The poem suggests that in order to win her Pandavas, her five elements, and her own being, a woman will have to remain aware and vigilant to defeat society and politics.

In several other poems, Amrita has delineated an independent woman; and also a glimpse of the future of not just women, but entire humankind. The poem 'Mera Pata' reveals the address of a place where there is no right or wrong path, where there is no religion nor caste, no boon nor curse and where there is no boundary, wall or shackle.

> Today, I have wiped off the number of my house…
> On the forehead of the street –
> ….
> And wherever you glimpse an independent soul
> Think that is my home
>
> (95).

Amrita revolved around the idea of love all her life – both human and spiritual. She never drew a line to divide love – personal and universal. For her, love was an acceptance of life and she never refused to accept life. The acme of her personal journey of love is her iconic poem, 'Main Tainu Pher Milangi' or 'I Shall Meet You Again'. She had found her soul mate in Imroz; and lived a full four decades of her life with him that were filled with love; and her poem is, in fact, her significant legacy for Imroz. She appears to be freed of many of life's desires but is honour-bound by love. This is not a desire for rebirth; she does not speak of meeting him in a physical form. She talks of becoming one with the universe and meeting Imroz in that universe.

> As a spark of imagination perhaps
> I shall descend on your canvas
> Or perhaps as a mysterious line
> on your canvas
> watch you silently
> Or like the ray of the sun
> mingle with your colours
> …..

159

or like a cascade
bedew your body with droplets of water.

(Pritam 2013: 65–67)

Amrita did not know how long Imroz would live after her. She promises to stay in the colours of his canvas as long as he is alive. But she knows that every life comes to an end, therefore:

When this body dies, so does everything else
But strands of memory
Are specks of the universe
I shall pick those specks
And lace them together
And I shall meet you again.

(Pritam 2013: 65–67)

This is a hope for the future at a personal level as well as for a time when such pure unions would be acknowledged and appreciated. Her legacy as a writer has been published as 'Ibarat ton Pichchon Ik Hor Khat' ('Another Letter after the Writing') in Jasbir Bhullar's edited volume, *Sahan de Hisse di Maulsari*:

I love these dreams, these thoughts. They are dearer to me than my life. That is why I have tied them in a bundle and kept them close to me as I go along on my journey. This bundle carried on my shoulders makes the shoulders tired. A very mysterious thing is that when these shoulders get tired, this bag take on the shape of wings on my shoulders and carries me to soar close to the moon and stars for some time.

I have hung the bundle held in my hands ... and have freed my hand to pen this letter....

I am writing this letter to my heir to whom I have to give this bundle when I go away from this world. My heir shall be a writer of the next generation.... My entire life are some steps that I have taken in the journey of life to make imagination into reality; and today this letter of mine is addressed to one who has to walk beyond the steps I have taken to go further....

(Pritam, Bhullar 2001: 143–144)

References

Pritam, Amrita. 1990. *Chonvien Patre*. Delhi: Sahitya Akademi.
———. 2001. "Ibarat ton Pichchon Ik Hor Khat", in Jasbir Bhullar (ed.), *Sahan de Hisse di Maulsari*, pp. 143–144. Chandigarh: Punjab Sahit Academy.

160

———. 2009 (1975). *Aurat – Ik Drishtikon*. Delhi: Shilalekh Publishers.

———. 2013. *Main Tainu Pher Milangi*. Delhi: Shilalekh Publishers.

———. 2014 (1976). *Ekta, Annie, te Jebkatre*. Delhi: Shri Prakashan.

———. Ed. 2014. *Dastavez*. Delhi: Shilalekh Publishers.

———. 2016 (1968). *Kala Gulab te Hujre di Mitti*. Delhi: Shilalekh Publishers.

———. Ed. 2018. *Amrita di Diary*. Delhi: Shilalekh Publishers.

———. 2019. *Kaagaz te Canvas ton Pahilan*. Delhi: Shilalekh Publishers.

15

WOMEN OUT OF LOVE

Nirupama Dutt

How does one start writing about women out of love? A difficult task indeed! One is so used to the image of women in love. Poets have eulogised it, painters have painted it and storytellers have spun such yarns of pain and passion on the feminine lovelorn *nayika*. It is not very easy to write about women out of love for it breaks so many myths including the much-celebrated myth of womanhood. But one must begin somewhere. For, believe me, a woman falling out of love is no myth; it happens slowly and very painfully but it happens.

What better place could be there to talk of this reality of lost love but through a memory of a conversation held by Amrita Pritam's bedside in the beautiful home she had built with her soul mate, the painter Imroz: K-25 Hauz Khas, New Delhi, that was sold and levelled down by bulldozers a few years after her death.

Amrita, the poet, was considered the high priestess of love, a great romantic if ever there was one; referred thus in her lifetime and even today. This is so because love was a recurring theme in her poetry and prose. In her immortal poem 'Ajj Aakhaan Waris Shah nu' ('To Waris Shah') written on the brutal violence meted out to the women of Punjab: molested, maimed, sold from one hand to another or raped and killed in the name of one religion or the other, she turned to the Sufi poet who had penned the legend of Hir Ranjha which is considered to be the very epitome of tragic love. That the violence was unleashed on women in the land which boasted of love legends aplenty was what especially pained the poet. Summing up the tragic call to Waris Shah to rise from his grave and give words to the agony of thousands of daughters of Punjab, Amrita writes:

The flute that played notes of love is now forever lost
Brothers of Ranjha have lost the hero's devotion, his charm

DOI: 10.4324/9781003214656-24

Blood rains on the earth, even the graves are oozing red
The princesses of love are now weeping midst tombs
Today all have turned into Qaidon, thieves of love and beauty
O where on earth do we go to look for a Waris Shah once more.

(Author's translation)

This everlasting poem by Amrita was the first dirge against the worst kind of horror wrought on the bodies, minds and lives of the daughters of her Punjab as the Radcliff Line cut the land of the five rivers into two on the basis of religion and the largest migration in the world took place.

Re-writing Stories of Women

The trauma was to translate itself in the story of Pooro some three years after Partition in the 1950 novel *Pinjar*, translated as *The Skeleton*, which once again looked at the communal wars fought over the bodies of women. Amrita the storyteller could not but look at women differently. This sequel to the ode to Waris Shah begins in the pre-partition years over a feud between two land-owning families – one Hindu and the other Muslim. Rashida, the son of the Muslim family, is assigned by his clan to abduct the young Pooro of the Hindus who is engaged to be married to a progressive youth, Ramchand. This is done to avenge the abduction of his aunt by Pooro's elders in the past; and Rashida abducts but does not violate her. Pooro escapes her abductor and reaches her parents' home but is not accepted. Pooro's parents deem the daughter dead because family honour considered an abducted daughter defiled and dead. She is forced to return to her abductor who then marries her.

Partition follows with all its ravages, and abducted girls begin to be restored to their families on both sides of the new border. Rashida and Pooro rescue an abducted Hindu girl who is her brother's young wife. Her brother Trilok and her ex-fiancé Ramchand, whom she had once cherished in the lost past, come to recover her and offer Pooro the life she had once dreamt of for herself in adolescent love for Ramchand. It is at this juncture Pooro surprises one and chooses to remain with Rashida whom she has grown to respect. This is a bold assertion of a woman's will in which she would not let bigotry, religion and convention force a decision on her and she exercises her own will.

Harking back to the Partition poem and her novella set in those turbulent times in the backdrop of the great divide, Amrita establishes the strength and determination of the writer in ascertaining a mind of her own, from 'To Waris Shah' in which fractured women wail over graves to Pooro exercising a choice of her own free will with grace.

At K-25 Hauz Khas: The Day Simone Died

With Amrita one shared a precious tie from the 1970s to her passing away in 2005 as a budding Punjabi poet, a journalist, and an admirer. I was among the many she nurtured and her home was nothing short of Mecca for some two generations of the Punjabi writers she published in her journal *Nagmani*, the path-breaking literary magazine in Punjabi that Amrita established with her partner Imroz in 1966. The doors were forever open to us all.

One encounter that I particularly cherish was on 15 May 1986. I recall the date after so long because the newspapers were full of the news of the death of one of the most influential women writers of the world, Simone de Beauvoir. The passing away of the cult French writer-intellectual, existentialist philosopher, feminist and more was deeply felt by those who had read her and followed her life that had broken many norms – rejecting her bourgeois background, pursuing a scholarship, telling anew the story of the 'second sex' and a lifelong companion of the giant existentialist philosopher, Jean Paul Sartre. When a literary icon passes away, a reader has the compelling urge to share that grief because somewhere the words have touched one's soul deeply.

The drawing room was used only for formal visitors; others were welcomed to her room which had chairs but most of us liked to sit on the fluffy rug by her bedside with cushions thrown all around. She already had a guest sitting on the carpet resting her back on a cushion when I arrived – the radical Urdu poet Fahmida Riaz, those days in exile in Delhi for opposing the dictatorial regime of the then Pakistan President, Zia-ul-Haq. It was the passing away of Simone the day before that had brought her to be by the side of our own home-grown radical Amrita.

The conversation over tumblers of tea, generously provided by her partner, Imroz, the artist, slowly veered to the life and writings of the French existentialist. Amrita, a precocious poet, had little formal education, remaining limited to the Punjabi 'Gyani' studies, but she had made up for it not only by reading world literature copiously but translating what appealed to her the most into Punjabi for the readers of *Nagmani* living in the towns and villages of Punjab. The conversation drifted from the courageous life that Simone led to her writings and then to her 1954 novel *The Mandarins* which had won her the Prix Goncourt award for the best and most imaginative prose of the year. Interestingly the protagonists, Robert and Anne Dubreuilh, were considered to be images of Sartre and Simone and their relationship. Theirs was a story that moved at least two generations into re-thinking the roles of women.

So conversation that morning moved from women in love to women out of love – an interesting reversal of *Women in Love*, the title of the

164

controversial English novel by D.H. Lawrence (1885–1930). When women writers took the pen in their hands with a sense of freedom that had once been only the right of men, they grappled with not just how to portray women in love but to look for ways out of unequal, destructive and abusive ties to achieve a state of being 'out of love' for their own sanity, well-being and survival. So we talked about the ecstasy of falling in love and then falling out of love with the person one cherished the most. Fahmida recounted that *The Mandarins* had cured her of an uneasy romance in college for she could not bear to see the pitiable state of Simone's Anne. I too confessed that although the novel did not cure me at once, it did make me feel ashamed of not being able to get out of an offensive relationship. Amrita stood for the concept of *ardha-narishvara*, a composite form of the Hindu deities Shiva and his consort Parvati to represent the male and female together. It was Amrita's interpretation of the myth that startled me, a small-town girl. She said that unison was essential yet Parvati exercised the right to her individuality by dalliance away from Shiva but returning to him each time. Amrita the woman and writer was never a votary of martyrdom in the name of man-woman love.

Love, Loss and Thereafter ...

Love and longing are a recurring theme in Amrita's fiction yet her heroines drawn from life do not choose destruction like Simone's Anne Dubreuilh in *The Mandarins*. True, set in the romantic mould, her heroines love too much yet they do take hold of themselves when the tipping point comes and decide not to cling to a tie that is bereft of love. Her women walk out with poise, no matter how painful it is, to face life and build something more enduring. In the journey, they recover their own self-esteem and even the joy of having found within themselves the strength they had yearned for.

Amrita travelled a long distance in her journey of women's freedom and search for love even in the worst of times. It is this courage which helped her to walk out of her own loveless marriage thrust upon her when she was but a girl and a budding poet in her teens. A woman's search for love is to be found in a confessional and courageous poem of her own marriage where she is all set to kill the searching virgin within and permit the fulfilled woman to live on. But when she glances at herself in the mirror the morning after the first night on the bridal bed, she finds to her shock that she has killed the married woman and it is the virgin who survives. This was the beginning of insisting on the feminine impulse and the assertion of a woman's heart to exert her fundamental right for love.

Penning the New Indian Woman

The novellas of the mid-1950s and 1960s, which Amrita wrote as part of her journey as a poet, supported her with an income of her own. Interestingly, her novels fetched her Rupees one thousand each from the publisher Hind Pocket Book. They were first published in Hindi and Urdu and later in Punjabi because remuneration in her language was negligible. There are several novels which dwell on a woman's journey from love and loss to fulfilment of her own and a blossoming of her identity beyond the world of love and longing. Many were based on real-life stories which her readers had shared with her. Amrita had a huge following of readers; of course, with women outnumbering the men. In the midst of many movements that coloured Indian literature across languages in the 20th century, starting with the spiritual and the devotional, the romanticism of her early endeavours, from the pre-Independence Progressive Writers' Movement, the experimental endeavour, the fiery revolutionary writing of the Left-of-the-road politics, the anthems of the women's movements, Amrita evolved her own individual oeuvre that had love at its core but not without freedom and dignity. Perhaps rightly slotted in the Progressive movement by critics whose business it is to slot writers under a given tag for literary analysis, she stood for change, for freedom, for dignity in a liberal and borderless approach.

Women's lives continued to interest her, as did the changes for the better that she saw emerging in them. The prima donna of Punjabi letters, who stood at par with writers of other developed Indian languages, being the first woman to win the national Sahitya Akademi Award, she never fought shy of speaking to, or even formally interviewing, whoever stood for change. In her prose, she recorded innumerable histories of women in fiction and non-fiction. The freshness and empathy of Amrita's own writings often drew women to her who wanted to share their own stories; and the author obliged by retelling them with poetic fluidity and grace.

Witness to the struggle for independence, an admirer of the radical poetry of the Urdu poet, Sahir Ludhianvi, and then fleeing home and hearth as a refugee to Delhi, the capital city of independent India, the woman with the pen in hand was quick to record the changes she witnessed. She saw women thrown into the workforce and girls going in for higher education because the new circumstances demanded it. With this she saw their gradual empowerment and the ability to make a choice and thus was born the new fictional heroine. The two novellas that one looks at as prototypes of her stories about women choosing dignity above dependence are *A Melody Called Annie* and *Ekta*. The names of the protagonists for the titles and their journeys are told in poetic prose that was a hallmark of Amrita's narratives.

Annie: From Frailty to Strength

Interestingly, the story of the pretty, dainty and supposedly frail Annie is told by her partner who is the fractured personality after the presumed fragile girl he abandons does not crumble to dust; instead, she rises to make a modest but independent life of her own without the man she loved and regarded as her saviour. He loved to call her lovely and foolish; in short a beautiful fool when she was dependent on him and lamented after she left him:

> A beautiful girl is like a melody. Others may have known her by some other name but to me she was just melody. What are you asking? Who was she to me? How can a melody be anything to anyone? Believe me I am not trying to evade your query. Well, a melody first enters the ears sans permission and travels through his veins to his entire being.[1]

Such was the story of the girl called Annie and the boy called Anwar who glanced into her luminous dark eyes and felt that he had reached the shore of the vast sea of life; the shore was always so alluring to Anwar: the shore was a wife, the canopy a home and the sea shell a child. Anwar had all of this – Annie, his wife, a three-bedroom flat at Worli in Bombay, and a seven-year-old son named Salaam. But Anwar, after diving in the deep sea of life, was filled with a sense of adventure. Even though, or perhaps because now he had found his shore, he no longer wanted to go near it. Anwar occupied his private secretary Liz's bed. The blue of her eyes spilled over to the curtains of her room, making Anwar feel that he was riding up and down the waves of a blue sea. His senses were filled with the enticing freedom of a vast expanse of water. With Liz in his bed, Anwar did not feel that he was with a woman. When her slim and fair arms and the firm mounds of her breasts touched his body, it was as though the silk of soft sea-fish were touching him.

Annie had run away from home in the dark of the night to marry Anwar, and he was all she had; she had defied her parents for she had loved him no end. Often Anwar would laughingly take Annie in his arms and say, 'I have never been able to understand how you were able to walk out of your parents' home. What if I had not been a good man and had left you in a matter of days?'

Over the years he started playing yet another game with her once again when she was in his arms. 'What if I had left you Annie?' Annie would curl up in his arms defenceless like a frightened little kitten and purr, 'Then I would have died.'

But after he was enraptured by the silky body of the lissome Liz, the wish of leaving Annie was no longer a threat but his desire. Perhaps to forget the shame, he once again asked Annie, 'What would become of you if I left you?' He was waiting for Annie to curl up in his arms like a frightened little kitten and purr, 'I would die!' Annie's reply, however, startled him, 'Whatever may happen but I will not die!' Shocked he continued, 'What if I was to divorce you?' The once demure girl, who had left her parents' home in the dark of the night to be with the one she loved answered, 'In the given circumstances that would be the right thing to do.'

Thus ended Annie's journey from being deeply in love to being 'out of love'. Without a word, she was left alone in the dark of the night. Although smitten by Liz, Anwar still tried to know what happened to the purring little cat who would curl up in his arms. What he heard was that she had bought a flat and sat all evening in a club. The truth however came from his own cousin Sultana, a friend of Annie, who revealed that the flat was bought with the money Annie's grandmother gave her after selling her house in Indore. She did sit in the club in the evenings because she was holding an exhibition of painted shawls and dresses and she had turned one room of her flat into 'Annie's Boutique'.

This is when Anwar's decline began. Shocked and ailing he summoned her once more. She came to see him, not as a wife would come to see a husband but as one person would come to see another. Anwar still looked for the shades of the old clinging Annie but could not find them. He asked her to come back and live with him as his wife. To this, her reply was,

> Anwar I can live with you but as a woman who is complete in herself. You may or may not give her the name of a wife. In our country the woman who goes by the name of a wife is never a complete woman.

But Anwar did not want a complete woman, for his ideal was a melody whom he could toy with; to sing it and then silence it.

Ekta: In Search of an Identity

One meets the beautiful Ekta, known for her Eskimo smile in her youth, at the Ratlam Junction railway station, forlorn and pondering as she waited to change trains to reach her parental home in the cantonment town of Mhow. Amrita describes her as 'feeling less of a woman and more of a road; a road that is always at a standstill yet comes from somewhere and reaches somewhere too.'² She then takes the metaphor from her own poem of the bridal bed to describe the plight of Ekta:

> There was a part of Ekta that was left virgin forever and there was the other part that was forever married. She had no idea why one part of her being was virgin and the other married. But she knew it was so and had known it for the past several years but now standing at the Ratlam Station she felt this more keenly.

She reached home in this state without giving any intimation of her arrival, and although her brother and his wife asked no questions, Ekta felt they were expecting her to offer some explanation. Maybe her husband Raghu had written to them and she wondered what he had said. If she were to have penned the letter she would have just said, 'The duration of the marriage of Ekta and Raghu was just ten years. That passed and now both of them are free.'

So Ekta starts exploring her freedom gently and slowly with girl friends of her college days. Like Ekta, the gentle Priya too had loved a young man but did not have the courage to go against her parents' will. Ekta turned her dreams into reality and lived them out. Priya suppressed her desires and in a way lived through Ekta. Surprised at this walking away after ten years of being married to the man of her dreams, she asks, 'Eki, you had struggled and suffered so much to marry Raghu.'

'I struggled and suffered just as much to break the marriage. In fact I suffered more and for a longer time. It took two years to get him but ten to get away from him,' Ekta replied. Then the layers of the decade of being lucky enough to be married to the man she loved start unfolding. Raghu was a happy man but the happiness was at the cost of Ekta. He would fall in love with a new woman every year and she would dismiss it as a passing fancy till she decided that she was no longer willing to bear the cost of his happiness. He had been in a hurry to marry her but soon after he said 'I had to marry you.' The child she had wanted was denied to her because he did not like children. Thus looking before and after the ten years of her marriage, Ekta finds that she can live on her own. Identifying with Ekta, Amrita takes her to Bulgaria for a business trip given as a gift to her. In the stopover at the Moscow airport gazing at the sea on one side and mountains the other, and the far-away woods, make her realise that there are joys greater than just struggling to be fulfilled by an unwilling man. She writes to her brother, 'I will not stay here forever but the world is wide and will give me another such space where I will be able to find a fragment of my own identity.'

Thus did Amrita conceive the idea of love – love not only for a significant other but for the beauty of one's whole, healed self.

Notes

1 From the unpublished translation by the author of the novella by Amrita, *A Melody Called Annie*. All subsequent quotes are from this work.
2 From the unpublished translation by the author of the novella by Amrita, *Ekta*. All subsequent quotes are from this work.

Figure 15 Nagmani 1st issue – Front Cover

ਨਾਗਮਣੀ—ਮਈ, ੧੯੬੬
ਸੰਪਾਦਕ : ਅੰਮ੍ਰਿਤਾ ਪ੍ਰੀਤਮ
ਚਿਤ੍ਰਕਾਰ : ਇੰਦਰਜੀਤ
ਪ੍ਰਕਾਸ਼ਕ : ਕਲਮ ਪ੍ਰਕਾਸ਼ਨ
ਬੇ-੨੫, ਰੇਡ ਖਾਸ, ਨਵੀਂ ਦਿੱਲੀ-੧੬
ਛਾਪਕ : ਸਿੰਘਾਸਨ ਪ੍ਰਿੰਟਿੰਗ ਪ੍ਰੈਸ
੬੬, ਆਜ਼ਾਦ ਮਾਰਕੀਟ, ਦਿੱਲੀ-੬
ਇਕ ਅੰਕ : ਇੱਕ ਰੁਪਿਆ
ਸਾਲਾ ਅੰਕ : ਦਸ ਰੁਪਏ

ਇਹ ਨਾਗਮਣੀ

ਕਰਮਾਤ ਉਹ ਘਟਨਾ ਹੁੰਦੀ ਹੈ ਜੋ ਅਸਲੀਅਤ ਤੋਂ ਇੱਕ ਇੰਚ ਪਰ੍ਹਾਂ ਵਾਪਰਦੀ ਹੈ। ਤੇ ਕਲਪਨਾ ਉਹ ਚੀਜ਼ ਹੁੰਦੀ ਹੈ ਜੋ ਅਸਲੀਅਤ ਤੋਂ ਇੱਕ ਇੰਚ ਅਗਾਂਹ ਹੁੰਦੀ ਹੈ। ਇਹ ਦੋ ਇੰਚਾਂ ਦਾ ਪੈਂਡਾ ਹਰ ਇਨਸਾਨ ਦੀ ਉਮਰ ਤੋਂ ਲੰਬਾ ਹੁੰਦਾ ਹੈ, ਕਿਉਂਕਿ ਹਰ ਅਸਲੀਅਤ ਜਦੋਂ ਵਾਪਰਦੇ ਮੁੜਦੀ ਕਲਪਨਾ ਵਾਲੀ ਥਾਂ ਉੱਤੇ ਪਹੁੰਚਦੀ ਹੈ ਤਾਂ ਕਲਪਨਾ ਉਸ ਤੋਂ ਇੱਕ ਇੰਚ ਹੋਰ ਅਗਾਂਹ ਨੂੰ ਜਾਂਦੀ ਹੈ, ਤੇ ਇਸੇ ਤਰ੍ਹਾਂ ਕਰਮਾਤ ਜਦੋਂ ਪੱਬਾਂ ਭਾਰ ਹੋ ਕੇ ਕਰਮਾਤ ਵਾਲੀ ਥਾਂ ਉੱਤੇ ਪਹੁੰਚਦੀ ਹੈ ਤਾਂ ਕਰਮਾਤ ਉਸ ਤੋਂ ਇੱਕ ਇੰਚ ਹੋਰ ਅਗਾਂਹ ਨੂੰ ਜਾਂਦੀ ਹੈ।—ਮਨੁੱਖ ਦੀ ਬੁਕ ਚੁੰਭੀ ਰਵਾਇਤੀ ਤੇ ਬਣਦੇ ਵਾਲੀ ਰਵਾਇਤੀ ਇਨ੍ਹਾਂ ਦੋ ਇੰਚਾਂ ਦਾ ਉਹ ਪੈਂਡਾ ਹੈ ਜਿਹੜਾ ਇੱਕ ਵੇਲੇ ਕੋਰਾ ਰਹਿਆ ਪੈਂਡਾ ਵੀ ਹੈ ਤੇ ਅਣਕੋਰਾ ਵੀ। ਪ੍ਰਾਪਤੀ ਵੀ ਹੈ ਤੇ ਆਪ੍ਰਾਪਤੀ ਵੀ। ਇਹਦੇ ਵਿੱਚ ਕੋਰੇ ਪੈਂਡੇ ਦਾ ਰੰਜ ਵੀ ਹੁੰਦਾ ਹੈ ਤੇ ਅਣਕੋਰੇ ਪੈਂਡੇ ਦੀ ਪੀੜ ਵੀ। ਇਹ ਦੋਵੇਂ ਰੁਜ਼ੀਆਂ ਵਿੱਚ ਦੂਜੇ ਲੋਕਾਂ ਮੁਖਾਭੜ ਹਨ ਇਸ ਲਈ ਇੱਕ ਦੂਜੇ ਦੀ ਭਾਂਖ ਹਨ। ਇਹੋ ਭਾਂਖ ਮਨੁੱਖ ਦੀ ਤਾਕਤ ਹੈ, ਇਹੋ ਤਾਕਤ ਉਸਦੀ ਹਰ ਰਚਨਾ ਦਾ ਭੇਤ, ਤੇ ਇਹੋ ਭੇਤ ਮਨੁੱਖ ਦਾ ਵਿਕਾਸ ਹੈ।

ਇਹ ਨਾਗਮਣੀ ਉਸ ਵਿਕਾਸ ਦਾ ਚਿੰਨ੍ਹ ਹੈ, ਉਸ ਭੇਤ ਦਾ, ਉਸ ਤਾਕਤ ਦਾ, ਤੇ ਉਸ ਭਾਂਖ ਦਾ, ਜਿਹੜਾ ਸਦਕਾ ਲੇਖਕ ਨਿੱਤ ਨਵੀਂ ਰਚਨਾ ਕਰਦਾ ਹੈ ਤੇ ਪਾਠਕ ਨਿੱਤ ਨਵੀਂ ਮੰਗ ਕਰਦਾ ਹੈ। ਚੰਗੇ ਲੇਖਕ ਰਚਨਾ ਦਾ ਮਿਆਰ ਉੱਚਾ ਕਰਦੇ ਹਨ, ਚੰਗੇ ਪਾਠਕ ਮੰਗ ਦਾ ਮਿਆਰ ਉੱਚਾ ਕਰਦੇ ਹਨ, ਤੇ ਇਸ ਤਰ੍ਹਾਂ ਇਹ ਦੋਵੇਂ ਹਮ-ਸਫਰ ਹੁੰਦੇ ਹਨ।

ਇਸ ਨਾਗਮਣੀ ਨੂੰ ਉਨ੍ਹਾਂ ਹਮ-ਸਫਰ ਲੇਖਕਾਂ ਤੇ ਪਾਠਕਾਂ ਦੀ ਲੋੜ ਨੇ ਹੋਂਦ ਵਿੱਚ ਆਂਦਾ ਹੈ, ਜੋ ਕੋਰੇ ਪੈਂਡੇ ਦੇ ਰੰਜ ਨਾਲ ਰੰਜਦੇ ਨਹੀਂ, ਅਣਕੋਰੇ ਪੈਂਡੇ ਨੂੰ ਭਾਲਦੇ ਹਨ ਤੇ ਉਸ ਦੀ ਪੀੜ ਨੂੰ ਆਖਣ-ਸੁਨਣ ਲਈ ਕੋਈ ਮਾਧਿਅਮ ਮੰਗਦੇ ਹਨ। ਇਹ ਨਾਗਮਣੀ ਵਿੱਚ ਮਾਧਿਅਮ ਹੈ—ਪਹਿਲੀ ਪੀੜ ਨੂੰ ਆਖਣ-ਸੁਨਣ ਲਈ, ਫੇਰ ਪ੍ਰਾਪਤੀਆਂ ਦੇ ਜੋਰ ਨਾਲ ਉਸ ਨੂੰ ਕੋਰੇ ਬਨਾਣ ਲਈ, ਤੇ ਫੇਰ ਨਵੀਂ ਪੀੜ ਨੂੰ ਆਖਣ-ਸੁਨਣ ਲਈ।

ਅੰਮ੍ਰਿਤਾ ਪ੍ਰੀਤਮ

Figure 16 Nagmani 1st issue – Back Cover

Imroz's drawing

Nagmani – May, 1966
Editor: Amrita Pritam
Illustrator: Inderjeet
Publisher: Kalam Prakashan
K-25, Hauz Khas, New Delhi-19
Printer: Singhson Printing Press
89, Azad Market, Delhi-6
One issue: One Rupee
The rest of the issues: Ten Rupees

This *Nagmani*

A miracle is an event that occurs one inch away from reality.
And imagination is something that is one inch beyond reality.
This distance of two inches is longer than the life of every human
being because when every reality arrives at the point of
imagination, yearning and struggling, imagination edges forward by
another inch; and in the same way when imagination traverses the
distance to reach a miracle, then miracle moves one inch forward. –
The past that is history and the future that will become history is
the distance of those two inches that is simultaneously the distance
traversed as well as not traversed. It is an achievement as well as
a loss. It embraces both the relief for the distance travelled and
the pain of the distance not travelled. Both these concerns are
opposite to each other and that is the reason they are each other's
yearning. This very yearning is the strength of a human being, this
strength is the mystery behind each of one's creation, and in this
very mystery lies human progress.

This *Nagmani* is the symbol of that progress, of that mystery, of
that strength, and of that yearning, for the sake of which a writer
creates something new every day and the reader makes a new demand
every day. Good writers elevate the quality of the creation, good
readers raise the standard of the demand, and in this way both
become fellow travellers.

This *Nagmani* has been born of this need of such writer and reader
fellow travellers who are not content with the distance travelled
but yearn to cover the distance yet to be crossed and seek some
medium to express and listen to this pain. This *Nagmani* is a medium
– first to articulate and listen to this pain, then to transform it
into contentment on the strength of its achievements, and then to
express and hear fresh pain.

Amrita Pritam

Figure 17 Transcript of the first editorial

16

LABOUR OF LOVE

Amrita-Imroz and *Nagmani*

Amia Kunwar
translated by Hartej Kaur Bal

It has been sixteen years since Amrita Pritam left this world and nineteen and a half years since her literary offspring, *Nagmani*, has seen the light of day. But even today the thought and image of both remain fresh in the memories of readers, fans and critics. *Nagmani* is a unique magazine and could only have been created by an extraordinary personality like Amrita; and both are transformed into living myths. Amrita first held the reed pen in her hand at a tender age while still under the umbra of tradition and religion, courtesy her father. Her adolescent writings are somewhat immature – religious, traditional and romantic. As she matured as a writer, she retracted her claim from more than half of her compositions. In a column titled, 'Meri Pehli Kitab' ('My First Book') in the Punjabi journal, *Samdarshi* (April–June 1987) published by Punjabi Academy, Delhi, she writes that her first anthology, *Thandian Kirnan* (*Cool Rays*) published in 1935 (she was all of 16 then), was merely a collection of childish rhymes that should not have been published. Further, she considers her first five anthologies a result of an immature craving to be published. But over the years, her experiences – good and bad – in life so nurtured her intellect that a certain steeliness filled her writings and her personality. When Amrita decided to start *Nagmani* in May 1966 she was nearly 48 years old. She maintained the journal's high stature consistently in consonance with her thoughts, choices and principles. Not only was *Nagmani* widely liked and accepted in the literary circles with the very first issue, for a writer to be published in it became equivalent to being certified as a fine writer. Mukhtiar Singh says that the role of *Nagmani* and Amrita can never be overlooked if one considers the growth of literature around the years 1976–1977. Short story writers Prem Gorkhi and K.L. Garg felt that they wouldn't have been such good writers had they not got the support of Amrita and *Nagmani*; as do Baldev Singh Sadaknama, Kirpal Kazak, Satti Randhawa, Vishal, Amia Kunwar and many others.

While editing *Nagmani*, Amrita established many new traditions. The paper used for the magazine was ordinary and of a rough texture, leading

 DOI: 10.4324/9781003214656-25

someone to quip about its low-grade quality that no shopkeeper could ever fashion into paper bags! Imroz responded by saying that it was a unique magazine whose pages could never be used to make paper bags. The title page and the colour of the back page kept changing from time to time – brown, yellow-ochre, grey, yellow, blue, peach and khaki. But its inherently simple look became its distinctive quality. Literary content was crammed into all its 28 pages (later expanded to forty), fulfilling a reader's literary cravings. The vocabulary was concise, sans superfluous embellishment. Not an inch of paper was wasted. Even the title and the back page carried literary pieces.

In the issues from May 1966 to December 1978, Amrita's name was written as editor with Imroz's name below it as the illustrator. But from January 1979 onwards the nomenclature changed; and on the title page of *Nagmani* came to be written – 'Workers: Amrita-Imroz' – till March 2002. In the last issue of April 2002, even the names Amrita and Imroz were dropped and only 'Workers Say Goodbye' was printed on the title page. This deliberate omission of a specific expected status of power indicated a certain humility and symbolised a renunciation of ego. Both Amrita and Imroz considered themselves as volunteers for the entire duration of 36 years of the journal's publication – from May 1966 to April 2002. Amrita selected the writings herself on the basis of their literary merit without considering the name or fame of writers. Initially, for almost 25 years, Amrita and Imroz would traverse the narrow by-lanes of the Old Sabzi Mandi (Azadpur) area in Delhi, sit on a stool in Sardar Balwant Singh's printing press and proof-read the manuscript. Offset printing machines had not yet arrived. It was the age of the letterpress printing. At times, the entire magazine would be proof-read and ready for printing, and suddenly a fresh submission would so touch their hearts that they would find it impossible to ignore it. Rather than wait to publish it in the next issue, they would resolve to publish it in the issue about to go to press. The aim was that the 'readers must get to read it *now*'. So, they would get into their car, drive to the printing press, have the press opened even late at night, remove the wooden printing plates of some odd text ready for printing, postpone it to the next issue, replace it with the text in hand and issue a command to have the proofs prepared. Kirpal Kazak relates an anecdote with great relish. Once when he was going to Delhi and was to meet Amrita, Prem Gorkhi sent one of his short stories with him to be printed in *Nagmani*. Kazak ji carried one of his own short stories as well. When he met Amrita, he said, 'Didi! I have written this with great effort. I hope you like it. Gorkhi's story is also there. If you think it worthy of publication, please do print it.' He sat chatting with Amrita and Imroz late into the night. Next morning when he was about to leave, he told Amrita, 'Please write a letter to Gorkhi ji to tell him whether his story will be printed or not.' Amrita laughingly turned to Imroz and said, 'Imu tell him.' Imroz then said, 'Dear Kazak, after you had gone to bed, Amrita read both the stories. She liked Gorkhi's story so much that she made me start the car right then; we went across the Yamuna to "Lok Printers" (*Nagmani* was printed there by then) and made the owner take out the wooden printing plate of one of her long essays and print Gorkhi's story instead. I did suggest that it could be printed next month but she said, "No, I can't deprive the readers of *Nagmani* of such a beautiful story for a whole month".' In another instance, he narrates that once when he submitted an article for the column, "Dus Kadam" ("Ten Steps"), an hour later he got a phone call from her saying, 'You've worked wonders. The article is long. I am replacing two compositions to accommodate it.'

Imroz would make sketches based on the compositions and also draw sketches of the writers. Either Imroz or Amrita would respond to the letters written by the readers. Their answers would be both crisp and relevant. After the magazine was printed, Amrita and Imroz would stick the requisite stamps on them, write the addresses of the members who had paid the subscription fee and themselves go to the post office to mail the issues. Thus, they truly justified their role as 'workers'. There was no room for the ego of a 'publisher'. Whenever they received a composition, they would read it quickly to make up their minds about whether to include it or not, then write a couple of lines on a postcard in their own hand and send it to the writer. Till today, writers like Jasbir Bhullar, Kirpal Kazak, Amarjit Kaonke, Vishal, Paul Kaur, Prem Gorkhi, Mukhtiar Singh and many others have preserved these handwritten postcards. If any one of their favourite authors remained absent from *Nagmani* for a long time, they would feel forlorn and contact them and urge them to send a fresh contribution at the earliest. For example, Kirpal Kazak received such a reminder when he could not send a contribution for a long time, 'Dear Kazak, what's the reason for being absent for so long? We and *Nagmani* are eagerly waiting for you and your story ....'

All that mattered was publishing high-quality compositions in *Nagmani*. It was immaterial if the writer was a friend or a critic. One story is quite well-known in literary circles. A pamphlet *Naag Nivaas* began to be published under the supervision of a publishing board composed of Ajmer Aulakh and a few other writers. Amrita was referred to in degrading language in some of the issues. Soon the pamphlet stopped. Subsequently, Aulakh thought of sending one of his stories to *Nagmani* and sent it under a pen name 'Aulakh Farmahi' and it got printed. Kirpal Kazak, Prem Gorkhi and a few other writers expressed their displeasure and objected to Amrita publishing it, even though it was under a pseudonym. The letter that Amrita wrote to Kazak as her reply was exemplary of the grace she exhibited as a publisher. She said, 'Dear Kazak, what you have reported to me was not in my knowledge. But even if I had known, it wouldn't have mattered because I don't know the Aulakh of *Naag Nivaas*, I only know Aulakh Farmahi, who is *Nagmani*'s and my favourite writer.

To be published in *Nagmani*, especially for budding writers, was a matter of great honour. They would carry around the issue in which their piece of composition was published like a medal. This phenomenon though also had a 'negative-development' effect. Writers left on the periphery for some reason or the other started accusing *Nagmani* of being an obscene and regressive magazine. Usually, the real reason for this was not having any means, excuse or chance to meet the charismatic Amrita. For example, a group of writers from Barnala, deeming themselves to be self-appointed guardians of social values, led a procession against Amrita and burned some copies of *Nagmani* at a road intersection in the city.

The attempt of Amrita and Imroz was always to present something fresh to the readers. The magazine had a column which was solely in the hands of a particular writer, wherein the writer expressed his thoughts and experiences. For instance, in the column 'Jung Jaari Hai' ('The Fight Goes On'), Amrita discussed characters from her novels in detail – Kamini and Nasir from *Dilli di Gallian*, Alka and Kumar from *Chakk No. 36* and other popular characters from her novels. Prem Gorkhi, honoured with the award of 'Outstanding Writer' twice, introduced his characters through 'Gairhaazar Aadmi' ('The Absent Man') and 'Jagde Sirran Vaale' ('Ones with Illumined Heads'). Gagan Gill shared several fine experiences in 'Sir Dhar Talli Gali Mori Aao' ('Come to My Lane with Your Head on Your Palm'). Devinder Kaur in 'Panjvan Chirag' ('Fifth Lamp') selected a particular poem for discussion. 'Kaale Tilliar' ('Black Sand-grouses') consisted of memorable letters of writers like Chandan Negi, Kirpal Kazak, Surinder Sharma, Paul Kaur, Dalbir Chetan, Shiv Batalvi, Dalip Kaur Tiwana and others. Similarly, when Amrita asked writers to write about 'Punj Baariyan' ('Five Windows') – windows into their inner consciousness – writers like Amia Kunwar, Gurdev Chauhan, Blaga Dimitrova, Dev, Swaranjit Savi, Jaswant Deed, Navtej Bharti and Ajmer Rode presented a peep into their inner selves. Even when she sought honest expression on forbidden subjects in 'Kaaliyaan Baagaan di Mehndi' (Henna from the Black Gardens), several writers wrote for it. In the column 'Satt Savaal' ('Seven Questions') writers like Khushwant Singh, Masood Munavar, Usha Puri, Harbhajan Singh, Raj Gill, Manjit Tiwana, Imroz, Dr. Lallan Prasad, etc. were asked seven questions about their life and creative bent of mind. Through the column 'Taare Bolde Hun' ('Stars Speak'), Urmil Sharma talked about astrology, palmistry and the changing planetary positions. In 'Mera Kamra' ('My Room'), Gul Chohan, Gurcharan Rampuri, Chandan Negi among others talked about the room they desired. Writers in 'Pichchle Boohe' ('Back Doors') declared secrets hidden in their minds rarely expressed; Kirpal Kazak, Ganga Prasad Vimal, Nirupama Dutt, Raj Gill, Pal Kaur, Rashim, etc. dared to give a peep through these back doors. 'Aakh Damodar Akheen Diththa' ('Describes Damodar the Witnessed Scene') directed writers to describe any first-hand experience, which writers like Jasbir Bhullar, Gulzar, Raj Gill, Kailash Puri, Prem Gorkhi, Kirpal Kazak, Dalbir Chetan,

Bhushan, Sara Shagufta, Amar Bharti, Prabhakar Machawe and some others did. In 'Chetarnama' ('Document of Love'), writers like Kirpal Kazak, Ajeet Cour, Devinder, Nirupama Dutt, Padma Sachdev, Chandan Negi and Amrita Pritam touched upon something close to their heart. In 'Prashan Kundli' ('Questionnaire Horoscope'), one question was posed to each writer as per planetary positions keeping their temperament and passions in mind (June 1997); and among the ones to answer were Prem Gorkhi, Kartar Singh Duggal, Amia Kunwar, Minder, Manjit Tiwana, Pal Kaur, Mohanjit, Bachint Kaur, Devinder, Ram Sarup Ankhi, Satti Randhawa, Baldev Singh, Amrita Pritam and Shanti Dev. In 1997, Amrita started a wonderful column 'Dus Kadam' ('Ten Steps'), in which she gave the story of the Hungarian poet, Bela Vihar, who had lost his way during the war and decided to walk ten steps for each of his family members – his mother, his wife, his beloved, his grandmother and his children – to ease the tedium of the long path. She asked writers to pen the names of people they would remember while taking the ten steps if they ever went through a similar experience. She published the 'ten steps' of Mahima Singh, Paul Kaur, Amar Bharti, S. Soch, Amia Kunwar, Madhu Sudan Sharma and others. There were other much discussed columns like 'Niazbo' ('Fragrant Basil'), 'Viaahnama' ('Document of Marriage'), 'Chautha Kamra' ('Fourth Room'), 'Navian Kitaabaan di Gull' ('Talk of New Books'), 'Sadaknama' ('Travelogue') (Baldev Singh), 'Meri Pehli Udasi' ('My First Pilgrimage'), etc. Some others were 'Zikre Yaar' ('Mention of a Friend'), 'Oh Ghadi Oh Ghatna' ('That Moment That Happening'), 'Shuk Suraahi' ('Pitcher of Suspicion'), 'Akkhar Bolde Hun' ('Words Speak'), 'Ik Khat Tere Naam' ('A Letter Addressed To You'), 'Pehla Chetar' ('First Love') 'Kandhaan De Kan-Kandhaan De Bul' ('The Ears Of Walls-The Lips of Walls'), 'Mein te Mein' ('I and I'), 'Dekh Kabira Roya' ('Seeing, Kabira Wept'), 'Dekh Kabira Haseya' ('Seeing, Kabira Laughed'), 'Sunno Ve Vehde Vaaliyo' ('Listen O My Neighbours'), 'Ik Savaal' ('One Question'), etc. Some like 'Dhooni di Agg Sekde Sain Lok' ('Holy People Warming Themselves on Bonfires') by Imroz, 'Barkate' (Blessings) by Amrita and 'Dindi Shah' by Devinder posed questions on burning social issues.

But the column that was different from all of these and can be placed above all these was 'Vaseeyatnama' ('Will') published in the July 1984 issue. Rather than mention any property or land, it was a will written about the dreams and thoughts of a writer. The wills of Babar, Nikosh Kazan Zakish, four friends from Pakistan – Masud Munnawar, Dr. Suhaib Ahmad Khan, Iftikhar Zaidi, Sabbir Shahid – along with poet Mohan Singh, Moon Meem Rashid, Kamala Das and Shiv Kumar were recorded. A part of Amrita Pritam's 'Will' reads:

> I desire ... now whenever it's time to say goodbye I can do so easily. I just want that those who were in no way connected to me while I was alive, should not be connected to me when I am dead....

There was no Punjabi newspaper or magazine that I could open without wondering who had spouted venom against me. (Some that were discovered by Imroz before me, he would tear away, hiding them from me) And after my death the 'obituaries' in those very newspapers would be a big fat lie.... Imroz had always saved me from such lies whilst I was alive. I can only appeal to him, that he must not let any lie get near my dead body....

The hands of Imroz and my children are enough for my mortal remains. Not just enough, they are a blessing. [With time, Amia Kunwar and Asma Salim also got this privilege]....

I desire Imroz to place my pen next to my body! ... the pen that remained with me throughout my long journey, I desire – it to remain with me till my flesh turns to dust.

(Pritam 1984)

Usually, publishers of magazines keep themselves insulated and aloof from all responsibility for any controversies arising out of any printed article; deeming the content to be the sole responsibility of the author. But Amrita ji took full responsibility for everything printed in it, saying, 'We print articles after giving them a thorough reading. We agree with the contents, only then do we provide them space in our magazine.' In this context, her views recorded in the column 'Hey Just Listen' in the January 1986 issue of *Nagmani* can be quoted:

The purpose of an epigraph is to broadcast the dictum of a king or preach the words of a great scholar by carving them on a rock, so that they can brace the storms of time. Comrades! The style of presenting 'Modern Epigraphs' is very endearing but the comment by the editor – 'the editor may not agree with the text published in it' – is like tainting the meaning of an epigraph with your own hands. If the meaning of an epigraph has to be sustained, we must steer clear of such comments filled with apprehension.

(Pritam 1986: 24)

Another distinctive thing about *Nagmani* was that she decided to give space neither to advertisements nor to any book review. But she would do any-thing for those she cared about. She broke her rule in the February 2001 issue by printing an extensive academic review of my anthology of poems written by Dr Beant Kaur, titled 'Amia Kunwar's Poetic Collection *Chhinna dee Gaatha* – A Feminist Perspective'. She was supposed to have written the foreword for my first poetic collection, but due to ill health had been able to write only four lines for the back cover; and asked Dr Mohanjit to write the foreword instead. Having borrowed the review to read, she pub-lished it in the very next issue of *Nagmani*. She thought this special effort to publish a review to be her duty towards her friends, writers and readers of *Nagmani*. She not only established many new writers through *Nagmani*, she also gave them new pen names which became their definite and lasting identity. Turning Satish Kumar Kapil into Satti Kumar, Rattan Kaur into Ratneev, Satwant Kaur into Satti Randhawa, Inderjit into Imroz, Kirpal Singh Aawara into Kirpal Kazak, Prem Niaana into Prem Gorkhi and Amarjit Kaur into Amia Kunwar, she published their writings in *Nagmani* and secured a special place for them in Punjabi literature for all times to come.

While working for *Nagmani* she also edited another journal for five years – *Samdarshi*, a quarterly magazine published by the Punjabi Academy, Delhi from 1986 to 1991. Prominent writers like Dr Harbhajan Singh, Mahinder Singh Joshi and Kartar Singh Duggal were on the editorial board of this magazine. The influence of *Nagmani* on this magazine was so obvious that readers started calling *Samdarshi* a deluxe version of *Nagmani*. Even in this magazine, Amrita chose to publish new poets, new writers and new artists under the columns titled 'Saadde Navein Shaayar' ('Our Budding Poets') and 'Saadde Navein Kalakar' ('Our New Artists'). She started many new columns, 'Aapne Sanmukh' ('Facing Oneself'), 'Dastavez' ('Documents'), 'Mehmaan Rachna' ('Guest Composition'), 'Sajjan Mainde Raangale' ('My Romantic Beloved'), 'Gull Dariyaon Paar Di' ('Talk of the World Across the River'), 'Ik Baithak' ('A Meeting'), 'Satt Kavitaanvaan' ('Seven Poems'), etc. She gave a different title to her editorial as well – 'Apne Khilaaf' ('Against Oneself'). But as it was a government publication, it did not fit in well with Amrita's sense of autonomy. Amrita lived life on her own terms and essayed the role of an editor in the same way. So, five years later, Dr Sutinder Singh Noor replaced her to serve as its Chief Editor.

For two decades of *Nagmani*, only the second page was reserved for the editorial. She even gave a title to the matter written on this page. For example, 'Bardo Hond' ('Liminal State between Death and Rebirth') March 1978, 'Aakhri Udasi' ('The Last Pilgrimage') October 1982, 'Kabaraan di Gawahi' ('Testimony of the Tombs') December 1979, 'Te Phull Murjha Gaye' ('And the Flowers Withered') August 1984, 'Ik Supna – Ik Aadesh' ('A Dream – A Direction') February 1987, 'Havan ho Reha si' ('Fire Worship Was Being Performed') September 1984, 'Chinnvaad' ('Symbolism') February 1987, 'Sajanaa dian Gallian' ('The Lanes of My Beloved') July 1985, 'Akkhar Kundli' ('Horoscope of Alphabets') March 1988, 'Bahi Roti' ('Stale Bread') November 1987, 'Na Koi Jaat Na Kabila' ('No Caste Nor Tribe') July 1996. In this editorial page, she touched upon historical, mythological, political, social, cultural issues but only where they were connected with writers and literature. This way the magazine stayed connected purely with good literature. An extract from one of her editorials (February 1978) is being presented as an illustration of her editorial prowess. In this, Amrita refers to many writers whose writing was either censored or confiscated:

Hello! Dear Mic!

Whenever the famous Russian man of letters, Boris Pasternak would be talking to his beloved Olga Ivinskaya, they would both always feel the presence of a third person between them. Their friends had cautioned them that microphones might be hidden in their walls. So, many a time Pasternak would laughingly remember the 'dear little mic'. This mic, in some form or the other, always hides between a writer and the world. It may have been placed by a society or a religion or politics. And from time to time many a poet and writer has had to deal with it....

Probably there never has been an age nor will be, when the thinkers of a time did not have to deal with the visible or the invisible mic. Yes, there surely was a time when according to a poem of Daagistaan, the first poet was born one hundred years before the creation of this world. Even though perhaps the poet regretted at that time that there was no one to listen to his poetry, he must also have felt reassured that there was no mic embedded in the wall to eavesdrop....

The Romanian poet Marin Sorescu writes, 'In the evening I go to the neighbour's house and borrow some chairs, and then I recite my poems to those empty chairs. It's a beautiful evening because the chairs neither pretend any enthusiasm nor do they censor.' This poem is a lovely one, even though it offers no solution to any problem, yet it points to that dreadfulness of problems which touches all of us. The only solution is that every thinker should be able to smile and with mental firmness say loudly, 'Hello! dear mic – Amrita Pritam'.

(Pritam 1978)

A valuable tradition that she put in place was an event called 'Nagmani Shaam' ('Nagmani Soiree') every month after the issue was published. This informal gathering was convened at her residence to hold critical discussions on the articles published in *Nagmani*. Writers were given an opportunity to read out their works aloud. If any contribution touched Amrita and impressed the others, she would select them for *Nagmani*. This not only provided fresh material for the magazine but motivated and encouraged writers. By sharing their work and also their difficulties in a group of peers, their inclination and resolve to write was strengthened.

Amrita started another initiative to inspire writers. In April 1983, *Nagmani* started the practice of '*Nagmani* Library', wherein every year on its anniversary in May, *Nagmani* would present a token sum of Rupees 501/- to any one of its eminent writers to help augment their library. Every year one of the *Nagmani* writers such as Kirpal Kazak, Devinder, K. L. Garg, Jasbir Bhullar and others were awarded this honour. The three-member committee for it comprised Amrita, Imroz and Surinder Sharma.

Amrita made another appreciable effort. She never limited her relationship with writers to merely that of an editor and writer but expanded it to bond with their families too. She was always concerned about their joys and sorrows and made every effort to help anyone in difficulty. When she went to Kolkata in 1982 for a programme, despite the organisers having arranged for their stay and sumptuous meals in a five-star hotel, Amrita and Imroz chose to traverse the narrow by-lanes of Kolkata to Baldev Singh Sadaknama's house and savour a traditional Punjabi meal of *saag* and *makki di roti*. Whenever Kewal Sood, Ramesh Bakhshi, Satti Randhawa, Amia Kunwar or anyone in her circle was in difficulty, even when unwell herself, she would go over to their houses and seek their welfare.

The failing health of Amrita ji filled one of her readers with anxiety. In the April 1999 issue, his letter was published, 'On reading *Nagmani* I first laughed and then cried. I was happy to know that we had *Nagmani* with us to raise the standard of journalism to this level, and sad to think what would happen when *Nagmani* wasn't there anymore – A reader dyed in the hues of *Nagmani*' (Pritam 1999).

Nagmani was published for 36 years and reached its readers without fail. This was a fulfilment of Amrita's dream and a promise made with her own conscience that she fulfilled till the very end. It was a purely personal initiative, undertaken on her own conditions and based on her own principles. When the day finally arrived when Amrita felt that publishing *Nagmani* was beyond her capacity due to failing health, she did not waste time in sentimentality. The magazine did not pass into anyone else's hands. It was neither transferred from one generation to the next nor sold. Nor did it come under the purview of any institution.

However, Amrita did not consider herself free from her editorial responsibilities just by stopping the publication of *Nagmani*. In November 2001, I had gone to Kurukshetra University for a refresher course. Some of my course mates there had sent with me the subscription money for *Nagmani* for a full year. But they had received only five issues till then. Amrita ji made me sit down, calculated the outstanding amount and had it returned to them. Surinder Sharma from Patiala says that he has had such a remarkable experience only twice in his life. Once upon stopping his subscription of the *Reader's Digest* he received the balance amount, and the second time was with *Nagmani*, along with a letter from Amrita ji saying, 'This is your outstanding amount (around Rupees 36.50/-), please accept this. Thank you! – Amrita.'

This is not all. Taran Gujral wrote that once on not receiving an issue of *Nagmani*, she quarrelled with Amrita ji and told her to take as much money as she wanted, 'but please for God's sake don't withhold my copy of *Nagmani*. Imroz ji said, then please buy a life membership. I was ready to do so, but Amrita stopped him … no-no … not now, I don't know how long my life is, and for how long it can continue, I can't take extra money for no reason, please just give her the issues she hasn't received….' She ensured there were no pending dues in her account. Many editors are indifferent to such obligations. The submissions by writers stay wilting on their tables for months on end. They neither reject nor return nor publish them. Sending a letter is even more unlikely. Some may even stop delivering issues after receiving the subscription money. But Amrita and *Nagmani* are memorable and unique because of the finesse they brought to the Punjabi literary tradition and social courtesies.

Nagmani's final issue was published in April 2002. Not too many pages were wasted in revealing the reasons for its closure, nor lengthy explanations offered. Importance was given only to creative articles. On the title page, where it used to be written – 'Workers: Amrita-Imroz', were written the following words – 'Workers Say Goodbye'. And then on the limited space available at the bottom of page thirteen were written these lines:

- Goodbye O fellow travellers
This will be the last issue of *Nagmani*
Because my health no longer supports my mind – Amrita
(Pritam: 2002: 13)

432
Regd. No.
DL-15002/2002
ਕਾਮੇ ਅਲਵਿਦਾ ਆਖਦੇ ਹਨ
ਅਪ੍ਰੈਲ 2002
10 ਰੁਪਏ

ਨਾਗਮਣੀ

ਵਰੁਣ ਕੇਤੁ

ਰਾਵਣ ਦਾ ਜਨਮ ਨਾਮ ਵਰੁਣ ਕੇਤੁ ਸੀ । ਉਹਦੇ ਦਸ ਸਿਰ ਦਸ ਦਿਸ਼ਾਵਾਂ ਦੇ ਗਿਆਨ ਦਾ ਪ੍ਰਤੀਕ ਹਨ ।

ਵਰੁਣ ਕੇਤੁ ਦਾ ਵਿਆਹ ਜਦੋਂ ਮੰਦੋਦਰੀ ਨਾਲ ਹੋਇਆ, ਰਾਜਾ ਮਹੀਦੰਤ ਦੀ ਬੇਟੀ ਨਾਲ, ਤਾਂ ਰਾਜਾ ਉਦਾਸ ਸੀ, ਕਿ ਜੇ ਉਹਦਾ ਲੰਕਾ ਦਾ ਰਾਜ ਅੱਜ ਕਾਇਮ ਹੁੰਦਾ ਤਾਂ ਉਹ ਬੇਟੀ ਨੂੰ ਬਹੁਤ ਕੁਝ ਦੇਂਦਾ । ਵਰੁਣ ਕੇਤੁ ਨੇ ਰਾਜਾ ਨੂੰ ਖੁਸ਼ ਕਰਨ ਲਈ, ਉਹਦੀ ਲੰਕਾ ਮੁੜ ਕੇ ਜਿੱਤ ਕੇ ਰਾਜਾ ਨੂੰ ਦੇ ਦਿੱਤੀ । ਉਸ ਵੇਲੇ ਰਾਜਾ ਮਹੀਦੰਤ ਨੇ ਉਹ ਲੰਕਾ ਵਰੁਣ ਕੇਤੁ ਨੂੰ ਸੌਂਪ ਦਿੱਤੀ ।

ਰਿਖੀ-ਮੁਨੀ ਇਕੱਠੇ ਹੋਏ ਵਰੁਣ ਕੇਤੁ ਨੂੰ ਰਾਜ-ਤਿਲਕ ਦੇਣ ਲਈ । ਇਹ ਰਾਜ-ਤਿਲਕ ਕੁਰਤੂ ਮੁਨੀ ਨੇ ਦੇਣਾ ਸੀ, ਪਰ ਉਹ ਸਭਾਪਤੀ ਦੇ ਆਸਨ ਤੋਂ ਉੱਠ ਗਏ, ਤੇ ਕਿਹਾ—"ਵਰੁਣ ਕੇਤੁ ਰਾਜਾ ਬਣੇਗਾ, ਪਰ ਮੈਂ ਉਹਨੂੰ ਰਾਜ-ਤਿਲਕ ਨਹੀਂ ਦਿਆਂਗਾ, ਕਿਉਂਕਿ ਉਹਦੇ ਮਸਤਕ ਦੀ ਰੇਖਾ ਕਹਿੰਦੀ ਏ ਕਿ ਉਹ ਰਾਜਾ ਹੋਣ ਦੇ ਯੋਗ ਨਹੀਂ ।"

ਫਿਰ ਰਾਜ-ਤਿਲਕ ਹੋਇਆ, ਵਰੁਣ ਕੇਤੁ ਲੰਕਾ ਦਾ ਰਾਜਾ ਹੋਇਆ ਤੇ ਉਸ ਵੇਲੇ ਉਹਦਾ ਨਾ ਰਾਵਣ ਰਖਿਆ ਗਿਆ, ਜਿਹਦਾ ਅਰਥ ਹੁੰਦਾ ਹੈ—ਮਹਾਦਾਨੀ ।

ਵਕਤ ਪਾ ਕੇ ਰਾਵਣ ਨੇ ਆਪਣੇ ਰਾਜ ਵਿਚ ਗਿਆਨ-ਵਿਗਿਆਨ ਅਰਜਿਤ ਕੀਤੇ ਤੇ ਕੁਰਤੂ ਮੁਨੀ ਨੂੰ ਜਾ ਕੇ ਕਿਹਾ—"ਰਿਸ਼ੀਵਰ ! ਇਕ ਵਾਰੀ ਤਾਂ ਮੇਰੀ ਲੰਕਾ ਵਿਚ ਆਓ !" ਕੁਰਤੂ ਮੁਨੀ ਆਏ । ਰਾਜਾ ਨੇ ਗਿਆਨ ਸ਼ਾਲਾ ਵਿਖਾਈ, ਵਿਗਿਆਨ ਸ਼ਾਲਾ ਵਿਖਾਈ, ਯੰਤਰ ਸ਼ਾਲਾ, ਪ੍ਰਯੋਗ ਸ਼ਾਲਾ, ਅਸਤਰ ਸ਼ਾਲਾ, ਸਸਤਰ ਸ਼ਾਲਾ, ਯੁੱਧ ਸ਼ਾਲਾ, ਤੇ ਕਿਹਾ—"ਮੁਨੀਵਰ ! ਇਹ ਮੇਰੀ ਪ੍ਰਾਪਤੀ ਏ । ਅੱਜ ਮੇਰੇ ਜਿਹਾ ਪ੍ਰਤਾਪੀ ਰਾਜਾ ਹੋਰ ਕੋਈ ਨਹੀਂ ।"

ਕੁਰਤੂ ਮੁਨੀ ਮੁਸਕਰਾਏ, ਕਹਿਣ ਲੱਗੇ—"ਹਾਂ ਰਾਜਾ ! ਪਰ ਇਹ ਪ੍ਰਾਪਤੀ ਹਮੇਸ਼ਾ ਖ਼ਤਰੇ ਵਿਚ ਰਹੇਗੀ ।" ਤੇ ਹੈਰਾਨ ਹੋਏ ਰਾਵਣ ਨੂੰ ਕਹਿਣ ਲੱਗੇ—"ਇਕੋ ਹਰ ਤਰ੍ਹਾਂ ਦੀ ਸ਼ਾਲਾ ਏ, ਪਰ ਆਚਰਨ ਸ਼ਾਲਾ ਕੋਈ ਨਹੀਂ ।"

ਤੇ ਕਹਿਣਾ ਚਾਹੁੰਦੀ ਹਾਂ ਕਿ ਸੁਤੰਤਰਤਾ ਨੂੰ ਆਪਣੀ ਆਚਰਨ-ਸਕਤੀ ਨਾਲ ਧਾਰਨ ਕਰਨਾ ਹੁੰਦਾ ਏ । ਜਿਸ ਤਰ੍ਹਾਂ ਲੱਕੜ ਪੱਥਰ ਦੀ ਦੇਵ-ਮੂਰਤੀ ਵਿਚ ਪ੍ਰਾਣ-ਪ੍ਰਤਿਸ਼ਠਾ ਕਰਨੀ ਹੁੰਦੀ ਏ, ਠੀਕ ਉਸੇ ਤਰ੍ਹਾਂ ਸੁਤੰਤਰਤਾ ਲਫ਼ਜ਼ ਵਿਚ ਵੀ ਪ੍ਰਾਣ-ਪ੍ਰਤਿਸ਼ਠਾ ਕਰਨੀ ਹੁੰਦੀ ਹੈ, ਜੋ ਸਿਰਫ਼ ਆਪਣੀ ਆਚਰਨ ਸਕਤੀ ਨਾਲ ਹੁੰਦੀ ਏ ।

Figure 18 Nagmani last issue – Front Cover

ਜਾਂਦੀ ਤੇ ਕ੍ਰਿਸ਼ਨ ਦੀ ਮੂਰਤੀ ਦਾ ਧਿਆਨ ਕਰਦੀ ।

ਹੌਲੀ-ਹੌਲੀ ਕਬੀਲੇ ਵਿਚ ਇਹ ਚਰਚਾ ਹੋਣ ਲੱਗੀ ਕਿ ਹਸਨਾ ਰੋਜ਼ ਗੁਫ਼ਾ ਵਿਚ ਜਾਂਦੀ ਏ । ਸ਼ੱਕ ਪਿਆ ਕਿ ਸ਼ਾਇਦ ਦੁਸ਼ਮਨ ਕਬੀਲੇ ਦੇ ਕਿਸੇ ਨੌਜਵਾਨ ਮਰਦ ਨੇ ਹਸਨਾ ਨੂੰ ਆਪਣੀਆਂ ਮੁੱਠਤ ਵਿਚ ਬੰਨ੍ਹ ਲਿਆ ਏ । ਉਹ ਸ਼ਾਇਦ ਉਸ ਨੂੰ ਮਿਲਣ ਜਾਂਦੀ ਏ । ਕਈ ਵਾਰੀ ਨਿਗਾਹਬਾਨੀ ਵੀ ਕੀਤੀ ਗਈ ਪਰ ਕੋਈ ਨਹੀਂ ਮਿਲਿਆ ।

ਆਖ਼ਰ ਇਕ ਦਿਨ ਕਬੀਲੇ ਨੇ ਬਹੁਤ ਜ਼ਾਲਮ ਫ਼ੈਸਲਾ ਲਿਆ ਕਿ ਹੁਣ ਜਦ ਹਸਨਾ ਗੁਫ਼ਾ ਦੇ ਅੰਦਰ ਗਾਈ ਹੋਵੇ ਤਾਂ ਬਾਹਰੋਂ ਹੀ ਗੁਫ਼ਾ ਦਾ ਦਰਵਾਜ਼ਾ ਬੰਦ ਕਰ ਦਿੱਤਾ ਜਾਏ । ਦੇਵੇ ਅੰਦਰ ਹੀ ਤੜਪ-ਤੜਪ ਕੇ ਮਰ ਜਾਣਗੇ, ਫਿਰ ਲਾਸ਼ਾਂ ਕੱਢ ਕੇ ਦਫ਼ਨਾ ਦਿਆਂਗੇ...

ਇੰਜ ਹੀ ਕੀਤਾ ਗਿਆ । ਹਸਨਾ ਗੁਫ਼ਾ ਵਿਚ ਗਾਈ ਤਾਂ ਬਾਹਰੋਂ ਘਾਤ ਲਾਈ ਕਬੀਲੇ ਦੇ ਲੋਕਾਂ ਨੇ ਗੁਫ਼ਾ ਦਾ ਦਰਵਾਜ਼ਾ ਇਕ ਪੱਥਰ ਨਾਲ ਬੰਦ ਕਰ ਦਿੱਤਾ, ਤੇ ਚਲੇ ਗਏ ।

ਹਸਨਾ ਜਦੋਂ ਗੁਫ਼ਾ ਤੋਂ ਨਿਕਲਣ ਨੂੰ ਹੋਈ ਤਾਂ ਵੇਖਿਆ ਕਿ ਦਰਵਾਜ਼ਾ ਬੰਦ ਹੈ । ਉਸ ਨੇ ਨਿਰ੍ਹਬੁਲ ਹੋ ਕੇ ਆਪਣੇ ਮਹਿਬੂਬ ਨੂੰ ਪੁਕਾਰਨਾ ਸ਼ੁਰੂ ਕਰ ਦਿੱਤਾ—"ਕ੍ਰਿਸ਼ਨ, ਕ੍ਰਿਸ਼ਨ, ਕ੍ਰਿਸ਼ਨ !"

ਫਿਰ ਖ਼ੋਰੇ ਕੀ ਕ੍ਰਿਸ਼ਮਾ ਹੋਇਆ ਕਿ ਉਹਦੀ ਕ੍ਰਿਸ਼ਨ ਪੁਕਾਰ ਸੁਣ ਕੇ ਗੁਫ਼ਾ ਦਾ ਇਕ ਪੱਥਰ ਰਾਉ ਦੀ ਸੂਰਤ ਅਖ਼ਤਿਆਰ ਕਰ ਗਿਆ ਤੇ ਉਹਦੇ ਥਣਾਂ ਵਿਚੋਂ ਦੁੱਧ ਸਿੰਮਣ ਲੱਗ ਪਿਆ, ਹਸਨਾ ਨੇ ਜੀਆ ਭਰ ਕੇ ਦੁੱਧ ਪੀਤਾ...

ਅਤੇ ਕਹਾਣੀ ਹੈ ਕਿ ਹਸਨਾ ਨੂੰ ਗੁਫ਼ਾ ਵਿਚ ਕ੍ਰਿਸ਼ਨ ਦੇ ਦਰਸ਼ਨ ਹੋਏ...

ਕੁਝ ਦਿਨਾਂ ਦੇ ਬਾਅਦ ਜਦ ਕਬੀਲੇ ਵਾਲੇ ਗੁਫ਼ਾ ਦੇ ਨੇੜੇ ਗਏ ਤਾਂ ਵੇਖਿਆ ਕਿ ਦਰਵਾਜ਼ੇ 'ਤੇ ਲੱਗਿਆ ਪੱਥਰ ਹਟਿਆ ਹੋਇਆ ਸੀ । ਅੰਦਰ ਗਏ ਤਾਂ ਹਸਨਾ ਕਿਤੇ ਨਹੀਂ ਮਿਲੀ, ਅਜੇ ਤਕ ਨਹੀਂ ਮਿਲੀ ।

ਬਸ ਇੰਨਾ ਹੋਇਆ ਕਿ ਉਦੋਂ ਤੋਂ ਦੁੱਧ ਸਿੰਮਦੀ ਉਸ ਗੁਫ਼ਾ ਦਾ ਨਾਂ 'ਰੌਕੁਲ' ਪੈ ਗਿਆ । ਉਹ ਰੌਕੁਲ ਗੁਫ਼ਾ ਕਾਬਲ ਵਿਚ ਅੱਜ ਵੀ ਏ...

ਇਸ ਤਾਰੀਖ਼ੀ ਸਚਾਈ ਨੂੰ ਪਹਿਲੀ ਵੇਰ ਸਿੰਧ ਦੇ ਸ਼ਾਹ ਲਤੀਫ਼ ਨੇ ਜੋਗੀਆਂ ਦੇ ਇਕ ਟੋਲੇ ਨਾਲ ਕਾਬਲ ਵਿਚ ਕਾਲੀ ਮੰਦਰ ਦੀ ਯਾਤਰਾ ਦੇ ਵੇਲੇ ਵੇਖਿਆ ਤੇ ਇਸ ਰੌਕੁਲ ਨੂੰ ਆਪਣੀ ਸ਼ਾਇਰੀ ਵਿਚ ਉਤਾਰਿਆ ਜਿੱਥੇ ਪੱਥਰਾ ਵਿਚੋਂ ਦੁੱਧ ਸਿੰਮਦਾ ਏ

...

ਹਸਨਾ ਅਲੋਪ ਹੋ ਗਈ...

ਪਰ ਅਸਮਾ ਸਲੀਮ ਨੂੰ ਵੇਖਦਾ ਹਾਂ ਤਾਂ ਕਹਿਣ ਨੂੰ ਮਨ ਕਰਦਾ ਦੇ ਕਿ ਆਖਾਂ—"ਹਸਨਾ ਇੱਥੇ ਹੈ—"

ਹਸਨਾ ਦਾ ਜ਼ਿਕਰ ਮੈਂ ਅੰਮ੍ਰਿਤਾ ਜੀ ਦੀ ਕਿਤਾਬ 'ਇਸ਼ਕ ਅੱਲਾਹ ਹੱਕ ਅੱਲਾਹ' ਵਿਚ ਪੜ੍ਹਿਆ ਸੀ ।

ਇਕ ਦਿਨ ਮੈਂ ਅੰਮ੍ਰਿਤਾ ਜੀ ਨੂੰ ਕਿਹਾ—"ਕਾਬਲ ਵਾਲੀ ਲਾਪਤਾ ਹਸਨਾ ਮੈਨੂੰ ਮਿਲ ਗਈ ਏ ।"

ਉਹ ਕਹਿਣ ਲੱਗੇ—"ਅੱਛਾ ! ਮੈਨੂੰ ਵੀ ਮਿਲਾ ।"

ਮੈਂ ਕਿਹਾ—"ਉਹ ਤੁਹਾਨੂੰ ਮਿਲਦੀ ਰਹਿੰਦੀ ਏ ।"

"ਮੈਨੂੰ ਮਿਲਦੀ ਰਹਿੰਦੀ ਏ ? ਕੌਣ ?"

ਮੈਂ ਕਿਹਾ—"ਅਸਮਾ ਸਲੀਮ !"

ਅੰਮ੍ਰਿਤਾ ਜੀ ਦੇ ਮੂੰਹੋਂ ਆਵਾਜ਼ ਨਿਕਲੀ—"ਹਾਏ ਅੱਲਾਹ ! ਕਿੰਨੀ ਪਿਆਰੀ ਗੱਲ ਕੀਤੀ ਜੇ ਰਾਜੇਸ਼ ! ਇਹ ਆਪਣੀ ਅਸਮਾ ਸੱਚੀਮੁੱਚੀ ਹਸਨਾ ਏ...

ਅਲਵਿਦਾ ਐ ਕਾਫ਼ਲੇ ਵਾਲੇ
ਨਾਗਮਣੀ ਦਾ ਇਹ ਅੰਕ ਆਖ਼ਰੀ ਅੰਕ ਹੋਵੇਗਾ
ਕਿਉਂਕਿ ਮੇਰੀ ਸਿਹਤ ਮੇਰੇ ਮਨ ਦਾ ਸਾਥ ਨਹੀਂ ਦੇ ਰਹੀ—*ਅੰਮ੍ਰਿਤਾ*

Figure 19 *Nagmani* last issue – Back Cover

Part V

WORD, IMAGE, IDIOM

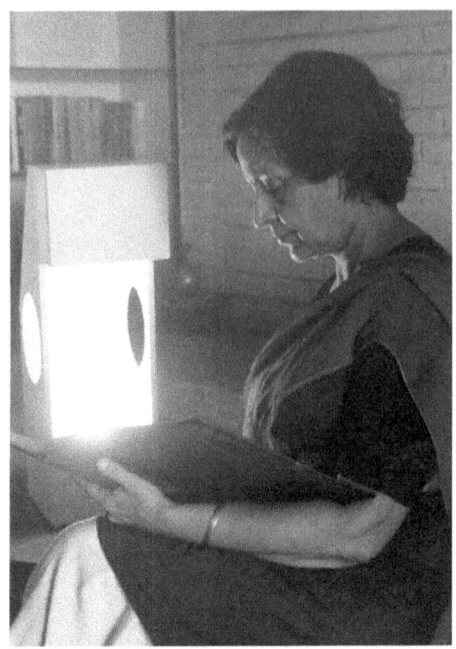

Figure 20 Amrita reading a book

Figure 21 Amrita at K-25 Hauz Khas: A Mecca for Artistes

17

AN ACHE INHALED

The Poetic Sensibility of Amrita Pritam

Sutinder Singh Noor
edited by Vanita
translated by Madhuri Chawla

Amrita Pritam expresses her poetic sensibility as 'an ache inhaled silently as a cigarette' from which she flicks off a few poems 'like ash'. As a poet who wrote poetry for over seven decades and witnessed not just successive movements in literature but massive upheavals in national and international politics, this ache or sorrow was an inherent part of her being and was reflected recurrently in her poetry – sometimes at personal and sometimes, universal levels – and often indistinguishably. This is linked inextricably to the other dominant emotion in her writing – that of love – love for a significant other as well as for the whole of humanity; in fact for the entire universe and its creation. Her long poetic journey was fraught with several changes along the way and her poetry may be viewed from an evolutionary perspective. This chapter examines the various nuances of her poetry to see the growth of her thematic and poetic sensibility.

She was in her sixteenth year in a pious and devotional household and a traditional world when her first anthology of poems *Thandian Kirnan* (*Cool Rays*) was published in 1935. Punjabi poetry at that time was dominated heavily by poets like Bhai Vir Singh and Dhani Ram Chatrik. The tradition of romantic poetry of the Middle Ages was woven into the poetic sensibility of the times; the tone and tenor of contemporary Punjabi poetry was spiritual, mystic and invariably imbued with a moral message. Amrita was influenced by these diverse streams of thought as well as by her father's teachings; together they shaped the form and content of her poetry. Initially, she used the *beint* and other traditional metres to write her poems. There was ethical correctness in her writing; and right from the beginning she was concerned about women, their ideals, occupations and lived reality in a patriarchal society but was affected powerfully by the traditional notion of womanhood as is evident from the lines:

> If women were like that of yore
> Homes would be happy again

DOI: 10.4324/9781003214656-27

Sorrows of the country would disappear
Would not see that face again.

Cast away the empty fashion
Embrace the simple style of yore
Life as it was earlier for women
With God's grace may be as before.

(qtd. in Noor 2010: 15)

She also exhorted her fellow countrymen – Muslim, Hindu and Sikh to not get divided so that they could see the dawn of freedom together.

Her second anthology *Amrit Lehran* (*Immortal Waves* 1936) brought her wide recognition. Her father Kartar Singh Hitkari and established poets and scholars like Dhani Ram Chatrik and Bhai Kahan Singh Nabha praised this anthology and wrote the foreword for it. Chatrik called the anthology 'not a mere meaningless exercise in rhyming' but 'a treasure of refined ideas' with cogent thought hidden in every fold. Following the beaten path, she began her anthology with a traditional invocation to the Gods. It included several short poems about the Punjabi language and a somewhat longer poem about her contemporaries listing their distinctive characteristics. This bore witness to the influence of the poetry of her contemporaries and the inspiration she drew from them. The first group of poems exhorted the Punjabis to love their language in the same vein as did poems by Chatrik and others. In the poem about her contemporaries she spoke about Mohan Singh, Harnam Kaur Nabha, Maula Baksh Kushta, Teja Singh, Jodh Singh, etc. Like Bhai Vir Singh and Chatrik she wrote most of the poems in this anthology in the Persian verse form of *rubai* consisting of four-line stanzas. At times she adopted the traditional poetic metre *chhand* or other poetic forms such as *dohra*, *korda*, etc. And like Bhai Vir Singh, Amrita too depicted nature in figurative language. At several places, her poems used the same question-answer format. The occasional manifestation of passion in her poems was not in the vein of *ishq majazi* (worldly love) but as *ishq haqiqi* (spiritual love) as in Bhai Vir Singh and other religious and Sufi poets.

When Amrita moved towards realism, it led to the emergence of two themes in her poetry. The first was a concern with the condition of women in contemporary times. Amrita felt that women were deeply influenced by western civilisation which led to fissures in the domestic space, in relationships, and she alerted women about this – at times through a dialogue between a husband and a wife. This tenor of her poems, visible in the collection *Thandian Kirnan*, is further elaborated in *Amrit Lehran*. During this phase, she advocated the subservience of women to men, believing that docile women reaped abundant rewards. The second theme that emerged in her poetry of this time was the idea of communication of moral values

190

and principles. Her constant refrain is to follow an ethical mode of life. The language of these didactic poems is similar to the language of traditional poetry and folk songs.

Between 1939 and 1943, several more anthologies of poetry by Amrita – *Jiunda Jeevan* (*An Exuberant Life*), *Trel Dhote Phull* (*Dew-Drenched Flowers*), *O Geetan Valiya* (*O the One with Songs*), *Badlan de Palle Vich* (*In the Lap of Clouds*), *Sunjh di Laali* (*The Crimson of Dusk*) – were published. The hues of her poems in these anthologies were considerably different from the first two collections. Doubt and satire started to emerge in the faith reposed earlier in religion and spirituality. 'Enough, enough! I have seen through/ The tears in your wrap, in the name of religion' (qtd. in Noor 2010: 20).

The foreword to *Trel Thote Phul* was penned by Gurbaksh Singh 'Preetlari', a tall figure in Punjabi society whose ideas had inspired a revolution in realism. Balwant Gargi, Ishwar Chitrakar and Kartar Singh Duggal also lauded Amrita's poetry which now evolved with the awakening of love in her poems. Expressions related to the tenderness and ardour, and longing and desire of love emerged in her poetry; and the identity of a woman merged into that desire. Various facets of a woman's being and emotions became the focus of her poetry – whether she spoke about the courtyard of the mother, or about the tenderness of children and maternal affection, or about a lover or a woman's love – what was paramount in her mind was an integrated identity of a woman's being.

To accommodate this new sprouting of thought and expression, she moved beyond the traditional *chhand* and began to write in free verse. Even when she used popular metres or picked words from local traditions and folk songs, she did not remain bound to any one particular metre. By and by, a more profound intellectual strain, beyond the romantic, fused with her poetry. The reason behind this growing consciousness was an awareness of the reality of the material world around her – its social, cultural and political facets – and the worldwide turmoil in the wake of the Second World War, and hard ground realities of destruction and deprivation impacting social, cultural and political life all over the world. This impinged upon Amrita's consciousness as well. From this experience was born her next collection *Sunjh di Laali* which represented the broadening of Amrita's sympathies to move beyond the self and immediate society to encompass the suffering of the world. She sought solace in the words and philosophy of Nanak, Buddha, Lenin, Gandhi, Iqbal, Tagore, Shakespeare and Dante and sought their inspiration and guidance in a war-torn world and invoked the birth of another such great soul to redeem the world. While Amrita comes close to the world of reality in this collection, her inclination towards intellectualism even in romantic verse is greater. In poems like 'Meghdoota' ('Cloud-Messenger') she expressed the emotion of love in a mystic mode; beautifully demonstrating an awareness of the aesthetics of poetic language. By now

191

her reputation as a poet was firmly established and several songs written in this phase were repeated in later anthologies.

Progressive Orientation

The next two anthologies *Lok Peed* (*Anguish of the Masses* 1944) and *Patthar Geetey* (*Stones and Pebbles* 1946) show further evolution. The world had already experienced the violent desolation caused by the Second World War, the Bengal famine had devastated a large population and new signposts of the freedom movement had emerged. The struggle against British imperialism had intensified; in the post-1936 era, the influences of the Progressive movement and Socialist Realism, along with an exposure to Russian literature, brought about an ideological change in society all over the world, and consequently, in world literature. Writers now focussed on presenting contemporary reality in their works and became resistant to writing poetry about 'beauty' and 'love' – issues that suddenly seemed trivial and frivolous. Punjabi literature could not remain untouched by these ideological concerns and Amrita's poetry, like that of several others, reflected these influences. Her themes broadened in scope, and in addition to writing about these calamities, she also expressed her anguish at a nation in which 'religion wields a sword', or where a woman is harnessed like a cow and is considered to be a childbearing machine, where there are caste distinctions or where new ideas are forbidden. This poetic voice linked her to a progressive vision. Her deep sense of pain was manifested in greater use of rhetoric in her poems. Her tone was more strident and prominent than the use of symbolism and imagery in her poetry. Though she did write love poetry during this phase, it was replete with reproaches and complaints; for example, 'beauty and love o' boy, are meant for idle times'. Thus, Amrita's poetry during this phase underlined a conflict in her poetic sensibility. Several critics have referred to this tendency as an example of romantic progressivism.

Of all her works during this period, *Patthar Geetey* was the most popular. Later when Amrita published her collection *Kaagaz te Canvas ton Pahilaan* (*Before Paper and Canvas*), she began with the poem 'Patthar te Geetey'. In the preface she said that she was claiming ownership of only seven of her works published before 1955; brushing aside earlier collections as irrelevant. This might be considered debatable from a critic's point of view because early works of any artist are important as a foundation on which the artist builds later works, while *Patthar Geetey* becomes imbued with even greater significance in the development of Amrita's poetry due to her own acknowledgement of its importance.

Amrita's intellectual maturity was clearly discernible in *Patthar Geetey*. Whether she talked about society or about love, there was an intensity of passion in her poetry sans any sentimentality or emotionality. Her poem

'Annadata' ('The Provider') from this collection received a great deal of scrutiny and appreciation. The poem reflected her deep awareness of the feudal character of Punjabi society wherein patriarchal values treat woman only as a commodity; and the same values are adopted in the shift to capitalism later in Punjab where again a woman does not have any identity of her own. This poem also heralded the first ideological perception of the individuality of the woman – a subject of prominent concern in her later poems. Both the feminist consciousness and use of satire in the language contribute to this poem being acknowledged as one of her most significant ones.

> O Provider!
> I am a doll of flesh
> Use me, abuse me,
> A cup of blood
> Drink, serve
> I stand before thee
> A commodity
> Use as you wish....

(Pritam 2019: 11)

In the poems in *Patthar Geetey*, the woman had an individual identity, a consciousness, an understanding of the manifold layers of love and other emotions. Towards the end, she expressed her insight about the social structure as well. The compilation thus marks a movement to more mature poetry.

Partition, History, Woman

Amrita's first book of poetry post-Partition *Lamiyaan Vaataan* (*Long Journeys* 1949) was divided into three sections. The first section engaged with the catastrophe of Partition of the nation into India and Pakistan in 1947. Like every Punjabi writer, she was deeply affected by the violent massacre in her beloved state. Amrita's most popular poem 'Ajj Aakhaan Waris Shah nu' that invoked Waris Shah, the cultural hero of Punjab, to lament the anguish of countless daughters of Punjab and captured the imagination of traumatised Punjabis on both sides of the border was first published in this anthology. Her poem 'Punjab di Kahani' ('The Story of Punjab') from the same collection, songs like 'Saanu Mili Jaana ho' ('Meet Me O before You Leave') and several other intellectually mature poems offered an analysis of the disastrous impact of the happenings between 4 March 1947 and 15 August 1947 as she unequivocally criticised the bloodshed in the name of religion and cursed sectarian regimes. This catastrophe coloured even her perception of love and she admitted in an anguished voice, 'Owing to the piercing pain of humanity's blood-soaked pages my love today is speechless' (qtd. in Noor 2010: 30). Thus, love and pain are inextricably linked in the poems and the love poems in the second part of this collection bear the imprint of this sorrow.

In the third part of 'Viautah Naar' ('The Married Woman'), she narrated the stories of women who suffered indignity and humiliation and how 'love' was crippled by social traditions. A woman abducted by a man from the enemy community found her return to her husband's doorstep impossible in a society shackled by religious customs and beliefs; and the hapless woman had no option but to seek death. As in *Patthar Geetey* earlier, Amrita questioned the slavery shackling a woman in 'Kanyadaan' ('Giving the Daughter Away'); and through the symbol of a cowshed in 'Gaushala' ('Cowshed'). She satirised those self-appointed guardians of society who were more bothered about the activities of a neighbour's daughter or son without introspecting about their own morals. In Amrita's world, the possibility of love in such an environment did not exist. She says:

> Purse your blood-stained lips, O unbeliever
> Who will listen to words you utter?
> The society is a bit deaf
> They can hear the din of savagery,
> But can never hear
> The sweet-soft melody of truth.

(qtd. in Noor 2010: 31)

In 1950 Amrita wrote a long poem titled 'Main Twareekh Hoon Hind Ki' ('I am the History of India') in which 14 August 1947 is called an eventful night. The dawn of 15 August when the nation was gaining freedom after witnessing the catastrophe of 1947 was in the offing. The ecstasy of freedom compelled everyone to forget the preceding tragedy. To celebrate this long desired-for dawn, she wished to write a poem that would impact the entire world. The poem reflects the conflict between the pain of Partition and Punjab's misfortune and the euphoria of the countdown to the dawn of a free nation.

Besides anguish at this historic tragedy, she is also alive to the wretched economic condition of Indian society mired in problems of capitalism, unequal distribution of resources, entrenched imperialism, etc. The Progressive movement connected Amrita to a vision of socialist structures for post-independent Indian society. The newly-independent nation also infused the heart with an idealistic spirit. Her eyes had hope and she dreamt of the future; she had faith in humanity which she felt could create a new society even after undergoing grave calamities. Romantic progressiveness of the time was linked with this idealism.

Romantic Idealism and Consciousness

Amrita's poetry now took an idealistic turn, within which was blended a consciousness of romantic progressiveness. Its mark can be seen in *Sargi Vela* (*Before Dawn* 1951). Amrita divided the poems of this collection into four parts. In the poems of the first part, the dreams of love again started budding as she narrated the memory and emotion of love which created music, and she urged the winds to flow in her direction. There is rich imagery of the beauty of the stars and the moon glowing in the folds of dark nights. In the second section was an awareness of the 'fake elements of society'. The image of the agony of love was deeply etched in her subconscious. She recollected tragedy in the entire history of love. Thus, again one sees the blend of love and pain in her poetry.

In the third section, she returned to poems which evoked the catastrophe of 1947. The condition of women who suffered indescribable atrocities crystallises as she portrayed a woman's pain of being abducted and commodified, and depicted the enormity of the violence that led to a total breakdown of ethics and values governing inter-personal relations among the various communities. Unspeakable horrors were being perpetrated all over Punjab at a time when the happy event of gaining independence from nearly two centuries of colonial rule was about to bear fruit. Amrita expressed these paradoxical emotions bursting in the hearts of people with a consummate blend of artistry and irony. While she lamented the moral and religious sacrilege and called the sovereign a 'lifeless statue' as he was unable to stop such atrocities, she also exhibited a growing consciousness of history, culture and aesthetics. Her approach was both futuristic and idealistic, as she wrote lyrically about the blooming youthfulness of the fields, the swaying of the tall, standing crop, the night of promises and of breaking into a joyful dance. Her poetry now assumed the voice of folk songs as she wrote about Punjabi folk dances like *gidda*, *sammi*, *jhummar* and *bhangra*; from there she progressed to writing poetry about ushering in peace and tranquillity – a theme that resonated across the globe.

The emotional anchor of Amrita's anthology *Sunhede* (*Messages* 1955) that won her the Sahitya Akademi award was the world of love. In her own words, she wrote these poems 'while she was thinking of Sahir Ludhianvi, or when she met him, or while she was pining for him'. The poem 'Sunehde' was the representative piece and its inter-related dual message of tragic love fused with messages of peace indicated her progressive outlook. Her poem brought alive the memories of the *qissas* of the Middle Ages which were still deeply embedded in the subconscious mind of the Punjabi reader. By referring to legendary icons of love like Hir, Sassi and Sohni and their lovers, Ranjha, Punnu and Mahiwal, she connected her own emotions and reality with these heroines of Punjabi romantic tradition. It drew tradition into its fold, and familiar signs and symbols evoked easy reception, as with the contemporary poet Shiv Kumar Batalvi's poems. The poem evoked the language of empathy that enabled a ready acceptance for the reader, as did its inherent compassion. The structure of this poem was different from the others written during this phase. The poem consisted of a blend of progressive thought and of the memory of love which has always been an integral part of Amrita's poetry; later in *Ashoka Cheti* (1957) too she juggles with her consciousness of Punjab while dealing with love.

Two different aspects of pain in Amrita's poetic credo are love and its expression in her poetry, and the yearning in these poems as a consequence of that love. These lines reveal this aspect of her poetic theory:

> Love of a lifetime is voiceless
> Each of my songs is my voice
> My words writhe in a manner
> As the stars smoulder through the night
> ....
> Each song of mine
> like a letter I go on writing,
> Surprised am I, not a single verse
> Doth reach you.
>
> (Pritam 2019: 82)

Her verses are in the form of a letter and connect the ache stemming from love with the history of her poetry.

> The reed went on writing the call of time
> Bloody pages in the sacred book of love.
>
> (qtd. in Noor, Mohanjit 2002: 217)

In her next anthology *Kastoori* (*Musk* 1959), she expresses the extent to which she undergoes throes of love for Sahir in her poem 'Raat Meri Jaagdi' ('My Night is Awake'), as in her anthology *Main Jama Tun* and autobiography *Rasidi Ticket* (*The Revenue Stamp*).

> One day burning with grief from the fire of the heart I was writing a poem, 'My night is awake, thoughts about you have dozed off ...' and in the contemplative time between moving from one line to another, with the pen held in my hand I unconsciously kept drawing some lines on my legs and arms. Then having completed the poem I became conscious and realised that on my arms and legs I had scribbled Sahir ... Sahir about a hundred times.
>
> (Pritam 2019: 145)

Amrita wrote, 'I had lived fourteen years of my unsuccessful love with Sahir.... When I met Imroz even my dead years began to speak about living'

196

(qtd. in Noor 2010: 41). Songs like 'Chaanan di Phulkaari' ('Embroidery of Radiance') rose out of this state of mind, which became a part of *Nagmani* (*The Serpent's Gem*) – her next collection of poetry in 1964.

Reflective Transformation

The years leading to *Nagmani* were also years of sadness for her. *Nagmani* was born out of her fragmented consciousness arising out of inner conflict. The Progressive phase in her poetry was replaced by a phase of the travails of love, of rumination and sadness. She now turned to symbolism to express this state. At times the over-use of symbols led to the fragmentation of the poem, reflecting her splintered consciousness; an extensive use of embellishments and figures of speech also indicated that her poem was in search of a new poetic style.

Modernist Approach

In the decades before and after Romantic Progressivism, there were discussions about experimentation and modernism in poetry. Poetry was bidding adieu to traditional practices and a new idiom was emerging. Amrita's *Kaagaz te Canvas* (*Paper and Canvas* 1970) indicates the drifting away of Punjabi poetry beyond Romantic and Progressive phases. This phase was marked by the experimental position of Jasbir Singh Ahluwalia, Ravinder Ravi and Ajaib, S.S. Misha's realistic, anti-romantic poetry, Harbhajan Singh's modernism, Jaswant Singh Neki's neo-mysticism, Shiv Kumar's lyricism, the revolutionary poetry of Pash and others, etc. In this context, Amrita's *Kaagaz te Canvas* represents a transformation of her earlier style towards modernism. The symbolic was discarded, excessive embellishments dropped and she became inclined towards writing in the simple, straight language of modern poets. Her satire also became sharper and more focussed while the lyricism of her poetry began to decline. She used words earlier forbidden in poetry, to reflect and emphasise bitter reality. Even when she wrote her poem 'Ishq' ('Love'), she expressed love and reproach in an unromantic language, given her new modernist tendencies.

Besides, in this phase, Amrita wrote poetry which was deeply connected with history and contemporary reality, but its tone was different from that of earlier progressive poems. The earlier idealism was dissipating. She made an unbiased assessment of socialism and the empire and gauged their limits. The blend of pain with every other emotion weaves this collection with the earlier ones. Amrita presented this through her introduction to *Kaagaz te Canvas* which she called the 'Saga of an Eclipse', 'Pain has so many colours, and the one who dons them, God knows how many colours and how many Gods he endures ... I can say whatever I have penned

197

till date is a long saga of an eclipse' (Pritam 2018: 9). Under the influence of modernism, existentialism and the absurd, the city emerged in her poetry. However, she did not accept modernism uncritically; her references to urbanisation and the city were satirical in 'Ik Shahar' ('A City') and 'Shahar' ('The City') where mankind was all too easily lost and human values were tangled and ambiguous.

The rebellious woman inside her burst out in revolutionary poems like 'Kumari' ('Virgin'). She rubbished the sham values of society and her language became bitter. Her poem 'Gali da Kutta' ('The Street Dog') was born out of this protest. Her horizon expanded to consider the role of a human, a writer, and of a thinker in wider terms. Now her idols were Martin Luther King, Kazantzakis, Genet, Van Gogh, Nietzsche, Ayn Rand, Henry Miller, Marilyn Monroe, who were all rebels in one way or another.

A study of *Kaagaz te Canvas* is incomplete without a perusal of the poem 'Nau Supne' ('Nine Dreams'). Never had such a poem been written about Mata Tripta, Guru Nanak's mother. In beautiful poetic language, Amrita described Mata Tripta's nine dreams from the moment of her becoming pregnant through the nine months of the changing Indian seasons – *magh* to *phalgun* to *chaitra, vaishakh, jyesth, aashadh, ashwin* and *kartik* (months as per the Hindu calendar). She portrayed Tripta's state of mind in these nine months using other symbols such as butter, a big milk vessel and a sweet ball of the sun. This poem came to epitomise Amrita's rebellious spirit and revolutionary poetry. The uniqueness of *Kaagaz te Canvas* won her the prestigious Jnanpith award.

Dream Sequences and Memoirs

In Amrita's last collection of poetry *Main Tainu Pher Milangi* (*I Shall Meet You Again* 2004), each poem was accompanied by a sketch made by Imroz; one experiences two different forms of art in this anthology. A few of Amrita's dreams can be discerned in her lyricism which carry some memories or reflect a consciousness of imminent separation.

The idea of separation is integral to poetry right from the very beginning for the strong affect that it carries. Baba Farid spoke about it, so did the *gurbani*. Sufi poets sang about it and various schools of philosophy pondered over it. Punjabi folk songs too have narrated it, as have celebrated poets like Batalvi. The world of myths too is woven around the idea of separation. In Amrita's poetry, one finds a celebration of the concept of separation; it was not presented with either pity or pain. The language of this collection used popular linguistic and cultural symbols quite liberally.

As Amrita circled the idea of the moment of separation, the memories that rise before her include those of Afzal Tauseef; and Mazhar-ul Islam, Illiyas Ghuman, Fakhar Zaman, Taureeq are present too in conversation with her, as are the memories of Manto. There was an acknowledgement of their blessings and of the flame burning inside her. The moment these memories and symbols surrounded her, she observed the 'play' of the universe and pondered over the idea of death. She solemnly remembered the entire creation in the philosophical style of Buddha that runs parallelly in her consciousness. In these memories were also mingled moments of love even as she looked at death; also present were the moments when 'my breath drew upon your breath and several epochs passed by in the mind' (qtd. in Noor 2010: 52). Separation here was a consciousness of the eternal journey and not a final goodbye at the time of parting. In the play of that eternal yet joyous journey, at some places, the flute of Krishna beckoned her, while at other places, it was a vision from a myth entrenched in her subconscious which created a world of fantasy. The lamp that she had kept hidden within herself was a symbol that was realised in this poem. The worlds of dreams, nature, universe, myth, consciousness were all fused together. The beauty of this dream poetry emanated from this rich fusion. This dream vision rose from that 'oriental' consciousness which she had observed, examined, safely interred and nurtured in the crevices of her heart, and which was responsible for her multi-layered creativity. Several sages and saints who were aware of this often visited her for discussion and debate. She moulded this experience into the subject matter of her poetry, and that too in a dream-like simplicity, wherein the distinction between prose and poetry vanishes. The poem written on one page fuses with the picture drawn on the opposite page and thus becomes moulded into a new form of art.

One is accustomed to reading poetry in a rigid frame and according to a singular meaning entrenched in one's mind without bothering to understand the structural and literary specificities of a poem. But to understand Amrita's poetry, it is essential to keep all these myriad factors in mind. She creates a unique paradigm and the entire spectrum of her poetry can be understood through it. For Amrita good poetry empowers one with a sense of freedom. She says in *Rasidi Ticket*:

> Many poems I had penned.... After I finished writing the longest poem, all the poems titled 'Chetar', (The month of 'Chait' as per Indian calendar) and one last poem titled, 'Aag di eh Baat Hai, Tuhein eh Baat Pai Si' (This Tale is of Fire, You only Narrated it), I felt as if having suffered a fourteen-year exile I was now finally liberated.
>
> (qtd. in Noor, Mohanjit 2002: 221)

Thus does Amrita Pritam's theory of poetry stretch from that initial pain to a feeling of liberation and her symbolic structure is an expression of this poetic paradigm.

References

Pritam, Amrita. 1976, rpt. 1998. *Rasidi Ticket*. Delhi: Shilalekh Publishers.
———. 2019. *Kaagaz te Canvas to Pahilan*. Delhi: Shilalekh Publishers.
Noor, S. S. 2002. "Amrita Pritam da Kaavi-Shaashtar", in Mohanjit (ed.), *Goode Akkharan vali Varanmala*, pp. 216–221. New Delhi: Punjabi Academy.

Source

The chapter is excerpted from Noor, S.S. 2010. "Amrita Pritam di Kavita," *Amrita Pritam*. New Delhi: Sahitya Akademi, 2010, p. 15–54.

18

BEYOND THE WORLDLY

Mysticism in Amrita Pritam's Later Writings

Amia Kunwar
translated by Harmeet Kaur Jhajj

The poetic genius of Amrita Pritam – a poet par excellence, a living legend, a fragrant presence – blossomed at a very young age and she wrote in different forms of literature over a period of almost seventy-five years. However, after ten years of publishing poetry, her self-reflexivity about her own creative process led her to separate herself from all her poetry written prior to the anthology *Patthar Geetey* published in 1946; disregarding nine earlier anthologies and acknowledging only four poems even from *Patthar Geetey*. One needs to understand this conscious choice although from a critical point of view her earlier poetry may illuminate her poetic career more fully. The usual insights that readers seek into female consciousness, women's experiences and issues or current social problems in her writings seem transient, impermanent and inconsequential, however; upon a perusal of the entire body of Amrita's work from 1946 to 2004 when she published her anthology *Main Tainu Pher Milangi*, what appears stable, eternal and constant in her work are two experiences – one, the expression of love that has remained the primary source of Amrita's poetry from the initial stage for about 50 to 55 years, and the other, the expression of philosophical thought and insight into past and future lives; perhaps a natural progression accompanying advancing age.

Amrita's work published during her last ten years or so, notably, *Darveshan di Mehndi* (*The Dervishes' Ecstasy* 1996), *Utth ni Sahiba Suttiye* (*Wake up, Slumbering Sahiba* 1998) and *Main Tainu Pher Milangi* (*I Shall Meet You Again* 2004) are not pure poetry. She has also used prose to elucidate the reasons behind her feelings and experiences which inspired these poems to enable the reader to comprehend the subtle and delicate nuances contained in the complex imagery of her poetry. These compositions proclaim the philosophy which Acharya Rajneesh, Sri Aurobindo and many other philosophers have given the name of 'Three Dimension Theory' of the conscious, subconscious and unconscious mind. It is believed that everything is contained in the seven layers of consciousness and the layer which an ordinary human being is aware of lies in the middle, with three levels below and three above. This thought has been

DOI: 10.4324/9781003214656-28

reflected in her later writings. It is a state where nothing is impossible, but it is a state which can be reached only in unconsciousness or in a trance of ecstasy. Most people cannot access this easily, perhaps because this is a mystical, mysterious world beyond simple faith. Her poem 'Nakk da Moti' ('The Nose-pin') can be taken as an example:

> Hey, I was standing on the bridge of breath ...
> The pearl in my nose pin fell off ...
> When I came to, I stretched my hands to catch it
> But it slipped from between my fingers.
>
> (Pritam 1996: 21)

In this poem, Amrita compares her consciousness to her nose pin and just as the nose pin slips from between her fingers and is lost from sight, her consciousness too leaves her body, slips from her grasp and passes into the unknown to a place where, according to the poet, the lord of her heart observes her state and smiles gently. Amrita elucidates the emotion at the back of the central theme of the poem:

> The known and the unknown both dwell within this body, and one felt ... that the steadfast and unwavering point lies beyond the horizon of the known in the unknown – where I am unable to reach ... but somewhere there was a connecting thread – and I seemed to be connected with it ... and involuntarily some part of me would slip away and go there ... far away ... these were very difficult years, some image would appear like an illusion, visible and tangible to me, but then it would smile and vanish ... this feeling one day translated itself into words....
>
> (Pritam 1996: 20)

The final stanza of the poem states:

> Hey, this is a mirage – the beatitude of silence
> All that I spoke, uttered, wrote
> Is merely a tear drop
> That fell from my eyes....
>
> (Pritam 1996: 21)

This reminds one spontaneously of another of Amrita's short poems which encapsulates the pain and philosophy of her entire life:

> There was a pain
> Which I inhaled in silence
> like a cigarette.

Only a few poems flicked off
Like ash from a cigarette.

(Pritam 1970: 60)

One can glean from the very titles of these poems that they are different from the experiences of ordinary life, for example, 'Beej Braham di Leela' ('The Universe in a Seed'), 'Beej Deekhya' ('Initiation of a Seed'), 'Teejey Pir di Mehndi' ('The Passion of the Third Pir'), 'Aali' ('The Wise'), 'Havankund di Mitti' ('The Ash of the Oblations Urn'), 'Nabhi Naad' ('The Music Within'), Gufa Darshan ('Insight'), 'Gufa Chittar' ('The Image of Darkness'), etc. The books *Darveshan di Mehndi* (*The Dervishes' Ecstasy*), *Hujre di Mitti*, (*The Soil of the Cloister*), *Satt Kirnan* (*Seven Rays*), *Lal Dhage da Rishta* (*The Bond of the Red Thread*), *Chiragan di Raat* (*The Night of the Lamps*) are also associated with the experience of the unknown and the spiritual, and span a diversity of themes.

Similarly, the title and subject matter of Amrita's book *Utth ni Sahiba Suttiye* also stirs our consciousness; exhorting all those asleep to wake up and become an awakened soul. When Bibo, a peasant woman in *Mirza Sahiban* comes to Sahiba as Mirza's aunt, all she tells Sahiba, languishing with the pain of separation from Mirza, is, 'Wake up, slumbering Sahiba, get up and show yourself'. This is the crux of the contemplation of centuries where the one who wants to 'see' becomes the one who is 'seen', or one can say, the one who desires becomes the one who is desired (Pritam 1998: 10).

These poems delineate an image of a sensitive, subtly conscious soul. Secondly, they take one into an ineffable state where the difference between diverse states of mind is erased. This is a condition where one attains oneness, where the disease and the cure become one and the same thing; a state that the Punjabi balladeer, Damodar expressed as, 'Chanting the name of Ranjha, I am now one with Ranjha / Call me Dhido Ranjha now, let no one call me Heer now'. Amrita's poem, 'Ve Sain' ('O Seer') in *Utth ni...* may be understood from this perspective.

O Seer, your spinning wheel
has spun – the spinner.

(Pritam 1998: 30–31)

The female protagonist spins the spinning wheel of a spiritual guru. At first, she spins the wheel with enthusiasm and then with a patent effort, but gradually she becomes immersed in its rhythm and falls into a trance. It soon seems that it is not she who is spinning the wheel, but the wheel that is spinning her; and this transformation appears utterly natural. While the mortal body continues to dwell in this world, one's consciousness resides elsewhere. The poem takes us through the entire process of spinning as something that goes on within one's mind without the intrusion of any outside ritual, consideration or contemplation.

203

It is important to remember the legacy of Sufism that Amrita had inherited. The inspiration behind these lyrical expressions is the poetic techniques of the Sufi saint-poets. Although the poet, Shah Hussain, uses the images of spinning and a bobbin in a different context mostly to offer pearls of wisdom for damsels in this world, for Amrita they define one's very being. She uses a distinctive idiom to convey her thought through new, truly original and unique images. A poem published in the April 1999 issue of *Nagmani* equates Kabir with a writer – both as far as caste and occupation are considered. A glimpse of this is presented here:

> Who sat me down at the loom of words
> I am Kabir ... weaving words
> Into my bones seeped the icy chill of lifetimes
> And lightning bolt of eons struck me too
> I sobbed uncontrollably
> Now my weaver's soul laughs with gay abandon
> 'Twas just one garment that I wore
> The garment of words that I weave.

> (Pritam 1999: 1)

In these final compositions, Amrita has embarked on a journey to pure inner consciousness and in this process, her articulation of experience also undergoes a spontaneous transformation. Renouncing appellations like 'beloved', 'friend', etc., the 'you' that she addresses now is in reverential epithets like 'Sain' or 'Aali'. So much so that she even addresses her partner Imroz as 'Sayian Baba' or 'Beloved-Saint'. By appending the word 'baba' (saint) to 'sayian' (beloved) she transforms the normal connotations of these ordinary words. She says:

> Entering the cloister of the sky
> I shut the door upon the world
> And smearing the sacred ashes of love
> My God became a sanyasi.

> (Pritam 1998: 82)

The word 'cloister' is employed for that dark cave or chamber where one sits in meditation for years on end, and the very soil of that space becomes redolent with holiness, making that place worthy of being worshipped. However, in the above-mentioned lines 'cloister' connotes Amrita's contemplative journey into inner consciousness. But Tantra science goes beyond this. It advocates a technique in which instead of some outer edifice, one's own body becomes a cave or a cloister, in which this mortal body becomes resonant and is able to feel the vibrations to transform itself into a hallowed chamber of God (Pritam 1998: 87).

At this point, another transformation occurs in Amrita's writing. She rises above the experience and sensitivity of womanhood and feminism to become purely a human being. In fact, Amrita's compositions are associated with non-dualistic, introverted contemplation. These actions are beyond the traditional or older social and material experience. Her poems depict the effort and conscious attention that is required in order to lose oneself in contemplation.

But, for Amrita, the strands of existence in the here-and-now cannot be extricated from those of the life beyond; they continue to remain tangled. A spiritual guru, 'Mohan', christened 'Swami Krishna Chaitanya' came in contact with Amrita upon being initiated into the spiritual order. She induced a mystical transformation in his personality and renamed him 'Sain Kaka', a title that he is known by in the whole world even today. While the word 'sain' indicates someone untouched by the material world, 'kaka' is steeped in material and human relationships of attachment.

This is characteristic of Amrita's complex personality. Ailing, bed-ridden for a long time, Amrita returns to live this very life once again. Shackled by her travails of pain, fear, insecurity, renunciation of this world, doubts, agitation and what-ifs, she continues to chant the name of 'Ima' or Imroz even in a state of unconsciousness, believing him to be her first and last constant, the pole-star of her life, living life in the belief that she would surely meet him in some form or the other, yet again. Though the 'where' and 'how' is not clear, she is confident that she will find Imroz once again – 'one the flame, the second, the image' is a belief that is evident in the poem 'I Will Meet You Again' in the anthology with the same title.

> I know nothing but that
> Whatever Time ordains
> This life shall walk with me.
>
> (Pritam 2004)

Thus, Amrita views *ishq majazi* and *ishq haqiqi*, that is, worldly, material love and spiritual, mystical love respectively as one and not separate from each other. Even while she immersed herself completely in the spiritual in the last few years of her life, she continued to hold the fringe of the worldly between her fingers. This is what is unique about her creative world and achievements.

References

Pritam, Amrita. 1996, rpt. 2017. *Darveshan di Mehndi*. Delhi: Shilalekh.
———. 1998, rpt. 2012. *Utth ni Sahiba Suttiye*. Delhi: Shilalekh.
———. 1999. Ed. Nagmani. Delhi: Nagmani.
———. 2004. *Main Tainu Pher Milaangi*. Delhi: Shilalekh.

19

LINGUISTIC DISCOURSE OF AMRITA PRITAM'S WRITINGS

Manjinder Singh
Translated by Harmeet Kaur Jhajj

Socio-cultural existence is an indicator of humanity that is far beyond a human being's mere biological existence and this identity is expressed and defined through language. In modern Punjabi literature, Amrita Pritam is a symbol of the struggle of the Indian woman for a separate, independent identity and is credited with the creation of a new language to lend a literary voice to woman's concerns. Hence, a formal analysis of the discourse of her innovative literary language is mandatory in order to understand the flow of the existential structure in Amrita's literary work. This can be discussed in two ways: by considering Amrita's language as an object and studying it according to the established rules and principles of the philosophy of language and linguistics to identify distinctive features of her literary language; or rather than look at her creative literary work merely as an object of study, accept it as a source of knowledge through which the emerging shape of the philosophy of language can be identified. The chapter will attempt to understand the linguistic discourse of Amrita's work through both these methods.

Language is not just a collection of sounds, words, or sentences but a complete culture in itself; meaning in language is implied in socio-cultural contexts. Just by analysing sounds, words or the grammar of sentences, one cannot understand the mystique of the language of literature. It is important to understand the technical and scientific meaning of grammar in Amrita's work, to investigate the grammar of its creativity and recognise the grammar of its aesthetics. In order to understand the linguistic discourse of Amrita's creative work, one must keep in mind the creative character of literary language and look beyond its morphology and syntax and understand its expanding semiotics. Literary language is not merely intellectual discourse; its literariness is strongly inspired by instinct. The first point regarding Amrita's language is that it has not one axis but two – intellect and instinct. Intellect is logical behaviour or praxis, while instinct is the powerful flow

DOI: 10.4324/9781003214656-29

of natural energy in the human mind. Usually, there is no similitude in the intellect and the instinct of man. Human utterance is inspired by intellect, while deeds are inspired by instinct. Consequently, one's words and deeds are at variance with each other. However, in Amrita's literary language, intellect and instinct are united and her words and deeds are one and the same. Unlike most other literary personalities, there is little difference in her life and creative output; her life and her work are in tune with each other and her work reflects her life. Perhaps if a difference had existed, her language would not have been able to generate that allurement and appeal that it does. As another celebrated Punjabi poet, Surjit Patar says:

> A conversation also goes on inside me,
> Where my blood moulds itself into words
> Where my argument is with my own self
> Where my descendants and forefathers stand facing one another.
>
> (Patar 2008: 13)

Amrita's own blood is moulded into her language, and her words become a manifestation of the anguish experienced by her body and soul. She is herself acutely conscious of this kind of creative process of her language. Indications of this can be seen in her writings, for example in the play of metaphor in her poem 'Chetar':

> The soul knocked on the door
> Today's song was formed thus
> As if words formed beads of sweat
> on the body of love ...
> The lips of the pen trembled
> Today's song was formed thus
> Some tears of sentences flowed ...
> All the pages of the heart opened
> Today's song was formed thus
> Like some stitches sewn on the
> wound of silence came apart.
>
> (Pritam 2006: 179)

Amrita's language impacts the unconscious of the reader because it is not inspired by intellect alone. Her intellectualism casts its magic spell on both body and soul by traversing instinctive emotiveness. The following excerpt depicting the mental condition of Pooro, the protagonist of her novel *Pinjar*, is an example:

> The sky was overcast. Pooro was shelling peas, a piece of sack under her feet. When she pressed open the pod to extract the peas

onto the palm of her hand, a white worm clung to her thumb. As when one's foot lands in a pit of muck, Pooro clenched her teeth in disgust. She jerked her arm to fling the worm away and pressed her hands under her knees .... Pooro felt as if her body from head to toe was like that pod in which instead of the pure peas an impure worm was thriving. She developed a hatred for her entire body. She felt like flinging off the worm growing in her womb; to hurl it away from her body, like plucking out an embedded thorn with one's nails, like throwing off a stinging swarm of bees, like dislodging the ticks on the udders of the cattle, like peeling off a clinging leech.

(Pritam 2011: 5)

In Amrita's poetic language, the conflict between nature and culture is clearly discernible. Language is a cultural achievement of human life. As culture evolved, humans took natural language from consciousness to build a system of cultural language. For humans, nature is innate, but culture is acquired. Natural language is the flow of desires, whereas cultural language is regulated by socio-cultural contexts. Under socio-cultural control, humans dismiss natural language from the conscious mind, but it is indestructible and inexhaustible and embeds itself into one's unconscious. Tears of laughter spouting from the eyes due to either boundless joy or intense sorrow are remnants of natural language in accultured Homo sapiens. The keening of a mother upon the death of a child is an expression of her unbearable grief and anguish in natural language and is extremely difficult to express in sentences of cultural language. Cultural language builds restrictions, whereas natural language is free from cultural taboos. Amrita's poetic language lives through the paradox of this conflict and descends into the realm of myth; the poem 'Oedipus' is a discourse on this conflict:

> This side of the threshold,
> My sin.
> The other side,
> my punishment ...
>
> Had thought it utterly pure
> This odour of milk
> But my lips were defiled ...
> The first sound from my lips,
> My first, lisping words
> Those words became sullied ...
> ...
>
> Now perhaps my whole life
> I shall search for this love

In the muck of carnal desire!
In forbidden or permitted flesh
Shall search for this fragrance
Shall search for this scent.

(Pritam 1970: 23)

Language is not just verbal; a large portion of it is non-verbal. The spoken is merely a sign of the unspoken. The philosophy of the Indian language discusses this unspoken form in detail. Indication about the conspicuous and the inconspicuous existence of word/language is recorded in the *Rig Veda*:

Four are the definite grades of speech
The learned and (the) wise know them
Three of these are deposited in secret
They indicate no meaning to the common man
Men speak the fourth grade of speech
Which is phonetically expressed.

(*Rig Veda* 1.164.45 qtd. in Rial 2004: 95)

As per the *Rig Veda*, there are four levels of word/language known to the learned and the wise. Of these four, three are located in the obscure realm of mystery and hold no meaning for ordinary humans who enunciate the fourth level of the word/language which originates at the level of sound. In Bhagat Kabir's *Baavan Akhari* (*Fifty-Two Letters*), these visible and invisible aspects have been given the notation of verbal and non-verbal forms of communication.

Where there is speech, there are words.
Where there is no speech, the mind can rest on nothing.
God exists in both speech and silence.
No one can know God as He is.

(*Shri Guru Granth Sahib*: 340)

The great linguist Bhartrihari has called these different levels of language *para*, *pashyanti*, *madhyama* and *vaikhari*. *Vaikhari* is the spoken/sound form of language, while the rest are its non-verbal facets. The real mystery of language lies in its unspoken facets and there is a lot that is unspoken in Amrita's language. In the realm of her consciousness, the spoken form of language, limited as it is by cultural boundaries and biases, is incapable of expressing her experience. That which Amrita wants to say is restricted in the language of 'culture'. The discourse of the poem 'Sabhayta' ('Culture') is very relevant in this context:

The thought that words cannot express
I have that thought

209

The word which lips cannot utter
I have that word.
Your culture
If you can ask, then do so
Or search when you can
Its clothes and belongings
Because a word of my unrestricted thoughts
Is lost.
And you well know
Who comes to this house except you!
No one comes, except you.
I birth the sun day after day
Your culture –
Which borrows light
from the outside sky
Sees my sun, my light
And scolds it every day
I birth the sun everyday
And every day is the sun orphaned.

(Pritam 1970: 13)

In the Indian knowledge tradition, the sun is a metaphor for knowledge. The sun that rises in the creative consciousness of Amrita is not acceptable to culture.

The language discourse of Amrita's writings is meaningful in the context of a woman's identity. She is in search of a new language in which woman is not relegated to the margin. The system of language and symbol that she inherited from her socio-cultural milieu does not enable her to express the experience of being a woman adequately. The inherited language and symbol system is male-centred; hence, an independent presentation of a woman's existence is not possible in this idiom. Creative imagination and a knowledge system based on male-centric language reduce woman to 'silence'. Under the pressure of man-centric language, at times Amrita's language turns into silence, while at other times it critically analyses the man-centric symbolic arrangement. In her book *This Sex Which Is Not One*, Luce Irigaray, a feminist thinker, has expressed the need to evolve a different idiom:

> I am trying as I have already indicated, to go back through the mas-
> culine imaginary, to interpret the way it has reduced us to silence,
> to muteness, or mimicry, and I am attempting, from that starting
> point and at the same time, to (re)discover a possible space for the
> feminine imaginary.

(1985: 164)

Just as Irigaray is in search of a possible space for woman-centric creative imagination, similarly, Amrita's poetic language discourse is in search of a novel language idiom to present woman's independent existence. According to Amrita, a woman's entire energy and intellect and language do not have an independent identity or pathway; they flow merely in the footprints of man. The innate vital force of woman is powerful, but male-centric culture has domesticated it. That is why now woman does not have either her own thought or her own language:

> The romance of some unknown men
> And that of the unknown texts of some books
> That my blood –
> Follows the scent of their footprints....
> This blood was very wild
> Roaring in the veins
> And with teeth – and claws – tearing down thrones
> But the nemesis of this blood is
> That it trots along sniffing the footprints of men and texts
> And sits in the veins like a pet dog, wagging its tail.
>
> (Pritam 1970: 39)

Language is not just a medium of communication but a complete culture in itself. Language and culture feed into each other, and both are traditionally male-centric. A sharp gender-based discrimination is discernible in a socio-linguistic analysis of any language when inanimate objects are divided. The bigger object is designated a masculine noun, and the smaller object of the same category is a feminine noun designate. One may derive the patriarchal character of Punjabi culture from a socio-linguistic understanding of the Punjabi language. For example, in Punjabi every living organism is divided into male and female as per the natural gender system, and in dividing inanimate objects, Punjabi assigns masculine gender to a bigger object and feminine gender to a smaller object in the same category. For example:

Masculine	Feminine
Pakkha (fan)	Pakkhi (smaller fan)
Manja (single bed)	Manji (smaller single bed)
Mota (fat man)	Moti (fat woman)
Kurta (long shirt)	Kurti (shorter shirt)
Ramba (gardening tool)	Rambi (smaller gardening tool)

In the Punjabi language, the primary forms of most nouns are masculine, with feminine gender nouns being modified from these masculine nouns. Masculine gender nouns formed by modifying feminine gender nouns are non-existent in the Punjabi language. From the cultural expanse of the

211

grammatical stratagem of word formation, the patterns of the collective unconscious of a people associated with a language or culture can be recognised. How this gender-based injustice in the grammatical strategy of Punjabi word formation came to pass may be understood in the context of the words of the noted critic, G.S. Rial:

> A method to belittle and demean woman is prevalent in grammar too. *Bihari* in Punjabi language performs the function of a suffix to indicate the measure of a lesser degree like *patti* which means a small *patta* or leaf. Nouns and adjectives of feminine gender are modified in the same way, for example, *buddhi* (old) is the feminine of *buddha* or old man or *madhri* (short) which is the corresponding feminine form of *madhra*. Overall, the scales are heavily tilted in favour of man. Man has been regarded as an image of God. According to the Bhakti viewpoint, God has been accorded the designation of husband who is worshipped by the devotee in a feminine form.
>
> (2004: 95)

In male-centric culture language, society, religion, politics, economy, etc. are defined by, and function from, a man's perspective. In the Indian, specifically Punjabi, culture the economy is headed by the male; sons, not daughters, inherit ancestral property. Equal rights granted as per law are a far cry from the existing reality in the collective mindset of the Indian or Punjabi social culture. Without economic equality, the social relationship of man and woman is that of a master and slave. In the conventional language of such a relationship, very respectful terms are determined for the wife to use to address her husband, but such respectful words are not used when a husband is to address his wife. Amrita's poem 'Annadata' ('The Provider') depicts this linguistic and cultural behaviour:

> Provider!
> Upon my tongue – is your salt
> Your name – stamped upon my father's lips
> And my father's blood runs in this body of mine!
> How can I speak!
> Before I speak, speaks your beneficence,
> There are some words, but we, the worms of the grain
> Sag under the weight of this grain – and they are buried too.
> (Pritam 2006:11)

The strategy of the male-centred Punjabi language and culture is similar. Hence, a woman's position in the Punjabi collective unconscious is lower than that of a man. This has also influenced Punjabi folk language, exemplified in the desire for, and joy in, begetting a son in the Punjabi mindset. Punjabi folk songs do not celebrate the birth of a daughter as it is regarded to be a cause for sorrow and sadness. The language of Amrita's writings is very conscious of this nature of Punjabi folk language. When Pooro goes to the fair in *Pinjar*, a group of Jat lads are singing *boliyan*, i.e. couplets. The text and the context of these depict the commodification of a woman's identity, and Pooro's reaction to these couplets depicts her desire for a novel language from which man's hegemony is absent:

> She sat at the well
> Brushing her teeth to polish them white
> They who take a fancy for you
> Will wed you, fear not.

'Alas! Would someone care to see the state these 'pretty' girls are in,' escaped softly from Pooro's lips....

Pooro kept thinking that all those songs were paeans to beautiful maidens, all hymns described true love. Will such songs be ever penned that lament the woes of girls like me? Will there be such hymns which have no gods to praise?

(Pritam 1958: 22-23)

The passage indicates the male gaze and the reduction of the female as only a desirable object to be available to a male. Just as God is the centre of the divine world, man is the centre of the human world. Jacques Derrida considers this assumption of the centre as deadly to human freedom; according to him, the entire western thought system is centred on a few specifics which determine and define all meanings. The problem of the centre is that it attains prominence for itself and prohibits others, and in doing so, it neglects and overlooks the marginalised others and suppresses them. Similarly, in a male-dominated society the male assumes the centre and the woman is reduced to being the marginalised 'other'.

However, folk songs are simple, spontaneous expressions of the collective mind and are capable of affecting the collective unconscious. A genuine poet is both an individual and a collective being. Amrita is conscious of the implied hegemony and injustice in the linguistic folk tradition, but the aesthetic charm and grace of innocent folk songs is an integral part of the consciousness of her poetic language. The appealing colours of Punjabi folk language are thoroughly dissolved in Amrita's creativity.

> Who can sew the phulkari of light!
> In the alcove of the sky
> I shall light the lamp of the Sun
> So high is the altar of the heart,

Who shall place the lamp there!
Had it been the galaxy glorious,
I would've filled my pitcher
But this is a river of sorrow,
Who will take even a sip!
This fervid fire
That is your parting gift
The burning embers in the heart
Who will ever endure the flames!
You have closed this chapter for good
Even then a sigh speaks of you!
Who can sew the phulkari of light!

(Pritam 2006: 148)

A special kind of philosophy of language emerges in Amrita's expression which is meaning-centred instead of being word-centric. Meanings are the unseen mystery of language; words are the vehicles of meanings. If words are not loyal to their meanings, then the aesthetic beauty and charm of words is meaningless. The import of meaning here is centred on deeds instead of words. If meanings do not translate into action, words are merely illusions. According to Amrita, when words do not behave in earnest accordance with their meaning, they violate them. Her literary journey, in its entirety, is in search of a fresh idiom which is free from every kind of hegemony. It is one in which there is unity of instinct and intellect; one which is free from discrimination and injustice created by culture; one in which glimpses of the charm and appeal of natural and socio-cultural diversity are seen, but this diversity is not defined in terms of high and low; one in which cultural control and checks do not strangle innate nature; words remain loyal to their meanings, and words and deeds are in harmony. That Amrita achieves this harmony is evidenced by the mythic stature she has acquired; she has taken root in the collective unconscious of the community, and her writings are deeply imprinted upon the mindscapes of the community.

To cover the nakedness of meanings
I draped the arm of words around their neck
Don't these words stay within the limits of decency?
Today the same words have returned
after raping the meanings
And stand shamefaced before me,
Not meeting my eyes.

(Pritam 1970: 39)

References

Irigaray, Luce. 1985. *This Sex Which is Not One*. New York: Cornell University Press.

Manmohan. 2006. *Derridian Vikhandan atte Bharti Gyan Shashtar*. Delhi: Punjabi Sabhyacharak Kendra.

Patar, Surjit. 2008. *Surzameen*. Chandigarh: Lokgeet Parkashan.

Pritam, Amrita. 1958, 2011. *Pinjar*. Delhi: Shri Parkashan.

———. 1970. *Kaagaz te Canvas*. Delhi: Navyug Publishers.

———. 2006. *Kaagaz te Canvas Ton Pehlan*. Delhi: Shilalekh Publications.

Rial, G. S. 2004. *Shabadan Diyan Likhtan*. Ludhiana: Chetna Parkashan.

Shri Guru Granth Sahib. https://sggsonline.com/guru-granth-sahib-page-340 (accessed on 20.12.2021).

Part VI

ROMANCING THE MEDIA

20

DEMYSTIFYING THE 'LEGENDARY':

Re-visiting Amrita Pritam through Her Interface with Popular Indian Media (1947-2005)

Guntasha K. Tulsi

For any woman writer born in the pre-Partition phase of a newly developing 20th-century Indian nation-state, the avenues and modes of representation were limited. One could either be a woman or a writer – usually trapped in meaningless stereotypes and undesirably marginalised or, on rare occasions, an agent of gradual, albeit, much required and meaningful change. Amrita Pritam falls in the second category – a feisty woman and an unapologetic writer – who refused to be silenced or sidelined and became an unstoppable force of feminist imagination on India's literary landscape. Interestingly, her maturing into one of India's finest writers parallelled a radical transformation in the nation's destiny as well; a country that began its journey as an economically under-developed and a socialist nation-state after its independence in 1947; eventually formulating a responsible post-independent policy of non-alignment and self-preservation which ensured its distinctive character and unique spirit.

The Indian story was premised on Gandhian idealism, Nehruvian progressivism and an altering socio-cultural and politico-national character. It came to be reflected in popular media of the day as well. Significantly, Amrita's evolution into one of Punjab's finest writers coincided with the growth story of the nation's media. This essay examines Amrita's complex and discursive interface with popular Indian media platforms – popular press (newspapers, magazines, journals, periodicals, etc.), television, films and documentaries, interviews, radio content, theatrical production and, in the current times, the digital 'boom' and cyberspace.

In endorsing the orthodox socio-cultural character of India in the 1950s and the 1960s, the media continuously negotiated with the multiple layers of Amrita's personality, and both celebrated and censured aspects of her life and literature. To explore the elaborate terrain of Amrita's interface with the Indian media through subsequent decades, this chapter is divided into three parts:

Part I: 'Early Media Interactions' captures Amrita's fascinating and candid interface with the media during the earliest three to four decades of her

DOI: 10.4324/9781003214656-31

career (1940s to 1970s) through her numerous interviews to print media and her tenure at All-India Radio (AIR). Part II: 'Later Media Interactions' assesses her interactions with the Indian media after the mid-1970s. This can be considered as the mature phase of her blossoming into a memorable woman writer who resolutely refused to wear a façade in public. Here, along with print, the focus is on her interaction with the electronic media, which was growing rapidly in a gradually liberalising Indian economy. Part III: 'Film Adaptations' looks beyond her conventional media interactions to focus on the various film adaptations in Hindi made on her select works and her collaboration with this medium. This part provides a perspective on these adaptations and is followed by the conclusion.

Part I: Early Media Interactions (1940s to Early 1970s)

For a woman who was engaged to be married at the age of four and lost her mother at 11, Amrita Pritam's journey (1919-2005), of becoming one of India's finest known writers, has been a fascinating one. Numerous accounts, interviews, testimonies and autobiographical renditions paint a picture of her loneliness as a child and a teenager. Her father, a poet and a scholar, fluent in many Indian languages, passed on his love for language and literature to his daughter and encouraged her to write poetry.[1] These early years of artistic experimentation were the foundation of a memorable career of almost seven decades in which, apart from poetry, she wrote copiously in various other genres – essay, novel, biographical writing, short story, etc.

The devastating events related to the Partition of the Indian subcontinent (1947) compelled Amrita to leave Lahore and move to Delhi with her two children. By this time, she had made up her mind to be on her own and carve a niche for herself in a newly blossoming Indian nation-state. These years also marked the beginning of restrained public broadcasting in India. AIR and Doordarshan were at the centre stage during this era, and the elaborate print network comprised of a series of national dailies and weeklies, newspapers and magazines. Amrita was an early participant in this phase of the evolving Indian media industry of the 1940s-1960s, and her first job assignment in India (and also the first significant media interaction) was with AIR in Delhi between the years 1948 and 1961 and she began her public career by organising and hosting shows. In fact, her association with this medium can be traced to her brief stint with the Lahore radio in pre-Partition days. Her consistent interest in popular media of her times and her interaction with the masses from a relatively young age can be understood from her life as a precocious young girl who evolved much faster spiritually and intellectually than her peers. She would come to literally document and discuss her life in full public glare with unapologetic confidence.

However, her early experiences also reveal how the coverage by certain media platforms affected her adversely. In one of her earliest interviews for a popular print daily, the *Statesman* in 1968, she mentions that when she played the sitar for the Lahore radio station in the early 1940s, her photo published in the radio programme journals was used as a poster by the local shopkeepers of the area. This created quite a 'scandal' 'for no fault of mine' (Pritam 1968-69: 1). In the same interview, she also observes that people were 'furious' with her choices from the very beginning, and the 'chagrin of many' arose from the fact that 'a woman doctor is all right, not a woman writer' (Pritam 1968-69: 1).

Her confessional style was evident in her interviews of these early years. During one of her trips to East Europe, while responding to a question in an interview for a radio show, she resisted any specific political bracketing and stressed the importance of individualism over Marxism. Later, she realised that instead of representing her full-length opinion, 'they cut it out while broadcasting!' (Pritam 1968-69: 2) – the obvious reference here being to their issue with her avoidance of the term 'Marxism'. Thus, one sees that across her media interactions, both nationally and internationally – regardless of political or social constraints – she exhibited no hesitation about expressing what she felt was vital for a meaningful evolution of the human spirit. She reiterates this in an interview given to Carlo Coppola for the Asian Studies Center journal, Michigan State University, *Mahfil*:

> I wouldn't call myself a Marxist. I am too much of an individualist to be one. I can admire something when it's good for the welfare of the people. Of course, I admire Marxism … I admire some of the changes in the socialist countries, but not all, especially the lack of individual freedom. I have spoken about that freely there.
>
> (Coppola and Pritam 1968-69: 7)

This disenchantment with almost all political systems and scepticism regarding established religious axioms made her take refuge in love, compassion and a belief in humanism. She also candidly revealed in another interview that her marital home no longer provided her with the comfort that she was looking for as a writer and it was her husband, Pritam Singh, who encouraged her to follow her distinctive calling of becoming a passionate storyteller and an inventive thinker (Verma 1992).

Meanwhile, her interviews also touched upon the choices of her writing career, her wide international travel experience, her lament at the state of Punjabi writing and publishing industry, the defining impact of Partition and reflections on womanhood. In the interview with Coppola, Amrita talks about her visits to the Soviet Union and Central and East Europe during the 1960s (1968-69: 7). She encouraged experimental, trans-national and progressive literature and collaborated with numerous Hungarian, Bulgarian,

221

Yugoslav and Russian writers and poets for her literary journal, *Nagmani*, that she ran for over three decades.

Her writing in this phase is a testimony to multiple influences which shaped her – from her affiliation with the Progressive Writers' Association to her reading of romantic and Sufi artistes; she was a rare poet and a writer who insisted on writing in Punjabi when most of her contemporaries wrote in Urdu. In the interview with Coppola, she said that her concern about the lack of readership for Punjabi writers compelled her to publish in 'Hindi translation first, then in my own language afterwards' (1968-69: 15).

She acknowledged the influence of Punjabi writers and poets on her writing – from poets such as Mohan Singh, Harbhajan Singh and Shiv Kumar Batalvi to short story writers like Kulwant Singh Virk and K.S. Duggal. In fact, in several media interactions she fondly remembered Principal Teja Singh, who first noticed her writings and reviewed her works in popular journals and magazines of the day, thus making her a widely familiar figure within the regional literary circuit (Pritam 1968-69: 2). She also remained an important figure of dissent and experimentalism within the regional literary tradition across distinct phases of her writing. In her early interviews itself, she testified to 'emotions and not form', determining the pulse of her poetry (Coppola and Pritam 1968-69: 10). Additionally, Amrita's compositions are a testimony to the influence of non-Punjabi writers, a fact she herself mentions in the above-cited interview. From John Steinbeck, Edgar Allan Poe and Robert Frost to Kalidasa, Faiz Ahmad Faiz, Waris Shah, Krishan Chander, Bedi and Kamala Das – the influences on her were wide and eclectic.

In all her interviews given to distinct media platforms during this phase, Amrita has reiterated the one incident which affected her writing and psychology deeply – Partition. Witnessing the devastating riots first-hand, being rendered homeless herself and migrating eventually to Delhi deepened her distrust of all forms of political ideologies and added emotional and spiritual angst to her content as a radio presenter. A lot of her work germinated from this tragic unfolding of the communal divide and her migration through a train journey between the cities of Lahore, Delhi and Dehradun. Her best-known works – the poem, 'Ajj Aakhaan Waris Shah nu' ('To Waris Shah', 1947) and the novel *Pinjar* (*The Skeleton*, 1950) – arose out of these experiences, making her one of the most evocative voices on both sides of the border.

In one of the first interviews which she gave after winning the Sahitya Akademi Award for her poetic work titled *Sunhede* (*Messages*, 1955), she documents the pain of receiving mixed responses from the popular press:

> Men take women's writing lightly; they doubt a woman's sincerity. For example, when I got this Sahitya Akademi award, and with it fame, the leading English daily in Delhi wrote that I got my

popularity in Punjabi literature because of my youth and beauty. I was very sorry to read that. Why not talent? They can admire a beautiful woman, but not a talented one.

(Coppola and Pritam 1968-69: 11)

She adds that she also 'toasted an article' which was written against her, in a celebration of what was the 'Silver Anniversary of Abuses' by the media.

Clearly, this phase of her media interaction was both chequered and contentious as it focussed more on her non-conformist life choices than on the aesthetics of her work. However, she did not allow it to affect her courage and honesty and gradually learnt to deal with both praise and criticism with grace, good humour and courage.

Part II: Later Media Interactions

The post-mid-1970s phase of Amrita's life was a narrative of her magnifying legendary status after her being awarded a range of national and international honours, nominated for the membership of Rajya Sabha (1986) and admiring worldview of polarisingly different figures such as Indira Gandhi and Rajneesh Osho.[2]

Her interaction with the popular broadcasting platforms reflected the transformation of the Indian media of the 1970s-1980s and the 1990s, characterised now by the liberalising Indian economy, and the expanding and deepening influence of various media platforms (led by the advent of colour television, expansion in private radio and TV channels and diversifying print-media platforms) on the masses.

Amrita, by now a larger-than-life figure, was no stranger to the ambiguous role of popular media and related experiences are narrated through various incidents in her autobiography, *Rasidi Ticket* (1976), possibly the sincerest account of her life in her own words. She cites the objections of the print media and literary magazines to 'Ajj Aakhaan ...' written as a dirge on Partition but evoking universal elements of human suffering. While Sikhs complained that the poem should have been addressed to Guru Nanak instead of Waris Shah, Communists lamented that it wasn't addressed to their leaders (Pritam 1976: 25). She also mentions the hue and cry over the publication of her poem 'Nau Supne' ('Nine Dreams'), which described the period through which Mata Tripta carried Guru Nanak in her womb.[3] The poem led to a decree being issued against her by the S.G.P.C.[4] for having insulted the Sikh religion (Pritam 1976: 119). She says:

Punjab's newspapers said all kinds of things about me and even asked the Punjab Government to ban this poem. Kirpal Singh Kasel, of the newspaper *Ajit*, labelled me as a 'lustful pest' who had no right to write a poem on Guru Nanak.

(1976: 82)

223

Pritam also refers to the dismissive attitude of the writing fraternity when she won the Bharatiya Jnanpith Award in 1982 (119). Similar incidents are recalled in an interview given to Rama Jha in 1982. On being asked about the controversy related to her poem 'Annadata' ('The Provider'), she mentions that the poem was banned (Pritam and Jha 1968-69: 12). She rues the fact that her (now celebrated) novel, *Chakk No. 36*, was also prohibited by the Punjab government, as it was considered 'pornographic' (Pritam 1982: 195).

There is a sense of recurring sorrow in all these interactions that her works are treated reductively only to drag her into a controversy. Contrarily, her artistic mastery and audacity are evident from her range of experimental texts written during this phase – *Kari Dhoop ka Safar* (*Journey under the Blazing Sun*; a study of women poets of the world from the time of *Rig Veda* onwards), 'Shah di Kanjari' ('The Shah's Harlot'; a short story based on a confrontation of two women belonging to different social strata) and *Unninja Din* (*49 Days*; a psychological drama based on a passionate man-woman relationship).

The remarkable quality of her media interactions lay in the fact that she spoke on a variety of issues courageously and truthfully without being pedantic or superficial. She returned repeatedly to Partition and her writings on it in her interviews. A memorable interview is the one given to Andrew Whitehead as part of a radio series for the BBC World Service, titled *India: A People Partitioned*.[5] She talks about the genesis of 'Ajj Aakhaan', observing that she remembered Waris Shah while travelling from Lahore to Dehradun via train after being displaced during Partition. In another vein, the influence of Punjab's Sufi poets on her writings is also gratefully acknowledged during this interview. She says:

> Punjabi culture, their poets, their Sufi poets, especially – I love: from Waris Shah to Shah Hussain, Bulleh Shah to Hasham ... from the very beginning, I read these poems ... they were in my blood. They were above all religion ... so they spoke (in) the revolt of the blood.
>
> (Pritam, Whitehead)

She bemoaned the fate of the 'children' of those countless abducted women who became 'forced mothers'. Between the 1950s and 1960s, poetry became a mode of catharsis for her, and the moving influence of her works even across the border can be noted from her testimony to the historian Nonica Dutta in an interview. Here, she mentions that her friend Sajjad Haider, a Pakistani Urdu playwright, translated her *nazms* into English and published them in *Pakistan Times* (Pritam, Datta 2017: 70-71).[6]

Another remarkable undated video interview (possibly of the 1990s and retrieved as digital video footage) demonstrated her progressive views on the man-woman relationship. She says that for a man to deny the power of a woman is actually a denial of his own subconscious. Amrita invoked the concept of *ardha-narishvara* (half-man, half-woman) from Indian mythology and asserted that it was only when the two unite that a whole human being is born.[7] It is this radically liberating humanism of Amrita, so palpable in all her radio and television interviews, that makes her stand taller than the rest of the crowd. In her autobiography, she mentions her interaction with Ho Chi Minh (1890-1969), the Vietnamese president, who complimented her for being quite like him – she used the power of her pen as he used the power of his sword. She even wrote a poem about him which was published in a Vietnamese newspaper in 1958 (Pritam 1976: 39). She kept adapting to constantly evolving media and was always open to public interactions and participated in numerous public recitals of her own poetry. Her house welcomed interviewers, print and television personalities and numerous media figures.

Amrita did not escape unsparing criticism even after her death. Khushwant Singh, despite being her translator, reader and contemporary (having known her from her Lahore days), wrote some caustic articles after her passing away in 2005. In an obituary titled 'Thinking of Amrita: Much ado about mantras', while he praised Amrita's unusual charm, he also labelled her as parochial:

> Amrita was not a highly educated woman, nor exposed to good writing in languages other than Punjabi. Nor sophisticated enough to add new dimensions to her own. She was besotted with Bollywood and believed getting one of her works accepted by a filmmaker was the ultimate success. All her stories and novels were sob stuff and uniformly second rate.
>
> (2005)

For Singh, 'To Waris Shah' was her defining work; much of the rest was 'sheer atmospherics'. His criticism notwithstanding, one thing that cannot be ignored is that even he considered her writings significant enough to be translated and anthologised.

Part III: Film Adaptations

Amrita's most popular works have been adapted for cinema and theatre. Mainstream Hindi adaptations of her works have attempted to portray the trailblazing qualities of her female characters. One of the earliest films was H.K. Verma's *Kadambari* (1975). The simple plot focusses on the deeply embedded social, economic and religious divide in an evolving post-independent India and the angst of the young Indian generation through the love story of Chetna and Amit (the film changes the religious identity of the male protagonist, possibly to underplay the religious overtones of Amrita's actual narrative). Amrita's creative involvement in film projects based on her works is clear from a reading of *Rasidi Ticket*; she talks about her role in the composition of one of the most celebrated songs of this film, 'Ambar ki ek pak surahi …' ('From the pure pitcher of the skies …') – a translation of one of her own songs from Punjabi into Hindi (Pritam 1976: 96).

The other cinematic adaptation from the same period which looks at the perspective of the marginalised and the anti-social has been Basu Bhattacharya's lesser-known 1975 film, *Daaku* (*The Dacoit*) based on her work, *Unhan di Kahani* (*Their Story*). The menace of dacoity was a much discussed and prevalent phenomenon in India between the 1950s and 1980s, and popular media (most notably, Hindi commercial films), cashed in on this theme – some examples being the cult-film, *Sholay* (1975) and the internationally acclaimed *Bandit Queen* (1994). Amrita's novel delves into the underlying causes which create a 'dacoit' and the film explores at its centre, the prostitute-dacoit (Champa-Daku Raju) relationship, so as to evolve a subdued, but hard-hitting socio-economic critique of the metanarrative of development.

Pinjar (2003), based on her novel with the same name, is the most well received of the media adaptations of her works and created awareness about Amrita's core philosophy in a whole new generation of readers and writers. It has been a defining point in her relationship with contemporary media. Directed by Chandra Prakash Dwivedi, the film expresses her anguish at the loss of human values, communalisation of the civilisational ethos and stereotyping of social roles. Its commentary on the state of women before and after Partition and poignant representation of a communal Punjab created a set of disturbing and unforgettable images. Pooro's tragedy and the search for a meaning in a new life across the border resonated with generations of Partition victims who had suffered the angst of an illogical division of the subcontinent.[8]

All three films are exceptional for their portrayal of women characters, sans any artificial trappings of pseudo-feminism or imposition of high-sounding ideas on the viewer's sensibility. Revti Saran Sharma, Amrita's colleague from the Hindi writing fraternity and also one of her early interviewers, makes some interesting observations in his study, 'The Search for Feminine Integrity: The Course of Amrita Pritam's Fiction', and mentions that Amrita has never been a vindictively feminist writer who would go against men without a valid premise. In fact, in almost all her writings, from *Dharti, Sagar aur Seepiyaan* (*Earth, Sea and Shells*) to *Chakk No. 36* (*Village No. 36*), Amrita's endeavour has been to search for a voice which is independent, gentle, self-respecting, but at the same time, sceptical and scrutinising. The questioning of stereotypes and construction of 'feminine integrity' has often happened not necessarily through male bashing, but by foregrounding a memorable female consciousness (Sharma 1968-69).

Clearly, 'Bombay' – media and films – infiltrated Amrita's creative aesthetics in defining ways, as did her lifelong association with stalwarts like Sahir Ludhianvi, Imroz and Gulzar. These films also depict Amrita's sustained reflections on the circumstances and issues which shaped her milieu. Though there have been instances of her not always being satisfied with the film adaptations of her works, she never hesitated from collaborating in the process since she was sensitive to the reach and impact of popular media.

Conclusion

India witnessed a transformation in its media platforms from the 1950s to the new millennium through an expansion of commercialised fora and a transformation of the sensibility of the Indian masses. The highlight of the new millennial era has been the 'digital boom' with increasing penetration of the internet and related multimedia platforms. From the 1960s to the present day, there has been no dearth of documentaries, print and electronic articles and scholarship, interviews and film adaptations on Amrita's life and her works. There are also numerous theatrical renditions of her life, relationships and poetry, like M.S. Sathyu's *Amrita – A Sublime Love Story* or Salim Arif's *Main Tumhe Phir Miloongi*. Various eminent film and theatre personalities like Gulzar, Deepti Naval, Rasika Duggal, Shekhar Suman and Divya Dutta have lent their incredible energies and superb performances to showcase the timeless appeal of Amrita Pritam on the Indian and the international stage.

There are two more outstanding odes to her life and art. The first is Basu Bhattacharya's beautifully rendered documentary on Amrita's life, poetics and philosophy, titled *Amrita Today* (2006). Conceptualised under the aegis of Sahitya Akademi, the documentary (shot during a later phase in her life) takes viewers to her Hauz Khas residence and introduces them to her daily routine of writing, cherishing Imroz's companionship and spending valuable time with her children and grandchildren. It introduces us to Amrita's family, acquaintances and scholars of her work – from Gulzar to Indira Goswami to reputed academics and cultural critics from all over India. The film is a glowing tribute to a woman who stood for what she thought was rational and humane, who defied traditions and rituals and yet managed to become one of the most popular literary and cultural icons of the 20th century. The second ode to her is by the celebrated poet, lyricist and filmmaker, Gulzar, who dedicated an audio album to her in 2007 in which he recites Amrita's select poetry in his haunting baritone. Apart from these, her long-time associates and stalwarts of Punjabi literature like Ajeet Cour, Amia Kunwar and Jasbir Bhullar, to name a few, dedicated a lifetime of scholarship to her, while Google celebrated her 100th birth anniversary with a 'doodle'.

Amrita's remarkable life has been marked by unique instances, phases of experimental writing, social and political recognition, unconventional friendships, bold decisions, building of a self-contained home and a lifelong collaboration with Imroz, fruitful nurturing of her children and creation of an individualistic value-system. The range of her content across media platforms in the present day – from print and radio to television and the digital – makes her truly one of a kind; a woman and a warrior who lived with no regrets, except perhaps that not many looked beyond her 'cigarette smoking' and 'cut hair' to understand her 'suffering of the mind and agony of the heart'. While popular media celebrated her, it also constructed her in an 'image' in the light of prevalent discourses, trappings of viewership or pressures of commercial profit. However, her actual persona continues to amaze and resonate with successive generations, through the excellence of her timeless creations and a uniquely rendered spirit of self-expression.

Notes

1 Amrita's father, Kartar Singh Hitkari, was a poet and a prolific scholar who wrote in many languages, notably Sanskrit and Braj Bhasha, and was intensely spiritual.
2 Amrita followed the famous Indian mystic and spiritual healer, Rajneesh (1931-1990) while contributing for some of his publications like *Ik Onkar Satnam* and supported his worldview on various public fora.
  She was also highly influenced by the first woman and one of the longest-serving prime ministers of India – Mrs. Indira Gandhi (1917-1984).
3 Mata Tripta gave birth to Guru Nanak, the founder of the Sikh faith, in 1469 in Nankana Sahib, Talwandi district in present-day Pakistan.
4 S.G.P.C. or the Shiromani Gurdwara Prabhandhak Committee is an organisation responsible for the management and upkeep of Sikh places of worship, heritage and culture.
5 Amrita's interview with Andrew Whitehead titled, "The Tearing of the Veil" (under the overall rubric, *India: A People Partitioned*), August 1997.
  Amrita gave interviews to multiple TV channels throughout her writing career, most of them between 1960 and 1990. Most of them are unavailable; however, thanks to the digitalisation of information, a lot of video excerpts are available on platforms like Prasar Bharti Archives, Twitter, Facebook and YouTube. I have mostly relied on these digital media platforms to access these video interviews.
6 There are numerous instances of the popularity of Pritam's works on the other side of the border, especially the poem 'Ajj Aakhaan Waris Shah nu' (for the purposes of this paper, reference has been made to Amrita's personalised recital of the Waris Shah poem; YouTube video, 3:48, posted by 'LohKatha', 9 July 2010). Interestingly, Amrita's Pakistani T.V. show (*Darpan*) was also extremely well-received. Her popularity and presence in Pakistan can be testified through a reading of the newspaper article written by Pakistani writer, Fakhar Zaman: 'Remembering Amrita Pritam', *TNS*, 29 October 2017.
7 For a complete reference, see indiavideodotorg, 'A documentary.'
  In an interview to Rama Jha for the journal *Indian Literature,* Amrita mentions that 'men and women have not yet met as two independent human beings' (1982: 188).

8 *Pinjar* stars prominent Hindi film actors like Urmila Matondkar and Manoj Bajpayee and has indeed been revered as one of the modern classic adaptations on a Partition narrative.

References

Bhullar, Jasbir, ed. 2001. *Sahan de Hisse di Maulsari*. Chandigarh: Punjabi Sahit Akademi.

Coppola, Carlo and Amrita Pritam. 1968–69. *Mahfil*, Vol. 5, No. 3: Amrita Pritam Number: (1968–1969): 1–26. https://www.jstor.org/stable/40874236?readnow =1&refreqid=excelsior%3Aa1cae6f394f5f92f5acfd38485ed6f5b&seq=1 (accessed on 05.01.2021).

Datta, Nonica. 2017. "Reframing Partition: Memory, Testimony, History", *South Asia Chronicle* 7: 61–93. https://edoc.hu-berlin.de/bitstream/handle/18452 /19506/04%20-%20Focus%20-%20Datta%20%20Reframing%20Partition. %20Memory%2C%20Testimony%2C%20History.pdf?sequence=4 &isAllowed=y (accessed on 05.01.2021).

Dhingra, Deepali. 2007. "Gulzar Recites for Amrita Pritam", *The Times of India*, 07 May. https://timesofindia.indiatimes.com/bombay-times/Gulzar-recites-for -Amrita-Pritam/articleshow/2008708.cms (accessed on 21.12.2021).

Garg, K. L. and Amia Kunwar, eds. 2019. *Amrita jo hamesha rahegi*. Delhi: Shilalekh Publishers.

Kazmi, Sara. 2019. "Radical Re-tellings of Hir: Gender and the Politics of Voice in Post-Colonial Punjabi Poetry", *South Asia Multidisciplinary Academic Journal*: 13.

Kumar, Akshaya. 2009. *Poetry, Politics and Culture: Essays in Texts and Contexts*. London: Routledge.

Kumar, Keval J. 1994. *Mass Communication in India*. Mumbai: Jaico Publishers.

Kunwar, Amia. 2012. *Amrita: Ik Kainat*. Delhi: Shilalekh Publishers.

Pritam, Amrita. 2002. *Dharti, Sagar aur Seepiyaan*. Haryana: Hindi Pocket Books.

———. 1950, rpt. 2009. *Pinjar: The Skeleton and Other Stories*, trans. & adapted Khushwant Singh. Delhi: Tara Research Press.

———. 1968. Interview to the *Statesman* (Delhi edition) on 24 May 1968, reprinted in *Mahfil* 5, no. 3, Amrita Pritam Number (1968–1969): 1–3. https://www.jstor .org/stable/40874235?seq=1 (accessed on 05.01.2021).

———. 1975. *Unhan di Kahani*. Delhi: Nagmani Prakashan.

———. 1976, rpt. 2020. *Rasidi Ticket*. Delhi: Kitab Ghar.

———. 1979. "To Waris Shah", in *Alone in the Multitude*, ed. & trans. S. Kohli. New Delhi: Indian Literary Review: 11.

———. 2019 (2nd edition). "To Amrita Pritam", from *Punjabi Poems of Amrita Pritam*, trans. Khushwant Singh. Delhi: Star Publications.

Pritam, Amrita and Rama Jha. 1982. "Interview to Rama Jha", *Indian Literature* 25, no. 5: 183–195. https://www.jstor.org/stable/23331122 (accessed on 21.12.2021).

Sharma, Revti Saran. 1968–69. "The Search for Feminine Integrity: The Course of Amrita Pritam's Fiction", *Mahfil* 5, no. 3, Amrita Pritam Number (1968–69): 119–131. https://www.jstor.org/stable/40874276 (accessed on 25.01.2021).

Singh, Khushwant. 2005. "Thinking of Amrita: Much ado about *mantras*", *The Telegraph Online*. 12 November. https://www.telegraphindia.com/opinion/thinking-of-amrita/cid/1021835 (accessed on 21.12.2021).

———. 2005. "An Unstamped Ticket", *Outlook*. 14 November. https://magazine.outlookindia.com/story/an-unstamped-ticket/229205 (accessed on 21.12.2021).

Trilok, Uma, ed. 2019. *Amrita and Imroz: In the Times of Love and Longing*. Haryana: Penguin Random House.

Zaman, Fakhar. 2017. "Remembering Amrita Pritam". TNS. 29 October. https://www.thenews.com.pk/tns/detail/564277-remembering-amrita-pritam (accessed on 21.12.2021).

Audio/ Video Links:

Amrita Pritam. 30 August 2020. "I Wanted to Write at All Costs, and I Did", Interview by Mukti Verma, published via Shunali Khullar Shroff in *Live Mint*. https://www.livemint.com/mint-lounge/features/-i-wanted-to-write-at-all-costs-and-i-did-amrita-pritam-11598616240283.html (accessed on 21.12.2021).

———. 07 March 2018. "Amrita Pritam-Indian Writer and Poet – Jewels of Indian Literature", [Television series episode]. YouTube video, 29:00, posted by "Prasar Bharti Archives" (Directed and written by Madhulika/Compiled by Rajan Bharti/Narrated by Sanjay Pandey). https://www.youtube.com/watch?v=YtZfBfmj-rY (accessed on 18.12.2021)

(@google.com). 2019. "Amrita Pritam's 100th Birthday", 31 August 2019. https://www.google.com/doodles/amrita-pritams-100th-birthday (accessed on 22.05.2022).

A Documentary on Amrita Pritam, Part I. 10 December 2010. YouTube video, 2: 15: 30, posted by 'indiavideodotorg'. https://www.youtube.com/watch?v=-exmiwdMZoA (accessed on 21.12.2021).

Amrita Pritam (@AmritaPritam_). 2020. "If Someone Asks Why Poetry is Important…", Twitter, 20 June 2020. https://twitter.com/amritapritam_/status/1274342189175148544 (accessed on 21.12.2021).

Amrita Pritam. Recital of the Waris Shah Poem. YouTube video, 3:48, posted by "LohKatha", 09 July 2010. https://www.youtube.com/watch?v=lVO14VdgdSI (accessed on 21.12.2020).

Pritam, Amrita. August 1997. "The Tearing of the Veil- India: A People Partitioned", Interview by Andrew Whitehead, B.B.C. World Service, audio: 27:52. https://www.andrewwhitehead.net/india-a-people-partitioned.html (accessed on 21.12.2021).

Films

Bhattacharya, Basu. 1975. *Daaku*. Mumbai: Panchsheela Art Production. YouTube video, 1:58:39, posted by "Vintage Classics". 03 October 2018. Basu Bhattacharya's film adaptation has been accessed through a YouTube link. *Daaku*, YouTube video, 1:58:39, posted by "Vintage Classics", 03 October 2018 (accessed on 03.01.2020). https://www.youtube.com/watch?v=oUYVB2JwoWs (accessed on 21.12.2021).

————. 2020. *Amrita Today*. 07 May. Delhi: Sahitya Akademi, n.d. Facebook.1:00:35, posted by "Sahitya Akademi Archives". https://www.facebook .com/SahityaAkademi/videos/1190933447965023/ (accessed on 21.12.2021).

Dwivedi, Chandra Prakash. 2003. Pinjar. Mumbai: Lucky Entertainment. YouTube video, 3:08:50, posted by "Hindi Film Movies", 25 February 2016 (accessed on 26.12.2020). https://www.youtube.com/watch?v=GVN29vz3bYI (accessed on 21.12.2021).

Verma, H. K. 1975. *Kadambari*. Mumbai: Madhu Pictures. YouTube Video, 1:32:22. Posted by "Zindagi Gulzar", 30 June 2020.

21

PLAYING AMRITA

Deepti Naval in Conversation with Rekha Sethi and
Sukrita Paul Kumar

Deepti Naval, a well-known actor, artist and poet, shared a special rela-
tionship with Amrita Pritam. It is well known that Amrita was a mentor to
many budding writers and Deepti was one of them. Amrita helped Deepti
publish her first poetry collection. Later, after Amrita was no more, Deepti
played Amrita's character on stage in a play, Ek Mulaqat, which was based
on the special relationship between two poets: Amrita Pritam and Sahir
Ludhianvi. Though the play was staged only after Amrita's death, Deepti
Naval has special memories of Amrita as a person, as a writer and as an
enigma for her readers and admirers. We spoke to Deepti Naval about her
memories and impressions that helped us know Amrita a little more.

Rekha Sethi: It was wonderful watching the video excerpts of the play *Ek*
   Mulaqat. I wish we had seen the full play on the stage when it was
   performed. However, all that I have seen and read, along with reading
   reviews and some of your interviews, gives one a fairly good insight into
   the play which is almost like undertaking a journey into the lives of two
   great poets. The play has been done beautifully; particularly your portrayal of Amrita. I could feel her persona coming alive. You picked up
   her mannerisms, attire, her very soft tone, and her lyrical language…. It
   made a great impact.
Sukrita Paul Kumar: I would be interested in focussing on the points of
   identification you felt between yourself and Amrita. Did you see any
   gap between yourself as a person and her persona? What made you feel
   that you could do it, that you could be Amrita Pritam on the stage?
Deepti Naval: See, I am an actor, and one is used to getting under the skin
   of another personality and creating…. You know, that is what our
   training as actors is, and what better opportunity could I get than this,
   that I was asked to play somebody whom I had also closely known.
   Otherwise, one has to depend on one's imagination and use one's judgement to imagine that a particular person would react in a particular way
   in a given situation. And here, I was asked to play somebody not only
   whom I had known but also somebody I hugely admired as a writer.

232   DOI: 10.4324/9781003214656-32

SPK: But sometimes the admiration could come in the way. What if she were to be in the audience watching you play the role of Amrita?

DN: Well I don't know what would it be like if she were to be sitting in the audience and watching me. The play happened only after she was gone. But I think I would have been very nervous if she was there sitting in the audience, and I was pretending to be her.

RS: Did you feel that as the play evolved, Amrita's persona grew on you?

DN: I think not as the play evolved, but as we kept doing more shows, it became easy for me to become Amrita. Because I had gone through the initial fear of the fact that I had never done a play in my life earlier. So I went through this fear of what would happen if I forgot the lines or if I were to get the wrong cue or even that we might miss out the chunk of material that should have been there. You know the strange fears one may have.

But I was always confident that I was going to play Amrita ji one day. I used to sit and observe her. She would sit on the bed and there was a settee on her right side. I used to go and sit there and keep observing her. She would sit in a slightly tilted position with a glint in her eyes. She would narrow her eyes whenever she was probing something in her thoughts. Then she would explain very deeply, profoundly. She had a very gentle way of saying something. She would seem very demure in her appearance but if you listened to her thoughts, you realised that she was quite a rebel.

SPK: In fact Deepti, I think she seemed to carry within her a spirit of defiance, in life as much as in writing....

DN: Yes. For her this was defiance. Just think of it, in her times, she actually ended a marriage which did not mean anything to her. She was in a live-in relationship with Imroz Saheb for years and years together. She had found companionship. She stuck to that, she stuck to what was real for her and not just what was going to be acceptable in society.

RS: So, in a sense, do you agree that she was a woman who was ahead of her times?

DN: Oh yes, she was. Since very few women want to live by what they believe in. I mean a lot of women dream of it, strive for it but she was like one of the leaders, she was the one who cleared the path for many women. You know, we make many decisions hypocritically.... It's okay. We cannot run down women who have not transcended social restrictions and broken all rules because they may have had many other considerations. Whether it is because of their parents or their in-laws or children. It is not easy for a woman to break out of her shackles and say 'I will start all over again'. Which is what she did; and sort of ... paved a way for future generations. She, so to say, dared and demonstrated that despite being a woman, you can live according to your own convictions.

SPK: In your conversations with her – and you had many of them – did she express any resentment or bitterness about the society she lived in or the social constraints that are imposed on a woman?

DN: No, on the contrary, I never saw any element of bitterness in her. When it came to her beliefs and her love life, her equation with Sahir Saheb was so stretched out but she had found a comfort level with herself. Maybe she had gone through some period of strife earlier, but she was absolutely at peace later. And this wonderful relationship with Imroz Saheb. I used to admire the relationship between the two, Imroz Saheb and Amrita ji. Whenever she talked about Sahir Saheb it was with a lot of fondness, a lot of adulation and a deep intimacy, remembering … never with bitterness, never any regret. You know she enjoyed the fact that she could be so much in love with him (Sahir Saheb), even if it may have been a one-way love.

SPK: Everyone considered it to be an unrequited love.

DN: Yes, it was, as Sahir Saheb never actually expressed his feelings.

RS: In the play *Ek Mulaqat*, two progressive romantic poets talk to each other. It is not just any two people talking to each other. The whole play comes across as something which is emerging from the depths of their hearts. What did the whole social system mean to them? How did they perceive their own individual emotions? How did you see this relationship?

DN: Umm … between Sahir Saheb and Amrita ji?

RS: Yes, particularly in the context of the play. The way it has been enacted on stage.

DN: I will tell you something honestly, something that I have indirectly spoken about many times during my interviews for the play. When I first read the script it was fine. When they started promoting the play, they called it a love story. I knew the world was going to misunderstand this. It is not a regular romance, or an affair. It should not be called an affair, by any means. It was *not* an affair. It was Amrita ji who was totally, totally in love with Sahir Saheb and his poetry. It is because of his poetry that she was so much in love with the poet. There *was* a mutual admiration, but it was not an affair. So I would hate for Amrita ji and Sahir Saheb's relationship to be misinterpreted in any way. Our play was called *Ek Mulaqat – A Love Story* but it wasn't so. It did not reach the point where it could really become a relationship. Sahir Saheb was an introvert. The only way he expressed himself rigorously was through his poetry.

RS: I agree.

DN: Like he writes, 'Ye duniya agar mil bhi jaaye to kya hai' meaning 'how does it matter even if you get the whole world'. So all his intense emotions would be expressed in poetry or when he interacted with stalwarts like Balraj Sahni, B.R. Ishara, K.A. Abbas, etc. With them he was expressive but he was very shy with women.

SPK: Sahir Saheb was a strong progressive poet. And it is often said that under the influence of Sahir Saheb, Amrita ji too gradually became progressive. Did she ever talk to you about progressive ideals? Of course it was demonstrated through her anti-patriarchal position but did she ever discuss this with you?

DN: Not actually in that manner, but she was aware of being a kind of a torchbearer for the women in our society. She was also revered for that … Amrita ji received a lot of adulation for this. I had just come back from America. I did not know much about her poetry then. Basu Bhattacharya took me to meet her. He wanted to make a film based on *Nagmani*. Its Hindi title was *Nagmani* and it was about a young girl and an elderly painter … and her fascination for him.

SPK: Oh, why was the film not made?

DN: True, it was never made. Basu da wanted me to play the young girl. Those were the *Chashme Baddoor* days. He wanted Gulzar Saab to play the painter. He was around 40-45 at that time. Had that film been made it would have been a classic.

SPK: What a pity! Anyway, let's talk about Amrita ji and the publication of your first book of poems.

DN: Yes, that book happened because of Amrita ji. She was responsible for getting it published. Basu da told Amrita ji, 'I must tell you that Deepti also writes.' So she said, 'Go ahead, recite something.' I remembered just one of my poems which I recited 'Chalo door tak, ajnabi raaston par paidal chalen' ('Come let us walk a long way, on unfamiliar roads'). She liked it and asked me to recite some more. I told her I couldn't recall any but would bring my notebook the next time I came to Delhi.

On my next trip which was about a month and a half or two later, I came back to her with my notebook. She heard all my poems very carefully. Then she asked me to leave my notebook with her until the next day. When I went back to her the next evening, she said, 'You have wonderful imagery. These poems should be published.' Well, I said, 'I only know how to write, I know nothing about publishing.' On my next trip I was amazed when Amrita ji called her publisher and told him, 'She has written *nazms* – read them carefully. They have a depth of thought and powerful imagery.' I thought to myself, my poems must be good if Amrita ji is saying so.

SPK: In lifestyle or living choices, what kind of an impact did Amrita have on you? She was, after all, a legend of her times, an iconic figure and someone who lived in her own way, making bold choices….

DN: Oh yes. Her personality was such that one felt drawn to her and her ways. She would keep writing; and her body of work is immense. Also, she was such a gentle looking person. She was not a screaming feminist; I am not very fond of screaming feminists. 'Burn the bra' type of thing! I love being a woman and I always relished being a woman. And I loved that about her. She also, I think, relished being a woman. And yet being a woman does not mean being shackled and that is what I loved about her persona. She had so many different observations about life and that is what she wrote about in her literature, I would say, with all love. But I must confess, I started reading her work only after meeting her. Even her famous poem 'Ajj Aakhaan Waris Shah nu' … I had heard only a few lines of it earlier and read the whole of it only after meeting her.

RS: I was waiting to talk to you about that poem. You sang it so beautifully in the play. Actually, you could bring out the pain with which she must have written it. She wrote it on a train when she was coming to Delhi after Partition.

SPK: Yes it was written after Partition in the context of what women had to face during the riots. There are a lot of references to this poem in Partition literature. She must have spoken to you about her pain regarding the Partition; maybe that's an added reason why you could present it with so much feeling on the stage.

DN: It also comes to me from my family stories of Partition that my father used to talk about. He would often say, 'There is no house in Punjab which does not have the history of Partition.' These stories are often passed on to the next generation in the families.

SPK: I also read somewhere that during the rehearsal of the scene when you had to sing this poem, you broke down in tears.

DN: To tell you the truth I could hardly sing this song without breaking down. Quite inevitably, no matter how prepared I'd be, I would end up crying in every performance.

SPK: Actually, more than being just a poem of pain, it has become an epic. This poem was read so much and sung so widely on both sides of the border that it has acquired an extraordinary expression of the deeply shared cultural connections between the two countries…. And then came Amrita's famous novel *Pinjar* which was also a great success.

RS: I want to add another point here. When I read Amrita ji I find many of her poems to be political. Her tone takes on an anti-establishment stance, particularly when she's talking about democracy. At times I feel, too much stress has been laid on the romance in her life, so much so that other aspects of her literary persona get completely overshadowed that way. We hardly ever talk about her politics or about her being a cultural ambassador. The socio-political aspects of her writings have not been discussed enough.

DN: Yes, in fact I feel if those aspects are probed a little more we will find enough evidence to show her strengths in that direction as well. As a woman she articulated her views very well. Though I have not read enough on all these issues, I am sure that the artists and writers of those times were usually expressive of the times they lived in. Politically alert and socially conscious.

SPK: I have not seen the entire play, *Ek Mulaqat* but I am aware that it was presented in the flashback mode ....

DN: Actually this play is about an imaginary meeting between Sahir and Amrita. Yes, they reminisce about the past and their creative work. The whole thing is a recall about life. Through the play, a phone keeps ringing but one can't hear the message from the other side. At the end of the play, Sahir Saheb sings his famous *nazm* from the film *Kabhi Kabhi*. Finally, the phone rings and is received by Imroz Saheb. It is then revealed that Sahir had died the same morning and that it was his soul which wanted to speak to Amrita for the last time to its heart's content. It is then that Imroz Saheb gives Amrita the sad news, 'Sahir has passed away'. Amrita replies, 'But he is with me' and she turns her head and looks around to find that he is gone, indicating perhaps, that the man who was talking to her, was not Sahir in person, but it was his soul that had come to say his final goodbye!

RS: Beautiful imagination. There are many other songs in the play, which were written by Sahir.

DN: Yes, they recorded another song in my voice 'tum mujhe bhool bhi jao to yeh haq hai tumko / meri baat aur hai maine mohabbat ki hai' ('You have the right to forget me / but I cannot as I am in love'). This was to express Amrita ji's point of view. This song was originally sung by Sudha Malhotra who was also Sahir's love interest, but even this relationship did not go far. Many people discuss Sahir Saheb and feel there was no place for a woman in his life. He was wedded to his poetry. I believe, he may have thought and believed that if he would find someone to share his pain and sorrow, his poetry could lose its edge.

SKP: You mean the note of suffering in his poetry ....

DN: Yes, sometimes artists have to keep their pain alive to write.

SKP: But wasn't that also true of Amrita ... that same edge of pain in the romantic relationship?

DN: But she found her bearings with Imroz Saheb and she found love. I can't tell you how much Imroz Saheb loved Amrita. There was love, care, and affection in this relationship. Imroz Saheb completely lost his 'self' in this love. I've always felt that if a man wants to love a woman it should be like Imroz loved Amrita.

RS: Towards the end of her life Amrita became inclined towards spirituality too.

DN: Yes, age does that to you. With age you start feeling – she had started feeling and wondering – where life's journey is heading to. She tried to deal with it in her writings. I would love to read that more.

SPK: In her autobiographical pieces she offers little glimpses of spirituality while detaching herself from the ordinary.

RS: Was that the influence of Osho ... Rajneesh?

DN: I don't know what her influences were, but I know that she was greatly concerned about her spiritual journey in the end. She was at the last stage of her life, she was very concerned, very captivated to understand what is the essence of this whole journey of life.

SKP: Deepti, I would like to ask you if you have a special memory of maybe a serious conversation with her on her creative process?

DN: It was all about translating life into poetry. Her whole life was an expression of poetry and writing. She also encouraged young writers very much, many women writers from Punjab particularly.

SPK: Yes she brought out the magazine *Nagmani*, which featured many young writers. She had a strong commitment towards the next generation.

DN: Yes, that is the reason why she is so relevant today. She engaged with the younger generation, she wanted to know about their writings how they felt, and this in itself became her writing force. She told me many times that I should write in Punjabi. I don't know whether I'll ever be able to fulfill her dream or not.

SKP: How did you respond to her use of Punjabi? I believe that for you Punjabi became a different kind of language after listening to her speak it.

DN: Yes, absolutely. I do have a story about my relationship with the language. I did not care much about the Punjabi language when I was young. I used to be so self-conscious about being Punjabi as I thought this language was only for music and hard beats but now I am a proud Punjabi. It is so primarily because of two women in my life, my mother and later Amrita ji; both spoke Punjabi in a way that impressed me and reaffirmed my faith in the language.

SPK: She spoke Punjabi so lyrically, gently, and beautifully.

RS: In the end I would request you to share something about Amrita ji that is very close to your heart.

DN: Everything was special about Amrita ji but I really find Amrita and Imroz's relationship very, very unique. When I visited Amrita ji, Imroz Saheb would make tea for us. I would walk up to him and politely offer to help. I could feel that he was a man who had completely deflated his ego. When you love a person you don't exist anymore, you exist only in her existence. Many times, he would explain his and Amrita's relationship to me, and I could actually feel the depth and warmth between them. They were inseparable. Their relationship reaffirmed one's faith in love – you wanted to believe in love. You wanted to believe in that kind of complete belonging to somebody and you wanted to live that way. You might not be as lucky as Amrita ji, but you can at least have the aspiration. I was also lucky in a way that I found somebody, for a brief period, and we could live a little bit of the Amrita-Imroz chapter in our lives as well.

RS: Thank you, so much Deepti ji.

SPK: It was lovely to talk to you and also understand how and why you could play Amrita Pritam with such a strong sense of affinity. Thank you.

(Conducted on 14 June 2021.)

22

DIRECTING AMRITA

Salim Arif in Conversation with
Prem Kumari Srivastava

Salim Arif, an illustrious alumnus of the National School of Drama, New Delhi, is a well-known name in the field of Indian theatre, television and films. Being innovative in approach, Arif has directed several notable stage plays such as Kharaashein, Lakeerein, Atthanniyaan, collated from the famed Gulzar's stories and poems, Sunte Ho, Agar aur Magar, Aapki Soniya, Kachche Lamhe, Hum Safar, Paansa, etc. Having scripted and presented several plays based on letters, he has been a recipient of prestigious awards for his contribution to theatre. In a candid conversation with Prem Kumari Srivastava, Arif spoke about his experience of knowing Amrita Pritam and then directing the play Main Tumhe Phir Miloongi in Hindi. Using excerpts from Amrita's biography, her letters to Imroz, poems and short stories juxtaposed with writings by Sahir Ludhianvi and others; the letters between Amrita and Imroz form the primary narrative of the play. As Arwa mamaji, one of the founders of Urduwallahs, says:

> *Letters have had a significant role in the historical evolution of Urdu prose. When you read letters by writers such as Amrita Pritam, Mirza Ghalib, Safia Akhtar, Faiz Ahmed Faiz, Josh Malihabadi, Maulana Azad, you get a sense of place and the period they live in. You learn about what they were interested in, what bothered them, who had an influence on their art.*[1]

Salim Arif was much intrigued and impressed by the bond that Amrita shared with Imroz. Arif is clear that the play is not a work of fiction. It rather dwells upon the time of the late 1950s to the early 1970s – since they started living together.

Prem Kumari Srivastava: Why is the telling of the love story of Amrita and Imroz important? Could you give specific instances from your play, *Main Tumhe Phir Miloongi?*

Salim Arif: This story was important to tell because of Imroz, who agreed to live on Amrita's terms and remained a devoted companion till the end.

DOI: 10.4324/9781003214656-33

'Main Imroz ki peethh par Sahir ka naam likh deti thhi' ('I used to write Sahir's name on Imroz's back') was the line that remained with me for a long time. It made me think about Imroz and not Amrita and Sahir. While I was in New Delhi as a student in National School of Drama, one read and heard a lot about Amrita Pritam's personal life and how it overshadowed her literary work. A woman who openly professed her love and fascination for Sahir Ludhianvi (a very popular poet still alive then), agreed to a live-in relationship with another man Imroz, leaving her husband and father of her children, was sufficient to give her rivals and critics enough fodder to attack her bohemian lifestyle. Had it been a man writing about his life in the manner Amrita wrote about hers, it would have been seen as a normal life spent in the company of artists. But Amrita was a woman, an artist negotiating life on her own terms, something which is not appreciated in a society that still wants to patronise them. It was Imroz who got me interested in exploring this relationship. I could see an interesting story developing through Imroz as a narrator and participant in this relationship.

Sadly the unrequited love, the open admission of her fascination for Sahir has taken a larger mindspace in popular imagination about the Amrita Pritam saga than it deserves. At best it remained a one-sided longing without any proactive step from Sahir's side. Had Sahir wanted, Amrita could have been with him. It was a news item about Sahir's rumoured involvement with a new good looking singer that made Amrita abandon her mad fascination for Sahir. It closed all possibilities on her side as far as that relationship was concerned. She never asked Sahir to confirm that story, nor did she ever again think about Sahir as her life companion. She opted to live with Imroz. He was willing to take on the world for his love of Amrita and redeemed that commitment.

'Main Tainu Phir Milangi' is the title of a poem written by Amrita for Imroz and we thought this would be an apt title for the show based on letters between the two. I was always fascinated by Imroz Saab and his devotion to Amrita ji, which I had seen during my meetings with Amrita ji during the months of October-November 1986 when she was staying at her Hauz Khas bungalow. She was also a nominated member of the Rajya Sabha, then, and I had gone to invite her for the first 'Apna Utsav' poetry session. It was Imroz who would get us tea and snacks and then quietly vanish in the background of that house. For me it was interesting to meet Imroz Saab as I had read *Rasidi Ticket* (Amrita's autobiography) and was curious to see the man who was now with her as her live-in companion.

PKS: Where do you place this play in your journey as a theatre person and artist?

SA: Letters have a unique first-hand and personal element that is often missing in biographies or creative writings. Letters of Van Gogh, Manto,

Henry Miller, and several others make for great reading. I have tried to use them as material for the stage and very often edited and collated them thematically to make them into a context for their poems or writings. I tried this form of letter reading juxtaposed with a musical presentation of poems in *Ghalibnaama* in 2002 and that became an instant hit. It led to several poets being presented on stage in that manner by others too.

Main Tumhe Phir Miloongi was our fourth show based on the presentation of edited letters on stage. We had done *Ghalibnaama* with letters of Ghalib juxtaposed with his poems; *Aapki Soniya* as a sequel to *Tumhari Amrita*; *Gulon Mein Rang Bharo* based on the correspondence between Faiz and his wife, Alys during his prison days in the 1950s; and this became our fourth show a few years ago.

PKS: What aspects of Amrita's life and works were taken into consideration while scripting the play? Do give specific examples.

SA: We took portions of *Rasidi Ticket* wherever they could become part of the letters and Amrita's poems. There is nothing outside their writings and I have collated that material as I thought fit to bring forth nuances of their relationship for an audience.

PKS: How did you resurrect such passionate souls (Amrita-Imroz) on stage only through dialogue?

SA: I relied completely on their writings. In creating fiction on the writings of others you bring your own prism and end up with a subjective interpretation of that story without leaving much space for the reader or audience to arrive at their own personal version. Theatre gives me the scope to bring in a certain transparency in rendition and leave sufficient space for the audience to participate by igniting their imagination through adequate leads. I prefer not to add my own words but rather to piece the dialogues together from the original writings of the authors to present a certain authentic juxtaposition on stage. Both of them wrote intense, heartfelt words and I was sure they would work better on stage. Where would you find an expression like 'Rahi ... tum mujhe mere jeevan ki sandhya mein kyon miley?' ('Traveller, why have you met me in the dusk of my life?') by Amrita to Imroz ... and Imroz replying with 'Tum mera savera ho ...' ('You are my dawn') I found such evocative dialogues quite effective in creating the two personas.

PKS: Referring to the youth, you once said that 'to express thirty varieties of anger, they use just one cuss word. They are attracted to Urdu because of its finesse, beauty, and nuance'. Why did you choose Hindi instead of Punjabi? Do you think it had greater impact?

SA: Hindi-Urdu being mainstream languages have a much larger readership that includes the Punjabis who love Urdu as their own language. Sadly, we treat Punjabi, Malayalam, Bangla, and most other languages as regional languages, irrespective of the quality of literature available in those languages. If Amrita had written in Urdu instead of Punjabi; she would have had a far greater reach and popularity than she has now. After all, Allama Iqbal, Faiz Ahmad Faiz, Ahmad Faraaz, Qateel Shafai, Gulzar Saab, and several others opted to write in Urdu instead of their mother tongue Punjabi and the impact of their writings is there for all to see.

PKS: Is anything lost in translation on stage? Can you share some specific instances where translation was felt to be a limitation?

SA: Poetically it becomes difficult, and more so if you compose and sing. Amrita ji did her own translations of poetry and we used them in the show. It is true that the flavour of Punjabi would have added immense value to this production.

PKS: Do you think that this play puts unnecessary emphasis on the Amrita-Imroz relationship and in some ways takes the focus away from the rich, multi-faceted creative persona that Amrita Pritam was?

SA: Not really. It reinforces her personality in her own words. All the facets of her personality are present in this show. Letters since time immemorial have been one of the most intimate forms of literature. We restricted our research for this play to her writings in her books and letters. You as an audience are free to take it for whatever value it may have for you. We are not qualifying Amrita with any hyperbole nor calling the play the greatest love story of all times. We don't have to build a shrine for Amrita in the show, nor present her as a five-headed and ten-armed woman. We are not calling it a representative Amrita show either. It is essentially Imroz presenting his love story with actual words used by him and Amrita. Most shows till date have tried to do the Amrita-Sahir love story. I avoid that largely due to the fact that none of them are physically in a position to refute whatever is being said or written about them. It would be highly irresponsible if we start presenting shows about the rumoured relationships of Guru Dutt, Meena Kumari, and several others in the film fraternity just because they make spicy, saleable material.

PKS: Amrita's unconventional lifestyle and society's mixed reaction to her does not seem to affect the world that Amrita-Imroz had created for themselves. This is also suggested at several places in the play through their intimate talk. Is that a deliberate ploy used by the writer-director of the play?

SA: No ... my only concern was to present a beautiful relationship as it was experienced by the two. The controversies were created because Amrita was a woman in a man's world with more courage, fame, and calibre than most other people. And she did not allow any man to patronise or promote her. The relationship with Imroz deepened from friendship into a life-long companionship over a period of years. Amrita was not desperate for a man in her life. She was also conscious of the fact that Imroz was younger than she was and she was not at an age where she might remain physically attractive for long. So, she, in her own inimitable way, sought Imroz as a co-traveller in her life. Amrita chose Imroz after careful deliberation and laid out her terms openly to make him aware of what he was getting into; and gave him time to introspect and decide. Those moments of realisation in their lives as well as in the play make it special.

PKS: In the last decade of her life, Amrita was greatly drawn to spirituality, which seemed a natural progression of her engagement with life. Was this aspect considered while framing the play?

SA: No ... we did not use it as the show was based on excerpts from the correspondence between Amrita and Imroz, some excerpts from her other writings, and one or two interviews. Amrita was like a Sufi fakir and her inclination towards spirituality is quite evident in her writings. Sikhism, with Guru Nanak's stress on wisdom, has a quest for knowledge and the right path in its very foundations. Sufi thought is a very prominent strain in their religious practices and in Amrita's creativity too.

PKS: Salim Saab, it would be so nice if our readers could experience your writing through some passages from your play. Since the play is based on Amrita's letters, the readers would be able to get a glimpse of her relationship with Imroz too. It would further add verve to this interview.

SA: Certainly.

Excerpts from *Main Tumhe Phir Miloongi*

Translated by
Anupama Jaidev Karir

Amrita:

Your utterly beautiful letters, Jiti! Far more beautiful than even my imagination. I waited for these my entire life, even though that wait remained endless. And I would answer them in numerous poems. Today, they've come true. But today, I can't seem to govern my heart. My eyes are tearing up – why didn't the years of my age halt at one place to witness this truth? Why did they continue to ascend? They don't seem to match you today! Your look just dusted off the haze of bygone years from me.

Amrita:

Raahi, O fellow traveller! Why did you meet me in this fading dusk? My life's journey is about to end. If you had to, you should have met me in the mellow afternoon of life; we could have soaked in its sunlit warmth.

If there's anyone who has understood me, it's the mute paint bottles lying in the drawers of your table, whose bodies I would clean and caress every day. Those colours smiled into my eyes because they gleaned the secret of my vision's gaze; they understood that I am so much in love with your creative power. Those colours would ache for a touch of your hands, just as my eyes would for the images emerging from them. The reason they yearned for the touch of your hands was because *they wanted to justify their existence*. I sought your companionship because my existence finds meaning in your creations. I find these meanings in my works as well, but with you, these meanings expand and flourish.

Imroz:

I've just received your letter, my Empress! I don't know if you are my evening, morning, or afternoon; but you are my destination, my destiny. It's my fortune, my good fortune! If this is the enchanting evening, I will commit my afternoon to this evening with all the steadfastness of my heart and my passion. I will live.

Now, and earlier too, I have felt as if I have offended my queen by coming to Bombay. When this thought occurs, my heart feels disenchanted with everything – my work, my talent, just about everything. You may be an elegant evening, but do not forget that you alone are my morn and my noon; try living it. With your whole heart, with me, with your Jiti.

Imroz:

My poetess, you don't belong to any one land, any one country, any one language or any one race. You belong to the land that is as expansive as a heart bursting with emotions. You belong to every one of those countries where grace and culture flourish night and day, free from all restrictions. You belong to every language where they know how to hear, see, and recognise hearts. You belong to every race, whose people don't dwell in the past, but completely in the present, and like the present, they live and breathe amongst themselves as well as thrive in the midst of others. You belong to each of those nights and days, where every night slumbers with the seed of a new creation in its womb. And where every dawn ascends the steps of the day humming a new song. I will always be wherever you are. There are no barriers for me now, except the barrier of your consent. You will find my hue in every flower, and my fragrance in every breeze. You will know my depth in every lake and my flow in every river. And in every new thought of a lyric and every pulsating rhythm of every song, I will turn to you again and again. Maaja, my saviour! I will never let you tire. I will wake up as a new hope in your eyes every morning. And like a breathing, throbbing will to live, I will walk your steps throughout the day.

Imroz:

Often it happens that I repeatedly see that place on my shoulder that you would mark with your kisses. Those marks aren't visible on the surface now, but deep down the touch still lingers.

I am on your quest, Aashi. That dark Jiti is on your quest too! He who used to think differently earlier, is now free but he doesn't think of anything else now. He doesn't seek anything else either. Now he is ashamed. But do see that he is no longer dark now. He's the colour of Aashi. That table, that drawer, those bottles of colour; the wait every day for the touch of the one who loved them; who became their brilliance. That brush, that colour still seeks that face, that forehead, whose brow they adorned to stay fresh. Or they would have dried up by now. Those that I water with my wait for you, lest they parch and cake. But their lushness is with you alone; you know it. Lushness! I am waiting for you too! In colours as well as in life!

Note

1 Chintan Girish Modi, 9 February 2016. 'Noteworthy Missives from the masters', *The Hindu*. https://www.thehindu.com/news/cities/mumbai/entertainment/note-worthy-missives-from-the-masters/article8213507.ece (accessed on 19.12.2021).

Part VII

THE LEGEND LIVES ON …

23

CALL OUT, WHERE ART THOU …

Mohan Bhandari
Translated by Harmeet Kaur Jhajj

Like the rays of the Sun is the mind, O mother
Which Heaven do they come from today?
They come, having caressed the origin,
These born of the essence of the Earth.

– Amrita Pritam

For a long time, this write-up kept playing hide and seek with me. Lost in my thoughts and memories, I mused: Amrita is placed firmly upon the zenith of the literary firmament, myriad facets of her personality bespeak excellence, her name commands respect far and wide, an eternal flame illumines her intellectual brow and there is endless curiosity in her mind. Blithe at heart and lithe in thought, she is both a seeker and custodian of self-respect. She is a living embodiment of love and affection, devoid of cunning and spite; appreciative of noble values and deeds; compassionate towards the needy; a zealous sentinel of high principles; a seeker and practitioner of spiritual values; one who considers Sufi compositions as equivalent to the words of Hindu mystics, a passionate lover of life and so much more besides. Despite the luminosity of all these qualities, she continues to be an enigma and I was caught in the predicament of how to begin this essay. A search for that elusive opening sentence! She has nearly 200 books to her credit which have been translated in about 35 languages around the world. When an accomplished and gifted woman like her says with such humility, 'I trust pure love; I lay no claim to talent', then the tip of the pen hovers over a blank page, and one must invoke one's Muse in order to write about such a soul, be it Sadat Hasan Manto's 786 or Waris Shah's Invocation in *Hir*, 'I start with a song in praise of the Lord who made love the foundation of this world, Sir'. Only then will it be possible to say as Waris Shah does, 'I strung words together and arranged them beautifully'. As I contemplated these great personalities cast in the mould of rigorous practice and symbolising the rich experiences

DOI: 10.4324/9781003214656-35

of the times and the throbbing pulse of the people, in that instant it struck me like a flash of lightning that the essay has already begun!

Amrita epitomises an eternal journey, a deep reflection and a quest. She is a supreme ascetic artist who holds a treasure trove inside her ageless bundle, safeguarding the heritage of sweet and sour experiences of almost a century. She may not claim to be an accomplished scholar in Eastern, especially Indian, philosophy, mythology and history, but the essence and core of all these streams flows in her veins and is expressed brilliantly in her writings.

She has a dedicated readership that has assimilated the colours, ripples and mysteries of spirituality in its very being. Criticism and discernment, cause and effect are, for her, like the ceaseless flight of birds – an embodiment of the agility of her mind. She is a saga of emotions felt to the core of the heart. Her contemplative soul travels the path of her multiple past lives, while her consciousness traverses the vast, limitless expanse of the universe. Dear friends, reflect upon and absorb the essence of these evocative lines of Amrita:

> One night the Pir of the infinite came and bestowed upon me
> the amulet of the divine ray of light
> I wear the amulet
> and see His shrine suffuse the entire firmament.
> And I carry the sweet offering of my passion
> to pay homage at His shrine.

When I heard these lines, it instinctively struck me that we who have only insincere platitudes to offer and seek the easy way out know nothing about the dignity of passion. At times, her imagination soars high in the sky, and at other times, it dives deep below the earth to fathom the depth of the underworld. Then it speaks to the faithful about the sermons of saints and hermits, spreading the message of these enlightened souls.

> Chant the name of Allah with every breath
> This heavenly music shall become your pulse
> Cleansing and
> Itself doing the pooja and reading the namaaz
> The mind is the gardener, and curiosity its partner
> The soul blossomed
> I made an offering to the moon
> And meditated upon silence.

Amrita carries forward the legacy of the imaginative spectrum of the great Urdu story writer, Krishan Chander. She also writes about the deep philosophy and vision of Professor Puran Singh, a quaint Punjabi poet, who embraced shepherds, trees and vines and kissed the faces of cows, goats and lambs:

> When the sun spread a crimson glow as it set, he would wrap this glow around himself as if he were soaking in the colours.
> One day I asked him, 'What are you doing?' He replied, 'I am wrapping this golden-edged dupatta carefully.' Such is 'Puran leela' – the unique charm and appeal of the mysticism of Professor Puran Singh!

Amrita's demonstration of the exquisite charm and greatness of another writer shows her faith and self-confidence. One has to meditate in order to understand her; otherwise, it is not possible to grasp the depth of her work. Once the famous satirist, Bhushan Dhyanpuri, and I were talking about Amrita. He expressed a desire to write about Punjabi editors. Taking a sheet of paper, he wrote a feature with seven editors there and then. About Amrita, the editor of *Nagmani*, he wrote, 'A girl has bewitched the *ichcha dhari sapni* (shape-shifting serpent). All around the burrow sit the *jogis*; the snake-charmers'.

In the history of Punjabi publication, it will forever remain a memorable precedent that she published many special editions and, more than anyone else, encouraged, praised and published many promising writers. In this endeavour, Bhushan stayed at her place for a full seven days and was published in a special edition on satire, titled 'Dekh Kabira Haseya' ('Look, Kabir Laughed') in May 1979. The editors were listed as Amrita, Imroz and Bhushan. A couplet was published on the title page:

> We shall live and laugh together in the neighbourhood
> If offended, you can build a wall in the courtyard.

Beaming with proud gratitude, Bhushan said, 'She paid me too!'

Amrita blessed me, 'May your vision be forever protected from the evil eye'. But alas! My eyesight has become weak now and I can barely discern the alphabets printed on many issues of the magazine correctly and I end up seeing 'b' for 'd'. I know my eyesight will deteriorate further over time. Still, whenever I see an issue of her magazine, a blessing spontaneously issues forth from my heart, 'May it always thrive!' In order to read her article titled, 'Chiragan di Raat' ('The Night of the Lamps'), one's eyes need to be like beacons themselves and one's heart should be that of a true friend. A writer should have someone to regard him or her as one's beloved and articulate, 'The world holds no appeal apart from the pull of your eyes'. Given to citing great writers of the world, if she read these lines or heard them, then perhaps she might agree with Shakespeare who says that love looks not with the eyes, but with the mind. This mind is the cause of much trouble in this world. The wise and the learned warn against being guided by one's mind. Opinions change with every blink of the eye! Amrita is capable of seeing beyond what is perceived by the body, mind, heart and intellect. And her heart is immense; she is truly empathetic. Some time ago I read her interview by Mohanjeet and her poem on Pakistani writer Afzal Tauseef 'Tauseef Aayee Si'[1] ('Tauseef Had Come'). I wrote a congratulatory letter. She replied immediately, 'A time comes in life when you feel the same joy in another's achievement as in your own. With much love to your good heart'. In response to Tauseef's fearless article 'Sheher de Vichkaar Taareekh di Laash Payi Hai' ('The Corpse of History Lies in the City Square') written after the demolition of a Jain temple in Pakistan, Amrita penned a complete book in Hindi dedicated to Tauseef titled, *Doosre Aadmi Ki Beti* (*The Daughter of the Other Man*). Later, about the publication in India of a book of Punjabi stories by a new writer from Karachi, Tauqeer Chughtai, she says, 'Who is publishing this book? You must publish it under your care'. Who would not want to salute her for feeling such deep concern! I would for one because nature has blessed her with an affectionate and loving heart. There is purity in her hands and loyalty in her heart. In nothing is she guided by any ulterior motive. I say this based on my continuous interaction and correspondence with her in these past 35 years. If others have a different opinion or experience, let them recount their version.

Many literary merchants wandered onto the stage of Punjabi literature, practised their craft, packed up and left – lock, stock and barrel. And many others will follow suit. But her high shrine – or camp or ashram or whatever name you may choose to give it – endures and thrives till date and her abode in Hauz Khas, New Delhi, continues to resound with the musical notes of devotion. Music which emanates from deep within the soul and whoever listens to this music leaves with a heart made whole again. Artists from all over the world, be they writers, musicians or sculptors, pay obeisance at this holy shrine despite hailing from diverse linguistic backgrounds. In the words of Waris Shah, 'There is no place for the arrogant here'. She borders on stubbornness in her refusal to exchange even pleasantries with the loud-mouths and the charlatans. Rather than respond to the obnoxious din of despicable people, she prefers to retreat into the solitude and silence of her heart to carry on with her deep contemplation and writing. She accords the status of worship to writing. She frequently mentions the efficacy of the 'mantra of silence'. While reading Ayn Rand's English novel, *The Fountainhead*, that she had recommended, Amrita's stature seemed to me like that of a tall building. Where, and how deep, did the first brick of such a strong foundation lie? Quiet and reticent; perhaps her reticence was best understood by one upon whom she conferred the title of 'Beloved Poet of Punjab'; the one who spun the tale of 'Chup di Vaaz' or 'The Voice of Silence' – Shiv Kumar Batalvi. Try to understand the significance and feel

252

the pulse of his words: The voice of silence is heard in the echo of ruins or in the aching ardour of a lover.

When I heard these lines, I was reminded of Jack Griffith London, an American novelist, journalist and social activist who built a large building believed to have 90 rooms. It was his dream to have writers and artists live and work in those rooms. But his enemies burned down that magnificent building to ashes. He said, 'If I get a chance in my next life, then I shall be someone who builds and not burns'. Amrita also exemplifies such thinking. She remained forever tolerant and tender, an epitome of decency, courteousness and civility.

Nagmani is her own flesh and blood. If a flame touches it, it is Amrita who is singed. Once she wrote to me:

> Only those writers are dear to me and published in *Nagmani* who can write and send something worthwhile. Apart from them, no one is near or dear to me. Whoever thinks well, thinks high, is my friend. Whoever writes well, is a writer for *Nagmani*. If they are few in number and hence, are frequently published, I can do nothing about that.

She never sent *Nagmani* free of cost to anyone. Its subscription amount was 10 rupees. Rajinder Singh Bedi sent 11 rupees along with a message, 'Amrita ji, I am sending eleven rupees, ten for the subscription and one as *shagan*; a blessing for success'.

Amrita is an unparalleled achievement of Punjabi literature. Writing about myths, she has herself become one. Sadat Hasan Manto was mentioned earlier in the article. Had Pakistan not been created, Amrita would have presented the programme, 'Awaaz di Duniya de Dosto' ('Friends of the World of Sound') from Delhi's Radio Station, and Manto would have written her character sketch. Like the one he wrote of Ismat Chughtai; with the same affectionate candour and tolerance for Amrita as for Ismat.

Therefore, let us remember the worthy Amrita. 'Amrit vela sach naau' or 'her essence is imbued with truth'. Here it is pertinent to mention that writers published frequently in *Nagmani* were known as *Nagmani* writers. Perhaps they conducted programmes like 'Deeva Bale Saree Raat' ('The Lamp is Lit All Night') in emulation of 'Nagmani Shaam' ('Nagmani Evening'). A few days ago, I asked a gentleman, 'Is the lamp still lit?' He laughed and replied, 'No Sir, now the jagdiyaan jyotan wale have replaced them', that is, 'those with lit lamps have entered the arena'.[2] During our days the programme was free of cost and we did not receive any payment. Now sums of money fixed at handsome remunerative rates are bestowed on these *jagrata walas* – those who conduct these night-long programmes. I have always seen a glow on her face; decorum in her behaviour; and in her manner, the grace of a queen and the asceticism of a dervish.

She has unwavering faith in primordial concepts. And she has dreams. And the curiosity to interpret and construe these dreams. Whatever she sees and hears in her dreams, she pens them down first thing in the morning. An ordinary person may wonder if this is even possible. How can one remember a dream exactly as it transpired? Renowned Russian writer Dostoevsky suffered from hallucinations; long spells of fits would afflict him. Upon regaining consciousness, he would record all that he had seen, felt and heard in that state of unconsciousness. Nowadays, psychologists are researching and investigating this phenomenon. Amrita has written a book about her dreams; as a Hindi writer says, she is perhaps the first Indian writer to wield her pen on this topic.

At times even a great writer like her could experience mental upheaval. The mind begins to cloud over, even if fleetingly, and question one's own motives and actions. This is what leads her to say on one occasion that she shouldn't have written books like *Utth ni Sahiban Suttiye* (*Wake Up, Slumbering Sahiba*), *Darveshan di Mehndi* (*The Dervishes' Ecstasy*) and *Lal Dhage da Rishta* (*The Bond of the Red Thread*). It is this thought, fleeting though it may be, which makes her a beautiful soul – an inhabitant of both realms of heaven and earth; an angel who lives among mere mortals. Her flights of fancy may soar high in the sky and witness or present wondrous glimpses of unique and awe-inspiring experiences, but her central focus shall always remain an independent individual – in Ahmad Nadeem Qasmi's words, 'the unpremeditated and spontaneous state of a human being'. Then why should anyone try to prevent such a great personality from writing about the themes of her choice? Or, to speak with the utmost respect in the style of the most loyal followers, who shall tell the supreme writer, 'Write not like this, but like this'. I am reminded of a couplet that I dedicate to her, 'That there are divine beauties in heaven is a fact, but first let me deal with the beautiful people here on earth; only then shall I cast my glance heavenwards'.

Once Bhushan and I were sitting and chatting with Amrita. Later, Imroz also joined us. The company became livelier and there was plenty of laughter and fun. Amrita and Imroz were in their element. Amrita recounted a joke about an American and a Russian dog in the context of Russian censorship. We had a hearty laugh over it. I don't know what suddenly came over Amrita, to show her appreciation for me, she took out something from the pocket of her gown to gift to me. It was a packet of cigarettes which she had recently brought from abroad. Bhushan cracked one resounding joke after another about the temperaments of Amrita's literary contemporaries and we found ourselves in splits. Sahir's name also cropped up. Imroz became animated and said, 'D'you know what he writes – 'Come, let's weave dreams' – only a weaver can say something like this!' In that instant, Amrita's face lit up with humour instead of a frown, and a reminiscent smile, devoid of sarcasm, played on her lips; an artless pride suffused with affinity and affection. Then she looked at the palms of her hands contemplatively, as if making a wish. A moment later she ran both her hands over her face in the manner of one praying. During this interchange, numerous thoughts darted through my mind. Both personalities blossomed before my eyes, the angst of womanhood aching in the depths of their souls and dreams of spreading the message of peaceful coexistence to the entire world in their hearts. Amrita's soul cried out in anguish, 'I call upon Waris Shah today.... Today millions of daughters are distraught'. Sahir too lent his voice to this emotion, 'Woman gives birth to man and man condemns her to brothels...' / 'Nature bestowed one earth upon us; we divided it into China and Iran'.

These days Amrita makes no remarks about her contemporaries. For her they are like the proverbial nightmare. Like the merchants of literature, many of her contemporaries too have left us forever. As for the rest, one may refer to her Hindi book *Kainaat Se Aagey* (*Beyond the Universe*) and say that Amrita has covered a distance far 'beyond the universe', while others continue to dwell in their narrow time warp and talk about that girl with ribbons in her hair. Commend them for their memory and forget this line by the late Raghubir Dhand, 'They don't forget the old, nor learn the new'.

She may choose to ignore odious and distasteful criticism, but she herself has been responding to well-intentioned and thoughtful criticism. This is clearly a matter of courtesy on her part and not a deliberate intention to dismiss criticism by saying that 'it is a private matter' as those people on television pandering to the low taste of the audience to rake in a profit would have you believe. One example will suffice. Dhand wrote a severely critical letter to Amrita with utmost respect. He was sending her his Punjabi translation of Kamleshwar's popular Hindi story 'Itne Achche Din' ('Such Wonderful Days'). Here I am quoting only some part. He writes:

> But Didi, while I have infinite hatred for this system, I also feel angry with you when I read your column 'The War is Still On'. You, didi, who owe your identity to your adoring masses, you, who have given such poignant expressions to the pain of the multitudes, why are you writing like this?... The kind of abject poverty that exists in our nation and the depraved manner in which blatant and bestial pleasure is taken in crushing the meagre remnants of self-respect of these poverty-stricken and down-trodden people, is perhaps found nowhere else. What is it, didi? Don't you go amidst the people and interact with them? Or perhaps you too have not yet decided who these people are. But have you taken the side of the pimps and the prostitutes who believe the leader to be irreproachable but his coterie to be the root of all evil? But didi, such justifications were given during Bikramjeet's tenure. Are they relevant in today's context? Do you want to put history in reverse gear? Perhaps you have never written a more infamous column than this. (This may be too impertinent a word; what I mean is 'unpopular'). My purpose can

255

never be to say anything to defame you. I have only 'Dixi et salvavi animam meam' ('I Have Only Spoken and Saved My Soul').

Had it been any other editor, a deep frown would have descended on her forehead and she would have cursed him and torn the letter to bits and tossed it into the dustbin. But Amrita published this letter verbatim in *Nagmani* even at a time when her career and popularity were at their peak. She not just published it but responded to it too. It is only fitting that her reply be also mentioned in this chapter. Her response too displays the same humility as Raghuvir's:

> Raghuvir ji, I value and respect your work as much as I value my own work and understanding. Both are totally different perspectives but they share a sense of conscientiousness. 'The War is Still On' is an attempt to understand a personality. The truth of a person as observed up close. The realisation of the increasing suffering of the people is an anguish which I feel in the depths of my being just like you do; and in the next shoot I plan to discuss it. The story sent by you shall be published soon.

The personality that Amrita has spoken about was our country's prime minister at that time – Priyadarshini Indira Gandhi whom Amrita was close to. Mrs Indira Gandhi could share her personal joys and sorrows with Amrita like a confidante, perhaps because she knew that Amrita was not a self-seeker. During her political crisis, Indira Gandhi shared her pain with Amrita, saying 'I am left all alone'. Without any hesitation, Amrita replied fearlessly, 'Indira ji, you are surrounded by crooks and scoundrels'. That haughty woman, intoxicated with power and rendered blind with totalitarian authority, one who could still play havoc with the life of any good person as Aurangzeb had done with Sarmad, a Sufi mystic, replied, 'Yes, I know'.

Amrita never indulged in drama in her life. Perhaps she never even wrote one. She wrote screenplays for a couple of films, but with film director Basu Bhattacharya's death they never made it to the silver screen. They are included in the book *Aksharon ke Saaye* translated as *Shadows of Words*. Currently a lot of Amrita's work is being published in Hindi also.

She is a confluence of the word and the sound. There is a musical rhythm to her speech and style which is drenched in emotion. She goes through life at her own pace – seamlessly and effortlessly. Look at these lines: 'Who sowed these seeds of letters? I have grown old watering them....'

It was an expression as expansive as the four epochs, in which the specks of the skies spoke, and the universe heard and was written on the parchment of consciousness. One may be born in any era, but all my life I have kept talking about those people the fragrance of whose words permeates my heart, and in my opinion, mentioning them is akin to nourishing these sacred peepal trees of letters.

Born seven years after Manto, she is overcome with emotion when she mentions the figure seven, while for me it is the number eight with which I associate my sense of exhilaration and my emotional connect with Amrita. I was eight when I came across her book *Amrit Lehran*. She was eight when she penned her first poem, and when on her 80th birthday a Hindi writer brought her a gift, even at that ripe age her joy was akin to a child's; the same happiness that I had experienced upon trading a 10 rupee note for 25 paise coins. Seeing her glee, the Hindi writer wrote, 'I felt like removing the zero from 80'.

To make ends meet, she knitted sweaters for little children and sold them, sang on the radio, played the guitar and commuted to the radio station on a bicycle. Her lips tremble when she recounts all that transpired in the journey of her life from the bicycle to the airplane. Who has the luxury or the inclination to listen to this long story and empathise with it? Perhaps only Kamleshwar, the famous Hindi writer, understood this. Recently she was bestowed with the 'Poet of the Millennium' award by the Delhi government. About the language in which she would speak on the occasion, he commented, 'Amrita shall speak in the language of a story'.

I have written above that Amrita is an achievement of Punjabi literature. And her achievement is Imroz. Ask him to paint a portrait of any woman; the visage would always strike you as Amrita's. Amrita brought grace and glory to the many awards bestowed upon her and to those countries that bestowed these awards upon her.

On her birthday on 31 August, exactly at seven, I called her up and wished her in the style of Mirza Ghalib. She laughed and quipped, 'What shall I do with so many years? I am just a bag of bones now'. At that moment my thoughts went to Imroz whom she had proudly accepted as her own – her companion, her everything. Both lived together with love and mutual respect and set a unique precedent. We pray that this bond endures in all dignity till their dying breath and may this be as long as Mirza Ghalib's blessing. Then they may seek a boon similar to this folk couplet:

> May the last breath be in the arms of the beloved
> While to the heavens, proceed our bones.

Source

Excerpted from Mohan Bhandari, 'Aavaaz de Kahaan Hai', *Saahaan de Hisse di Maulsari*, ed. Jasbir Bhullar, Chandigarh: Punjab Sahit Akademi & Amritsar: Lok Sahit Prakashan, 2001, p. 62-74.

Notes

1 Published in *Main Tainu Pher Milangi*, 2004, 2016, p. 45-51.
2 This is to indicate that compared to the secular and poetic nature of the programme 'Deeva Bale Saree Raat', the programmes had taken on religious hues.

24

AMRITA! THE NONPAREIL

Vanita
Translated by Hina Nandrajog and Hartej Kaur Bal

Amrita!
The 20th century
remembers you
As does the 21st
These women – poets and artists –
Your name on their lips every other moment,
Venerate you; some adorn their brows
With a red bindi of consciousness
Style their hair like yours
Clink goblets
Inhale deep puffs of cigarettes
and emit clouds of smoke
....
Amrita!
You have become
The Voice of Asia and
The Statue of Liberty
For Punjabi women
For Indian women
For Pakistani women
And for women in other countries
You are immortal for centuries to come
....
Amrita! You are a nonpareil
None can equal you
To become like you one does not
Merely don the glory of your beauty
One has to stamp the revenue stamp as well
To toil and labour for *Nagmani* too
To pay obeisance to the soil of the cloister

DOI: 10.4324/9781003214656-36

To sink and float on a river of fire
To endure jeers and taunts of kith and kin
To awaken the courage of the soul
To churn the ocean and drink the poison
Only then is an amrit-like Amrita born after centuries

I wish! For the sake of the "daughter of words",
May the universal relationship of the writers
with you deepen.

Source

Excerpted from 'Amrita! Nahi Reesan Teriyan', *Sahitak Ekam* January–March 2020, ed. Artinder Sandhu, Amritsar, p. 4-5.

25

AMRITA PRITAM

My Inspiration

Rupinder Kaur Waraich

I was born in England, Birmingham. My parents would never have imagined that the land and the language they left behind would be the language I
would fall in love with and want to know more about. My journey began as
a confused 19-year-old in search of her purpose in life and, along the way,
I began writing poetry – first in English, then in Punjabi and finally in both.
On my journey as a writer, the one who made me fall in love with Punjabi
was Amrita Pritam, a name that holds many worlds of not just writing but
life. Over the past few years, I have explored Punjabi literature deeply, but
still the poet who transports me to a different world and fills my soul with
an indescribable feeling is Amrita (other than Shiv Kumar Batalvi). I am
often asked, 'But why … why do you love Amrita so much?' I fall short of
words to answer the 'why'. Not just me, Amrita inspired a whole generation of Punjabi female poets and still continues to do so. Her pen gave birth
to many female poets who, at a time, were known as *baagi-vidrohi aura-
tan*: 'rebel women' such as Manjit Tiwana, Nirupama Dutt and Shashi Pal
Samdura, to name a few.

Pure Love: 'Ik Geet' ('One Song')

Amrita started writing very early in life and once got a slap from her father
for writing a love poem to an imaginary 'Rajan'. Today young Punjabi poet,
Brar Jassi writes in her poem, 'Mai Sau Kudi Nahi Han' ('I Am Not a Good
Girl') 'mohabbat vali kavita / likhan valiyan kudiyan / charitraheen nahin
hondiyan', meaning that girls who write love poems are not wanton (2019).
It makes me wonder what it is about writing romantic poems that is seen as
an act of rebellion even in today's day and age.

Much is known, discussed and highlighted about Amrita's love life,
especially her highly romanticised relationship with Sahir. I, however, have
always felt that if one is ever in love, it should be like that of Amrita and
Imroz – unconditional and free. Sadly, the home that they built together
with love was sold and demolished. Supriya Kaur Dhaliwal, a poet based in

DOI: 10.4324/9781003214656-37

both India and Ireland, writes in her poem, 'Undesigning K-25, Hauz Khas' for Amrita and Imroz:

The autocorrect tells me Waris is not spelt so, it must be war is. / But that is what it has come to now. It is war in our homes; / in your home too – every inch of its walls bedecked in love and "bulldozed dreams".

(2021)

It is evident that even today people regard the Amrita-Imroz love story as yet another romantic folktale of Punjab.

In 'Ik Geet' from the Sahitya Akademi award-winning anthology *Sunehde* Amrita says, 'pyar mera ho gaya yaadan de hawale' (Pritam 2019: 77). Nikky-Guninder Kaur Singh translates this as, 'My love lies in the custody of memory / anchors have split from their banks / Oars lie severed from their boats / Waves rage in the river of my heart / Flooding down my cheeks' (2012). Coming from Punjab known as the land of five rivers (prior to Partition), it is perhaps natural to refer to water as it is the lifeline of Punjab (Sandhu 2019). Amrita laments, 'dil dariya vich kaanga aayiyaan' / 'Waves rage in the river of my heart' (Pritam 2019: 77).

In the second stanza Amrita goes on, 'At the feet of every woman / Flows a Chenab even today / The soles of every Sassi / Even today burn with blisters' (Pritam 2019: 77). Love, which means free choice of one's mate, constituted open defiance of patriarchal authority and interest and deserved condign punishment. Even today women who love outside caste, religion and social norms are shunned. Even today women revolt against society's disapproval of love outside one's caste, culture and religion. Even today there are songs sung and written about women who revolt and are termed bad; seen as *ghar di izzat* or the honour of the home, those who flout societal expectations are seen as besmirching their fathers' turban, a Punjabi idiom to indicate a loss of family honour.

I believe love has always brought about a revolution. In another poem of Amrita, 'Jhummar' she embodies Hir and voices the latter's desire for the fulfilment of her love. Amrita writes, 'My hands are coloured with henna / my wrists chime with bridal bracelets / O Ranjha I am all yours: See I belong to nobody else' (Pritam 2019: 58). A female writer giving voice to a heroine is radical for Amrita's time, especially talking about Hir's desires that nobody else thought of, perhaps not even Waris Shah. Even today, not much is written on this. In her much acclaimed poem 'Ajj Aakhaan Waris Shah nu', Amrita appropriates the role of Waris Shah and takes ownership of the centuries-old tradition of the Hir narrative (Kazmi 2018). She refers to the River Chenab as the river of blood due to Partition, though Chenab is noted as the river of love in Punjabi folktales.

261

Indian religious and cultural texts have created unforgettable characters from the medieval Indian era – from Radha to folk characters like Hir and Sohni who may be seen as manifestations of Radha in Punjabi and Sindhi poetry (Das 2003). Sassi also symbolises the human soul and Punnun, the divine beloved. Sassi symbolises the seeker for God and longing for union with him (Singh Shan 2000). Similarly, Waris Shah's Hir is seen as the human soul and Ranjha as the divine beloved, as also in the tale of Sohni-Mahiwal.

Like Amrita I also refer to Punjabi folk tales in my work. In one of my poems 'Swimming', I write, 'He sang meri jaan / I thought I was drowning / like the love in my blood / but I learnt to swim / when he lied, called me his jaan / and left' (2021). In the last verse I write about a love where it was easy to drown like Sohni-Mahiwal but instead of drowning like Sohni, I learnt to swim. I wanted to challenge the oft-told tale. In an essay Amrita writes that Hir, Sassi and Sohni are the symbols of that consciousness which exists in the social units of every region and country. The poison given to Hir, Sassi's death in the desert and Sohni's drowning in the Chenab are incidents that are direct reflections of will-driven consciousness (Pritam 1993).

Naresh K. Jain writes in 'Sahiban in Punjabi Literature' (Grewal and Pall 2005) that all Punjabi love legends are rooted in a patriarchal society in which the woman was a symbol of family and tribal *izzat* and was disposed of at the discretion of the male head of the family. Amrita's essence and quest for love is seen in almost all of her poems; in 'Daag' ('Stain') (Pritam 2019: 175-76) she refers to incomplete love as a stain – a stain seen on her father's back and she speaks about asking her mother about what she should do with this stain and where she could hide it. In recent times there has been a growing realisation that Sahiban is a victim of gender injustice and has been more sinned against than sinning (Grewal and Pall 2005).

Waris Shah writes in the opening lines of *Hir*, 'Love is the root of the universe'. In the fourth stanza of 'Ik Geet' Amrita writes, 'This life I offer you / That life is also for you / Those who love / Forsake both worlds' (Pritam 2019: 77). The afterlife, or life after death which nobody knows about, and this present life are forsaken by lovers. Lovers in the tragic love tales of Punjab like Hir-Ranjha, Sohni-Mahiwal, Sassi-Punnun and Mirza-Sahiban are said to be united in the afterlife as they were not able to meet in this life.

In the final stanza Pritam writes:

eh birha asa mang ke lita
eh birha sanu sajana ne dita
es birha de ghup hanere
kyu koi deva bale

This heartache I solicited
My lover granted me

In these dark clouds of pain
How do I light a flame?

(Pritam 2019: 77)

Pritam mentions the word *birha* (separation) which was later made hugely popular by Batalvi who became known as '*birha da Sultan*'. But even before Batalvi it was Sheikh Farid who used the term in Sufi poetry and *birha* made its way in Punjabi poetry forever. Moreover, the line 'pyar mera ho gaya yaadan de hawale' or 'My love lies in the custody of memory' echoes a haiku by Sonia Sanchez, 'if i had known, if / i had known you, i would have / left my love at home' (1999). Perhaps it is an act of self-realisation; the love that is no longer yours or is long gone is best left to memory; and a focus on the present is necessary, which for Amrita was Imroz. Her love for Imroz reflected in her poem 'Main Tainu Pher Milangi' has been popularised in the Bollywood movie *Manmarziyan* (2018). In a tribute to Amrita, the poet Priya Malik reinforces the notion that Amrita's words are as inspirational for women writers today as they were years ago.

Main tumhe phir miloongi
Kahan, kaise, kis tarah
Mujhe sab pata hai

(Malik 2021)

I will meet you again, yet again
How and where
I know everything

Feminine Energy: 'Kumari' ('Virgin')

'Kumari' from Amrita Pritam's collection *Kagaz te Canvas*, which won her the Bharatiya Jnanpith Award, looks at a virgin's first sexual experience and compares it to an act of self-annihilation. 'When I entered your bridal chamber / I was not one but two persons / One's marriage was consummated and complete / the other remained a chaste virgin' (Pritam and Singh 1982: 31). In these opening lines Amrita looks at the duality of being a virgin and a married woman. On one side is a chaste virgin and on the other, a woman who has to give up her chastity as she is married. The language of marriage is often a language of ownership, not a language of partnership (Adichie 2014). These lines show that the sexual act occurred only because she was now married. In South Asian culture, sex before marriage has mostly been seen as a sin and a woman expressing her sexual desires is rare.

263

The next verse follows these lines,

> To fulfill our union / I had to kill the virgin / And kill her, I did. / Such murders are sanctioned by the law / Only the humiliation accompanying them is illegal. / So I drank the poison of humiliation
> (Pritam and Singh 1982: 31)

She talks about the physical union of a husband and wife; the virgin in Amrita's poem has undergone an act of self-annihilation. The virgin who becomes a wife has no choice of her own and has to give in. She calls this a murder which is sanctioned by the law, a not-so-subtle hint to marital rape.

In the well-known feminist essay, 'Laughing Medusa' Hélène Cixous also talks about an act of self-annihilation, saying that we must kill the false woman who prevents the live one from breathing (Cixous, Cohen and Cohen 1976). Here Cixous refers to the many women who have another woman within that does not allow them to breathe or allow them to live their lives on their own terms. In order to break free and realise one's own self, one has to kill the false woman. In Amrita's poem, the virgin has no choice as a married woman but to kill her innocence. In an interview on YouTube, Amrita says that a man denies his own subconsciousness when he denies the power of women.

The opening lines from Amrita's poem 'Blasphemy' are 'Today I sold a world / And bought a religion. / It was an act of blasphemy' (Pritam and Singh 1982: 23). Amrita knew that what she was writing about was not what Indian women writers, especially Punjabi women writers, wrote about or were expected to write about. For Punjab, most noted for its Sufism, romance and *gurbani*, Amrita's work as a woman was different. Writing about female desire during those times was indeed a revolutionary act and it is still so. Desire is a normal aspect, also explored at length in Batalvi's version of *Luna*; however, one wonders if Batalvi's take on Luna would still be appreciated if he were a woman writer. Both men and women have their own desires, whether it is to do with their careers, sexuality or life in general (McTaggart 2012). It becomes a radical act for women to express their desires in a society that is patriarchal, constantly wanting women to silence themselves.

Anaïs Nin, an American-Cuban-French diarist and novelist, says that the language of sex was yet to be invented and the language of the senses was yet to be explored (2007). I spent some time thinking about how a woman's desire has been described in Punjabi. It has been described and explored through the long folk tradition of oral songs which are sung at weddings. Long before Amrita, Peero Preman (1832-1872), Punjabi Sufi poetess, wrote of being a low caste prostitute along with expressing her own thoughts and feelings towards love and religion. Her narrative was rebellious for her times – Peero could be a Sita to her Ram-like guru (Gulabdas) or a Hir questioning the Mullahs (Malhotra 2017). Years later, despite becoming very popular, Amrita was still disliked by many, and even today women writers are criticised malevolently.

Returning to Amrita's poem 'Kumari' the next lines follow, 'Came the dawn and / I saw the dawn / and I saw the blood on my hands / I washed them / Just as I washed off the odours on my body' (Pritam and Singh 1982: 31). The natural ease with which Amrita says this indicates that she had no choice; this was expected of her. She goes on to say, 'But when I saw myself in my mirror / there she was before me / The same one I thought I had murdered during the night' (Pritam and Singh 1982: 31). She talks about seeing herself in the mirror; she who was considered dead appeared in front of her. So perhaps she didn't kill her after all.

Amrita ends with, 'Oh, God! / Was the bridal chamber so dark that I could not tell / the one I had slain / from the one I did, in fact, kill?' (Pritam and Singh 1982: 31). Who does Amrita end up killing in her poem – herself, the virgin, the wife? Or maybe none of these, maybe it was just a hallucination and she didn't actually kill anybody.

This poem may seem outdated as one imagines women making their own choices about their bodies, sexuality, desire, marriage, etc. in present times. But even today women in many places are not allowed the choice of consent. Marital rape in India was seen as a crime only when the wife was below the age of 15. This merging of a married woman's identity with her husband is perhaps what Amrita wants to kill – an identity which has no acknowledgement in a male chauvinist society (Singh and Singh 2020).

The Essence of Freedom: 'Mera Pata' ('My Address')

'Mera Pata' portrays the free essence that Amrita embodied in her writings and her life:

> Today I effaced the number of my house and
> The name of the street at the top of the street
> (Pritam and Singh 1982: 177)

These lines for me read almost like a Sufi poem; Bulleh Shah comes to mind, 'Bulla ki Jana Main Kaun' sung by Rabbi Shergill: 'Bulla ki jana main kaun / Na main arabi na lahori' ('Bulla knows not who he is / Neither and Arab nor of Lahore'). Amrita's free soul is something that women even today aspire to be.

In a short poem titled 'Amrita Pritam' she writes:

> ik dard si
> jo cigarette di tarah
> main chup chaap pitta hai

Pain –
I inhaled it
Silently
Like a cigarette

(175)

Cigarettes were once seen as a social taboo and sometimes viewed as a 'torch of freedom' by rebellious bohemian intellectuals (Amos 2000). 1960s onwards smoking became almost a badge of a rebellious, outspoken, 'fallen' woman – artist or working woman depicted with a cigarette dangling from her hand.

Nirupama Dutt, who calls herself a daughter of Amrita, writes in her poem, 'Laughing Sorrow':

to cheer a sorrowing day fail
I will sit on the slope outside the girls' hostel
and light my cigarette
the ashes will mix for sure
in my poem today
and readers will get a chance
to say I am all wrong –

(online)

'Such are the constraints of women poets of Amrita's age, a cigarette is their only solace!' With Dutt's reference to Amrita, we can see the kind of comments that women smokers receive – being compared to Amrita herself.

In 'Mera Pata' Amrita's soul seems to travel everywhere; it now has no identity and is truly free. The last line remains my favourite, 'Te jitthe vi sutantar rooh di jhalak pavey / samajhna uh mera ghar hai' or 'And wherever the glimpse of a free spirit exists / That will be my home' (Pritam and Singh 1982: 177). This line reminds me of the concluding lines of Amrita's fiction on Partition, *Pinjar*, 'Whether one is a Hindu girl or a Muslim one, whoever reaches her destination, she carries along my soul also' (Pritam 2017: 80). Amrita really does hold onto this freeness throughout her work which inspires me in my writing to say, 'I have become the woman I have always wanted to be – / I have become azaad, free / Main azaad ha / I am free / I am free like birds' (2018).

Meri Amrita (My Amrita)

Towards the end of the Hindi film *Soni* which looks at crimes against women in Delhi, Kalpana gives a copy of Amrita's autobiography *Rasidi Ticket* to Soni to read, saying that if not all, it should answer some of her questions. Soni asks what *Rasidi Ticket* means and Kalpana tells her that it is a small excise stamp to collect tax on tobacco and liquor. Kalpana also narrates the anecdote that an esteemed writer (Khushwant Singh) once told Amrita that her life was inconsequential enough to fit on the back of a *rasidi ticket* (revenue stamp). This incident indicates how women in India still find Amrita empowering and are still able to relate to her.

The Sanskrit word *amrit* (nectar) implies immortality and today Amrita is immortal due to her words. When I think of her, I imagine a bird flying in the sky smiling not in search of its nest but just happy with its flight and seeing the whole wide world. Amrita for me represents a free soul in its true essence.

Amrita's creative work is celebrated for its sensuous imagery and evocative rhythm and is widely read and appreciated though it has also been criticised as vacuous and sentimental (Tharu and Lalita, 1995). Amrita's work needs revisiting and her lesser-known work such as her essays should be translated. The driving force in Amrita's writings is pure love, feminine energy and the essence of having a free spirit which has inspired countless writers after Amrita, including myself.

Amrita Pritam is a name that will forever hold power, love and freedom. She gave Punjabi literature worldwide recognition and became 'Awaaz-e-Punjab' ('The Voice of Punjab'). Most of her contemporaries were men and she dared to raise her voice when poetry itself was seen as unsuitable for a woman. She lived in her own world, and instead of clinging to multi-layered boundaries of social expectations, she broke free from them. The way Amrita lived as a free spirit, both in her life and in her works, was a major source of inspiration to me – to never think about others' perception of you but to simply follow your own he(art).

References

Adichie, Chimamanda Ngozi. 2014. *We Should All Be Feminists*. London: Fourth Estate.

Amos, Amanda. 2000. "From Social Taboo to "Torch of Freedom": The Marketing of Cigarettes to Women", *Tobacco Control* 9, no. 1: 3–8. https://doi.org/10.1136/tc.9.1.3.

Brar, Jessy. 2019. *Main Sau Kudi Nahi Ha*. 3rd ed. Patiala: Caliber Publications.

Cixous, Hélène, Keith Cohen, and Paula Cohen. 1976. "The Laugh of the Medusa", *Signs: Journal of Women in Culture and Society* 1, no. 4: 875–893. https://doi.org/10.1086/493306.

Deol, Jeevan. 2002. "Sex, Social Critique and the Female Figure in Premodern Punjabi Poetry: Vāris Shāh's "Hīr"", *Modern Asian Studies* 36, no. 1: 141–171.

Dutt, Nirupama. 1995. "Laughing Sorrow", *Poetryinternational.Org*. https://www.poetryinternational.org/pi/poem/7456/auto/0/0/Nirupama-Dutt/LAUGHING-SORROW/en/tile (accessed on 18.12.2021).

Grewal, Reeta and Sheena Pall. 2005. *Precolonial & Colonial Punjab: Society, Economy, Politics & Culture Essays for Indu Banga*. Delhi: Manohar Publishers.

Gurbachan. 1972. "Punjabi Literature in 1971 – A Critical Survey", *Indian Literature*, Sahitya Akademi 14, no. 4: 93–94.

Hustvedt, Siri. 2016. *A Woman Looking at Men Looking at Women: Essays on Art, Sex, and the Mind*. London: Sceptre.

Kaur, Rupinder. 2018. *Rooh*. Exeter: Verve Poetry Press.

Kaur, Rupinder. 2021. "Swimming", *Wild Court*. https://wildcourt.co.uk/new-work/swimming-a-poem-by-rupinder-kaur/ (accessed on 26.05.2022).

Kaur Dhaliwal, Supriya. 2021. *The Yak Dilemma*. Dorchester: Makina Poetry.

Kaur Singh, Nikky-Guninder. 2012. *Of Sacred and Secular Desire: An Anthology of Lyrical Writings from the Punjab*. New York: I.B. Tauris.

Kazmi, Sara. 2018. "Radical Re-Tellings of Hir: Gender and the Politics of Voice in Postcolonial Punjabi Poetry", *South Asia Multidisciplinary Academic Journal* [Online], Free-Standing Articles, Online since 20 May 2019, connection on 03 September 2022. URL: http://journals.openedition.org/samaj/5294; DOI: (accessed on 03.09.2022).

Kumar Das, Sisir. 2003. "The Mad Lover", *Indian Literature*, Sahitya Akademi 47, no. 3: 149–178.

Law, Lawyers, Nivedita Singh, and Rakshita Singh. 2020. "Unveiling the Paradox of Marital Rape in India", *Law and Lawyers* 1, no. 1: 1–8.

Malhotra, Anshu. 2017. *Piro and the Gulabdasis: Gender, Sect and Society in Punjab*. New Delhi: Oxford University Press.

Malik, Priya. 2021. *"Main Tumhe Phir Miloongi"*, Priya Malik ft Hasan. Tribute to Amrita Pritam. (UnErase Poetry) https://www.youtube.com/watch?v=vFIMenVQxS8 (accessed on 25.11.2021).

McTaggart, Anne. 2012. "What Women Want? Mimesis and Gender in Chaucer's "Wife of Bath's Prologue" and "Tale", *Contagion: Journal of Violence, Mimesis, and Culture* 19: 41–67.

Nin, Anaïs. 2007. *Delta of Venus*. London: Penguin Books.

Pritam, Amrita. 1982. *Amrita Pritam: Selected Poems*. Trans. Khushwant Singh. Delhi: Bhartiya Jnanpith Publication.

———. 1993. "Will-Oriented Consciousness: Poetic Musings", *World Affairs: The Journal of International Issues* 2, no. 2: 70–73.

———. 1994. *The Revenue Stamp: An Autobiography*, trans. Krishna Gorowara. Noida: Wide Canvas, Vikas Publishing.

———. 2017 (1950). *The Skeleton*, trans. Khushwant Singh. Delhi: Shilalekh.

———. 2018 (2006). *Kagaz te Canvas*. Delhi: Shilalekh.

———. 2019 (2006). *Kagaz te Canvas to Paihlan*. Delhi: Shilalekh.

Pritam, Amrita and Khushwant Singh. 2009. *Punjabi Poems of Amrita Pritam in Gurmukhi, Hindi, Roman and English*. New Delhi: Star Publications.

Sanchez, Sonia. 1999. *Shake Loose My Skin*. Boston: Beacon Press Books.

Sandhu, Amandeep. 2019. *Panjab: Journeys Through Fault Lines*. Chennai: Westland Publications.

Sircar Chibbar, Roopali. 1990. "Patriarchy and the Indian Woman-Poet", *Indian Literature*, Sahitya Akademi 33, no. 5: 165–178.

Tharu, Susie and K. Lalita. 1995. *Women Writing India: Volume II*. 1st ed. Delhi: Oxford University Press.

Films

Manmarziyan. 2018. Directed by Anurag Kashyap and written by Kanika Dhillon.
Soni. 2018. Directed and written by Ivan Ayr.

Other Links

Documentary Film: Bhattacharya, Basu. 2006. *Amrita Today*. New Delhi: Sahitya
Akademi. https://bit.ly/2KzdksN (accessed on 04.09.2022).

26

ONE'S SHARE OF THE SCENT OF *MAULSARI*

Jasbir Bhullar
Translated by Hartej Kaur Bal and Hina Nandrajog

Maulsari may go by any name
Bulle Shah maybe
Barkate, or perhaps Amrita
Or maybe the river Sandal
Alphabets alone cannot complete it.

"Complete" is only a word
If anything exists at all
It is naught but a scrap of time
Disordered pages of memories
The dream before the creation
And the full thought of unfulfilled romance.

Not with the breath of friendship
Nor in the embrace of love
does one feel complete
Or belong to anyone completely
It is merely lighting a few lamps
To illumine oneself
Turning a few pages
To carve one's identity.

Those, who are her friends,
Writers, and
audience and critics, too
Enraptured by her charm,
They are Amrita's lamps
And shine in the sparkle of stars
On the parapet of adoration.

DOI: 10.4324/9781003214656-38

Those close to her
Mistakenly thought
Drawing a collage of stars
would complete her picture
And recreate
the sky sprawling up to the horizon.
The soft drizzle of words
and wisps of emotions
the sparkling glow of lamps
and one's share of the scent of *maulsari*...
Can one paint the whole universe
With just these few strokes of the brush?

Time shall again walk in the company of colours
to etch a rainbow-hued portrait
And will turn
another page of enchantment
Well, this is the saga for now
Only a handful of pages
For the book on Amrita.

***

Source

Jasbir Bhullar, 'Sahan de Hisse di Maulsari de Baare', *Sahan de Hisse di Maulsari*
ed. Jasbir Bhullar. Chandigarh: Punjab Sahit Akademi & Amritsar: Lok Sahit
Prakashan, 2001, p. 11-12.

27

'TEA WITH AMMA JI'

Reminiscences by Aman Kwatra, Amrita Pritam's Grandson

It is four in the morning and the eight-year-old me is wondering whether grandma and baba ji (Imroz) would be up already. It would be lovely to get some tea and biscuits on this cold winter morning in Delhi. But is it too early? Everyone else is still asleep. I look around slowly and notice that nothing is stirring. So, I get up quietly only to find that Mum is now half awake and asking if I need anything. I whisper that I'm going upstairs to amma ji's place. She nods, perhaps half-listening to what I'm mumbling, but peacefully falls back asleep. No one else notices my movements and I pride myself on being as quiet as that mouse that I saw running through the house a few days ago. Spoken too soon. The ears of my dogs' twitch and their heads pop up from their cosy beds as they notice my stealthy movements towards them. I beseech them with a finger on my lips not to start barking and they seem to understand. With equal sneakiness, they decide to follow me out of the room. Now, like three ninjas, we venture out, across the corridor, past the dining room, and out through the inner doors of the ground floor apartment and start our ascent on the inside stairs of the house that link my granny's place on the first floor. The dogs now have the same idea as I do… well, about the biscuits anyway, perhaps not the tea. Twenty-four steps later, we reach my granny's abode and I put my right ear to the door. It's still very quiet and I don't hear any conversations or footsteps. Alas, I'm too early!

Not wanting to disturb amma ji or baba ji, I decide to wait, and all three of us make ourselves comfortable on the granite stairs, though they are rather cold. The thought of hot tea (and tasty biscuits) is enough at this time to stand the torment. The dogs make themselves comfortable too – and sit beside me – ready for some serious conversation. But first, they get gentle pats on their heads, and a good scratch around the ears; for you can't talk good philosophy unless you've made yourself quite comfortable. About twenty minutes later, having discussed our place in the grand scheme of the

DOI: 10.4324/9781003214656-39

universe, we move on to the topic of... but wait, what's that sound? My ear is back on the door. Footsteps. Definitely footsteps coming from inside amma ji's place. They're up! That can only mean one thing ... it's tea-time!

I gently knock at the door. Nothing happens. I knock again, this time a little louder. One of the dogs also lends a helping bark. I now hear the footsteps getting louder. Finally, baba ji opens the door with a big smile. It's like he's been expecting me. I wish him a good morning and we walk in, dogs first and then me. Baba ji goes to the kitchen to get some biscuits for the two hungry four-legged beings, while I head straight into amma ji's room. She is busy writing. I wish her a good morning, and she looks up to see me at the door. She is happy to see me and warmly calls me in. She puts aside her papers, as I snuggle into her bed. I ask her what she is doing, and she tells me that she's writing about a dream that she's just had. She asks me whether I had any dream in the night, and I begin to tell her about my own sleep journeys. Possibly something about dinosaurs, but one can't be too sure as dreams, like life itself, quickly fade way even though we may try our utmost to hold on to them.

Baba ji now walks in, having kindly done the delicate work of brewing the perfect pot of tea, bringing three teacups on a tray, along with an assortment of some delicious biscuits too. Our ritual wakes the sun, who soon peeks in through the window, curious, I suppose, about this pre-dawn gathering. The dogs enter amma ji's room too, wanting to be as much a part of this sweet company, as also wanting to try some of those sweet treats.

After the tea ceremony is complete, it's time to go out to the rose garden for a frosty morning walk. While amma ji and baba ji get ready, I go into her library to glance at some of my favourite books – mostly about unexplained mysteries of the world, mythological stories, and yes, about dreams – all of which were introduced to me by my grandmother. At that time, I had no idea how much her influence would shape the course of my life. Anyway, back to the library. In a few minutes, baba ji tells me they're ready to leave. I ask him if he has packed some food for the peacocks and the squirrels. He confirms that he has. Perfect, all is in order – but someone is missing! I walk the dogs back into my parents' room and tell my mum I'm going for a walk with amma ji and baba ji. I eagerly nudge my sister awake and tell her to come too. Promptly, she's ready and so, the four of us joyfully step out for our morning stroll. Curiously, when we are in the rose garden, I notice many people stopping by and wishing my grandmother a good morning. She always smiles and wishes them back. This happens many times during our walk and seems rather fascinating to me, for I simply can't understand how she knows all these people. After all, I for one, don't seem to recognise any of them. Yet, I forget to ask her about this, because my attention goes back to the peacocks and the squirrels who are waiting for their meal.

That was nearly 30 years ago, but such memories remain as clear as still waters, especially because we enjoyed many such pre-dawn tea ceremonies, and they were ever so meaningful to me. At that young age, Amrita Pritam was simply my lovable (and very huggable) grandmother and my under-standing of her was limited to what can be perceived through the eyes of childhood love. To me, she was a kind, gentle and very loving grandmother, full of life, laughter and compassion. She would listen to all my nonsensical stories and poems, and I had no idea about the depth of her own writings. Even during my early teenage years, I would have spent more time read-ing all the other books that she would recommend to me, rather than read her writings. It was only during my late teenage years that I became more acquainted with her works and felt mesmerised. Since then, I've been trying to reflect on the gem of her life and work both through my personal memo-ries of her and through a more mature understanding of her writings. It was only after her death in 2005 that I truly began to understand the extraordi-nary nature of her being and the magnitude of her profound wisdom and of her astounding courage.

More recently, it has been wonderful to see that interest in her being, her life and her literary works have received renewed critical attention from aca-demia and admiration from a whole new generation of readers. In light of the same, this significant volume is a much-needed introduction (or perhaps even, re-introduction) to different aspects of her life and works – ranging widely from poetry to storytelling, and from politics to spirituality. This is an important and much-awaited step forward in recognising and exploring the depths of one of the most important and enigmatic Punjabi writers of the 20th century. Amrita Pritam, a.k.a. 'Amma ji' to me, had and continues to have a profound impact on my life, and I would wager, also on the lives of so many of her readers. For the gift of this notable volume, I remain ever so grateful to the editors and contributors of this book and also thank them for giving me this opportunity to share this small personal note, this child-hood memory about having tea with a titan, who was also my grandmother.

LIFE EXTRAORDINAIRE
Biochronology

- **1919.** Born on 31 August; in her own words, born of a prayer expressed by her parents' students. Named Amrit (nectar) a Punjabi translation of the word 'Piyush', her father's pen-name. Her mother, Raj Bibi, was a schoolteacher and her father, Kartar Singh Hitkari, a *pracharak*, a preacher of Sikhism, with a deep interest in literature.
- **1923.** Engaged at age four to her bhua's son at her mother's desire.
- **1930.** At age 11, her mother fell ill and died despite Amrita's prayers. Led to a crisis of faith. Marked as 31 July 1930 in *Rasidi Ticket*. The seed of detachment that had attracted Kartar Singh to a religious *dera* before his marriage grew despite having a family, and the untimely death of his wife turned him to self-absorbed religious study. His lonely daughter immersed herself in studies and pursuit of literature, voraciously reading not just ancient and contemporary Indian texts, but world literature as well.
- **1932.** Cleared Punjabi Vidvani exam.
- **1933.** Passed Giani exam.
- **1935.** Marks the beginning of Amrita's literary journey. First anthology of poems, *Thandiyan Kirnan*, published in 1935 under her maiden name, Amrit Kaur.
- **1936.** Second collection of poems *Amrit Lehran* published. Began to be noticed as a poet in Punjabi literary circles.
- On 1 December 1936, at age 17, she was married to Sardar Pritam Singh Kwatra who worked in a shop in Anarkali Bazar, Lahore. On the evening of the wedding, she tried to tell her father that she didn't want to marry, but it was too late. She could never accept the marriage in her heart though she fulfilled her marital responsibilities. She has also never spoken against her husband or his family; she said that they were good people and it was she who could not become worthy of them.
  - Too young to articulate her aversion to the union, she was left with a haunting sense of her unfulfilled 16th year being mingled with every year of her subsequent life, and this provided her with much of her impulse in writing.

- • Interestingly, although she could never relate to her husband, Pritam Singh Kwatra, his first name is a part of her identity for all times to come.
- **1937-1938.** Began editing *Navin Duniya* (*New World*), a literary monthly in Lahore.
- **1938.** Beginning of her media journey. Started anchoring a programme 'Aavaaz di Duniya de Dosto' ('Friends of the World of Sounds') for Lahore Radio Station. People would keep staring at her when she recorded her programmes. Her audience loved her voice, too.
- **1939-1946.** Engaged in prolific writing, primarily poetry, but also stories and fiction.
- **1944.** Met Sahir Ludhianvi for the first time in Preet Nagar. In *Kala Gulab* she says that she probably dreamt of hearing from her father's lips asking if she recognised him and that he was her destiny. Her sense of loneliness was intensified by her unrequited love for Sahir Ludhianvi.
- **1947.** Eventful year. Her family fled Lahore to Delhi during the mayhem of the Partition of India and the creation of Pakistan.
  - • Iconic 'Ajj Aakhaan Waris Shah nu' was written on a train when she was returning to Dehradun from Delhi where she had come to look for work.
  - • January: Edited *Hitkari*, a quarterly magazine.
  - • 3 July: Birth of her son, Navraj.
- **1948-1961.** Supported her family by taking up a job at All India Radio (AIR), Delhi, with the help of Mahinder Singh Randhawa, an IAS officer and a close friend.
- **1948.** Regular meetings with Sahir Ludhianvi after Preet Nagar.
- **1949.** Her hugely popular novel, *Doctor Dev*, published (in Hindi in 1951).
- **1950.** *Pinjar* (in Hindi in 1952).
- **1955.** Poetry anthology, *Sunehde* published.
  - • M.S. Randhawa asked Amrita to write the introduction of his collection of Kangra folksongs and she stayed for a few days in Andretta where she met a pioneer in Punjabi drama and theatre, Nora Richard, and famous painter, Sobha Singh. Amrita says she learnt to make rotis there.
- **1956.** Became the first woman to win the Sahitya Akademi Award for *Sunehde*. She only regretted that the one for whom they were intended was oblivious of them. In the course of an interview, she kept writing 'Sahir' on a sheet of paper.
  - • M.S. Randhawa, who had helped her get a job at AIR, also made it possible for her to have 'a room of her own'. He deposited Rs. 1,000/- on her behalf with the purse received for the Sahitya Akademi Award to get a plot in Hauz Khas, a DLF colony. She paid for the allotted plot 'K-25' in instalments and built her house that became a hub of cultural and literary activity.

- **1958.** Won the Shiromani Punjabi Sahitkar Award from Bhasha Vibhag, Punjab.
  - Met Vietnamese President Ho Chi Minh in 1958. He told her that they were both trying to fight the evil values of the world, he with a sword, and she with a pen. She wrote a poem that was published in the Vietnamese paper *Nhan Dan* on 26 May 1958.
- **1959.** In chapter '1959 di Ik Kabar' ('A Grave of 1959'), *Rasidi Ticket*, she mentions a girl who betrayed the affection that Amrita had showered upon her. Says she wrote many stories about her as if plucking thorns from her body.
  - Towards the end of this year, she happened to see the news of Sahir's new love interest. Wrote the poem 'Saal Mubarak' about her broken dreams.
  - Had also met Imroz by then who had introduced himself as Dr Dev on the phone. He was an artist whom she met to discuss the design of a book cover. She soon began to perceive her Rajan in him.
- **1960s-1970s.** Travelled to the countries of East Europe and Central and South Asia. Received wide coverage by the international press.
- **1960.** Visited Nepal as part of an official government delegation in January.
  - 27 January 1960. Wrote her celebrated letter to Imroz, lamenting that he had met her in the dusk of her life and not in the bright afternoon.
  - During October-November, she walked out of her marital home.
- **1961.** Went to Tashkent, Uzbekistan and several other places. She met poets, including Zulfia Khanam, who was the first poet she translated into Punjabi. When it began to drizzle during a conference, Mirza Tursan-Zade, a major poet of Tajikistan, said that the sky had come to water the seed of their friendship. When asked about the river of lovers in her country, she answered 'Chenab' and they had 'Verziab' so even these rhymed. She also visited Russia at the invitation of the Writers' Union Uzbekistan, Tajikistan, Moscow and Azerbaijan.
- **1963.** Formally divorced on 8 January 1963.
- **1965.** Published novel, *Dharti Sagar te Seepiyaan*. Basu Bhattacharya's film *Kadambari* was based on this.
  - Honoured by Indian Women's Federation.
- **1966.** Influenced by the biography of America's famous journalist and writer, Anne Royall, written by Irving Wallace. Anne had started a paper at age 80 with very few resources and had led a life full of struggle, economic hardship and court cases. Amrita identified with her struggle. In an interview with Devendra for the radio that was published in *Dastavez* later, she says that in this oppressive world it is easy to malign a woman.

- Went twice to Moscow and then to Georgia and Armenia when Georgia was celebrating the 800th anniversary of Georgian poet, Shota Rustaveli.
- Also went to Nepal at the invitation of the Indian Embassy and then to Bulgaria and Moscow.
- **1967.** The government of India sent her to Yugoslavia (International Poetry Festival), Hungary and Romania in a cultural exchange, for three weeks in each country. Bulgaria West Germany and Iran also invited her.
- **1968.** Interview to the *Statesman*, a prominent English print daily.
  - 3 September 1968. Gives the context of the poem 'Mera Pata'. Inspired by Czech people who had removed the numbers from their doors, streets, etc.
  - Published autobiographical *Kala Gulab*.
- **1968-1969.** Interview to Carlo Coppola for the Asian Studies Journal, *Mahfil*.
- **1969.** Again travelled to Nepal.
  - Celebration of 500 years of Guru Nanak Prakash Utsav. A publisher asked her to write about Nanak, but she refused because she did not think poetry could be commissioned. But suddenly after receiving a phone call from her son from the hostel of Baroda University, she felt overcome with maternal love. (This is one of the three instances she quotes in *Rasidi Ticket* when she felt 'all woman', the other two being when she rubbed Vicks on Sahir's chest and when Imroz painted a red bindi with his brush on her forehead.) She wondered about Guru Nanak Dev's mother's feelings and wrote a poem 'Garbhvati' ('Pregnant'), later retitled 'Nau Supne' ('Nine Dreams') – the journey of nine months of pregnancy given as nine dreams. Punjabi media slammed her and asked the government to ban the poem. A Kirpal Singh Kasel called her a 'kaamuk cheenti' in *Ajit* newspaper and said that she did not have the right to write about the holy guru.
  - Awarded Padma Shri, the fourth highest civilian award in India.
- **1970.** Published *Kaagaz te Canvas*, dedicated to Imroz. Won the Bharatiya Jnanpith Award. Second Indian woman and first Punjabi woman to get the award. Second Punjabi to get the award.
- **1971.** Wrote 'Ek Dosti ki Maut' ('The Death of a Friendship') in the last week of March 1971, four months after the death of a friend who was born in 1933 and in whose living room the magazine *Nagmani* had been conceptualised.
- **1972.** Publication of novella, *Akk da Boota*. In *Rasidi Ticket*, she narrates that she added an incident about the protagonist being covered with a quilt by a fellow passenger on a train. Remembers how four years earlier in Bulgaria, a fellow passenger had put his overcoat on her on a train.

- Again sent to Yugoslavia (International Poetry Festival), Czechoslovakia, and France for three weeks each; she also went to London and Italy at her own expense. Cairo invited her for one week on her return.
- Interview to B.B.C. London where she was introduced to poet Sahab Qazalbash who was delighted to meet the author of 'Ajj Aakhaan Waris Shah nu' and said, 'I must embrace her.' They also met in Surinder Kochchar's house, where other Pakistani writers, Saqi Farooqi, Fahmida Riaz and Abdullah Husain, and singers Nazakat Ali and Salamat Ali were present. Nazakat Ali was asked to sing something, and although he did not have an instrument, he said, 'I have never sung without an instrument ... but for her who has written "Ajj Aakhaan Waris Shah nu", I shall sing even without an instrument.'
- **1973.** Attended 'World Peace Congress' in Moscow.
- Published novel, *Yaatri*. In 1973, when it was being translated into English, Amrita identified with Sundaran's character. Sundaran would pile up flowers in a temple, under which she would try to touch her beloved. Thinks she too is someone who piled words upon words to touch someone, which others would not be able to see.
  - 1973 D.Litt. conferred by the University of Delhi on 15 May 1973. Recalls that Devendra offered her a *shagan* of a silk kerchief, *mishri* and 21 rupees as a father or a brother. In her novel *Ek Savaal*, a similar incident had been written in.
  - 1973 D.Litt. conferred by Jabalpur University.
- **1975.** Published novel, *Unhan di Kahani* (*Their Story*).
  - This was also the year of the release of Basu Bhattacharya's *Daaku*, adapted from this novel.
  - Adaptation of Amrita Pritam's novel, *Dharti, Sagar te Seepiyaan*, into H.K. Verma's directed film *Kadambari*. The most well-known song of the film, 'Ambar ki ek pak surahi', is her song translated from Punjabi. When asked to write a song about the character winning his beloved, oblivious of societal norms, she says she remembered the song she had written about her mind's condition upon meeting Imroz for the first time in 1960.
  - Honoured by Vishva Hindi Sammelan Nagpur as one of 15 writers from other languages who were honoured.
- **1976.** First published her autobiography, *Rasidi Ticket*.
  - Attended Vishva Hindi Sammelan in Mauritius.
  - N.I.F. Award.
- **1977.** Visited Bulgaria and Yugoslavia.
- **1978.** *Amrita di Diary.* In her diary she wrote on 27 February 1978 that she read an interview of Mohan Singh in the paper *Main* which made her feel that the pure topic of love was being spoken about in the language

of the sewer. In the context of this interview, she wrote 'Ik Safa' in *Nagmani*, May 1978. When she came to Chandigarh for a function, this editorial was being discussed.

- *Dastavez* – Letters of Amrita-Imroz published.
- Honoured on the occasion of the 50-year celebration of AIR.
- Honoured on Kannada Sahit Sammelan.

- **1978-1980.** Amrita Pritam involved in creative assistance and writing work on Basu Bhattacharya's film on Indira Gandhi.
- **1979.** International Vaptsarov Award by the Republic of Bulgaria.
  - Cyril and Methodius Award from Bulgaria.
  - Honoured by Punjabi International Society.
- **1980.** Went to Greece and Bulgaria (World Writers' Conference).
- **1981.** Visit to Bulgaria.
- **1982.** She won the Bharatiya Jnanpith Award for the poetry anthology, *Kagaz Te Canvas*. First Punjabi writer to get it.
- **1984.** Dalbir Chetan went to meet her as she was ill. She said she would get well if Punjab got well.
  - Pakistani poet, Ahmed Salim wrote a beautiful poem on *Rasidi Ticket*, 'Kudiyan Pyar Kardiyan ne' ('Girls Fall in Love') (*Nagmani*, April 1984).
  - Published *Hardatt da Zindaginama*, a novel based on Shri Madan Mohan Haridutt's life, a colleague of well-known thinker, M.S. Rai. Haridutt was sent to the dreaded Siberian camp during the Second World War on being suspected of spying. He had been freed after 16 years of torture. The publication led to a civil suit that eminent Hindi writer Krishna Sobti filed regarding the use of the word 'Zindaginama'. After 26 interminable years, the matter was decided in Amrita's favour in 2011; author Khushwant Singh records that he sided with Amrita in this matter. He appeared in court on her behalf and said that there could not be any copyright on a title like 'Zindaginama'. He offered proof by collecting more than a dozen books from the Iranian embassy because 'zindagi nama' is a Persian phrase. In addition, he submitted his two volumes of Sikh history to show that Guru Gobind Singh's life story by him was also called 'Zindaginama'. As per his narration, Krishna Sobti lost her temper in court and told the judge not to believe a single word of what he said as he belonged to the same mafia of rich writers.
- **1986.** Invited to speak in a conference of chief ministers where with characteristic outspokenness she lamented that the horror of casteism was turning every state in the country a madhouse – a term used once by Swami Vivekananda for Kerala.
- **1986-1992.** After hearing the recording of this conference of CMs, Rajiv Gandhi nominated her to the Rajya Sabha. She raised several

issues related to language, literature, society and culture, and several were acted upon. She also raised the issue of capitalism, globalisation, etc.

- **1987.** D. Litt conferred by Visva-Bharati Shantiniketan.
  - Degree of Officer dens/Order des arts et des letters by the French Government.
- **Post-1990s.** Making of a documentary on Amrita Pritam's life by her close associate, Basu Bhattacharya. Titled *Amrita-Imroz* and shot exclusively at her Hauz Khas residence, it was released in Pakistan in 2003.
- **1995.** Autobiographical *Aksharon ke Saaye* published (originally in Hindi as *Aksharon ki Chhaya Mein*).
- **2000.** Shatabdi Samman – Poet of the Millennium 2000 – awarded by government of NCT of Delhi.
- **2002.** Discontinued *Nagmani*. Amrita fell very sick and Imroz had to take care of her. Many friends offered their services. But they did not want it to become an institution.
  - Punjab Government bestowed the 'Lifetime Achievement Award' with 15 lakh prize money for excellence in the field of art, literature, science, technology, culture and politics. Amrita was the first recipient of the award conferred upon her by Punjab Chief Minister Capt. Amarinder Singh.
- **2003.** 26 May 2003. World Punjabi Congress in Lahore decided to give the first Lifetime Achievement Award to Amrita Pritam. Fakar Zaman said the decision had been taken as a gesture although she did not need any award. According to him, she was very pleased with the news because it was to be given in Pakistan, but she could not visit the place where she was born and spent 28 years of her life.
  - Punjabi Akademy, Lahore, also gave her an award towards the end of her life, to which she remarked, 'Bade dinon baad mere maike ko meri yaad aayi' ('My natal home has remembered me after a long time'). As a token of respect and love, Punjabi poets of Pakistan sent her *chaddars* from the tombs of great Sufi poets, Waris Shah, Bulle Shah and Sultan Bahu. They were green silk covers edged with gold. The dying poet proudly had herself photographed with the *chaddars*.
  - Release of director, Chandra Prakash Dwivedi's landmark film *Pinjar*, based on Amrita Pritam's novella, *Pinjar* (1950).
- **2004.** Awarded Padma Vibhushan.
  - Celebrated anthology *Main Tainu Pher Milangi* published.
  - The 'Sahitya Akademi' (Indian National Academy of Letters) bestowed upon her 'Sahitya Akademi Fellowship', the highest literary award given by the academy.
  - Zee Cine Award for Best Lyricist – *Pinjar*.
  - Zee Cine Award for Best Story – *Pinjar*.

- **2005.** Honoured as 'Immortals of Literature' by Sahitya Akademi.
  - Died on 31 October 2005 at the age of 86 due to prolonged illness in her haven of love at K 25, Hauz Khas, New Delhi.
- **2007.** The audio album titled, 'Amrita recited by Gulzar' was released by celebrated lyricist, Gulzar, reciting Amrita Pritam's poems.
- **2015.** Release of M.S. Sathyu's theatrical rendition titled *Amrita – A Sublime Love Story* (one of the most well-received theatrical renditions of her life till date) – a tribute to her through his rare performance 'Ek Thee Amrita'.
- **2019.** 31 August was celebrated by Google as Amrita's 100th birth anniversary with a doodle by artist Vrinda Zaveri. In the doodle Amrita Pritam is seen sitting in front of a bunch of black roses as she writes in a diary. It is a reference to her autobiography *Kala Gulab* (*Black Rose*). The accompanying write-up reads, 'Today's Doodle celebrates Amrita Pritam, one of history's foremost female Punjabi writers, who "dared to live the life she imagined"'.

(The editors thank Dr Guntasha K. Tulsi for some inputs.)

BIBLIOGRAPHY

Anthologies of Poetry

1935. Amrit Kaur. *Thandiyan Kirnan*. n.a.
1936. Amrit Kaur. *Amrit Lehran*. Lahore: Amolak Ratan Bhandar.
1939. *Jiunda Jeevan*. n.a.
1942. *Trel Dhote Phull*. Lahore: The Commercial Printing Works.
1942. *O Geetan Valiya*. n.a.
1943. *Badlan De Palle Vich*.
1943. *Sunjh di Laali*. Lahore: Lahore Book Shop.
1944. *Nikki Jihi Sugaat*. n.a.
1944. *Lok Peed*. n.a.
1946. *Patthar Geetey*. Amritsar: Lok Sahit Prakashan.
1947. *Lamiyaan Vaataan*. Amritsar: Sikh Publishing House.
1950. *Main Twareekh haan Hind di*. n.a.
1951. *Sargi Vela*. n.a.
1955. *Sunehde*. Amritsar: Sikh Publishing House. Navyug.
1957. *Ashoka Cheti*. Delhi: Navyug Press. Lok Sahit.
1959. *Kasturi*. Delhi: Navyug Publishers.
1964. *Nagmani*. Dehi: Navyug Publishers.
1968. *Navin Saver*. Delhi: Navyug Prakashan. (For children)
1970. *Kaagaz te Kanvas*. Delhi: Bhartiya Jnanpith Publications. 2018. Rpt. Delhi: Shilalekh Publishers.
1977. *Main Jama Tun*. Delhi: Nagmani Prakashan. (An anthology of poems from earlier anthologies)
1983. *Chetarnama*. Delhi: Nagmani Prakashan.
1992. *Trinjan*. n.a.
1995. *Saaviyan Pariyan*. Delhi: Shilalekh. (For children)
2001. *Khamoshi ton Pahilan*. Delhi: Shilalekh.
2004. *Main Tainu Pher Milangi*. Delhi: Shilalekh Publishers.

Edited Poetry

1952. *Punjab Di Aawaaz: Punjab de Lokgeet*. Delhi: Navyug Press. (Folk songs)
1955. *Mauli te Mehndi*. Delhi: Navyug Publishers. (Folk songs)
1957. *Chonvi Punjabi Kavita*.

1960. *Ashuma*. (Folk songs of the world)
1972. *Ajj di Punjabi Kavita*.
1972. *Geetan di Changer*.
1974. *Dardmandan di Aahaan*.
1974. *Akkhar*. (Poems from other countries)
1980. *Main Sassi main Sahiban*. (Poems of women poets of the world)

Edited Poetry in English

1974. *Punjabi Poetry*.

Novels

1946. *Jai Shree*. Lahore: Amrita Publishing House.
1949. *Doctor Dev*. Amritsar: Sikh Publishing House.
1950. *Pinjar*. Amritsar: Sikh Publishing House.
1952. *Aahlana*. Delhi: Navyug Publishers.
1958. *Ashu*. Delhi: Navyug Publishers.
1959. *Ik Savaal*. Delhi: Navyug Publishers.
1960. *Bulaava*. Delhi: Navyug Publishers.
1961. *Bund Darvaaza*. Delhi: Navyug Publishers.
1963. *Rung da Patta*. Delhi: Navyug Publishers.
1964. *Ik Si Anita*. Delhi: Navyug Publishers.
1964. *Chakk No. 36*. Delhi: Navyug Publishers.
1965. *Dharti Sagar te Seepiyaan*. Delhi: Navyug Publishers.
1968. *Dilli di Galiyan*. Delhi: Navyug Publishers.
1969. *Ekta te Ariel*. Delhi: Nagmani Prakashan.
1970. *Jalavatan*. Delhi: Nagmani Prakashan.
1971. *Yaatri*. Delhi: Nagmani Prakashan.
1971. *Jebkatre*. Delhi: Nagmani Prakashan.
1972. *Pakki Haveli*. Delhi: Nagmani Prakashan.
1972. *Akk da Boota*. Delhi: Nagmani Prakashan.
1973. *Agg di Lakeer*. Delhi: Nagmani Prakashan.
1974. *Kachchi Sadak*. Delhi: Nagmani Prakashan.
1975. *Koi Nahi Jaan-da*. Delhi: Nagmani Prakashan.
1975. *Unhan di Kahani*. Delhi: Nagmani Prakashan.
1977. *Eh Sach Hai*. Delhi: Nagmani Prakashan.
1977. *Doosri Manzil*. Delhi: Nagmani Prakashan.
1977. *Adaalat*. Delhi: Nagmani Prakashan.
1977. *Ek Khali Jagah*. n.a.
1977. *Tehrevaan Sooraj*. Delhi: Nagmani Prakashan.
1978. *Unninja Din*. Delhi: Nagmani Prakashan.
1982. *Kore Kaagaz*. Delhi: Nagmani Prakashan.
1984. *Hardatt da Zindaginama*. Delhi: Nagmani Prakashan. (Biography of a Minor Revolutionary).
1984. *Na Radha Na Rukmani*. Delhi: Nagmani Prakashan.
1994. *Khabarnama*. Delhi: Nagmani Prakashan.

Autobiography / Letters, etc.

1968. *Kala Gulab*. Delhi: Navyug Publishers.
1976. *Rasidi Ticket*. Delhi: Nagmani Prakashan. 2019. rpt. Delhi: Shilalekh Prakashan.
1978. *Amrita di Diary*. 2018. Delhi: Shilalekh.
1978. *Dastavez* (Love Letters of Amrita-Imroz). Ed. Imroz. 2011. rpt. Delhi: Shilalekh.
1995. *Aksharon ki Chhaya Mein*. New Delhi: Aman Publication. (Hindi). 2017. *Aksharon ke Saaye*. Delhi: Rajpal and Sons. (Hindi originally).
1998. *Aavaaz di Duniya 2016*. Delhi: Shri Prakashan.

Short Stories

1943. *26 Varey Baad*.
1944. *Kunjiyan*.
1956. *Aakhri Khat*.
1960. *Gojar diyan Pariyan*.
1962. *Chanan da Hauka*.
1968. *Jangli Booti*.
1970. *Ajnabi*.
2000. *Sassi Punnu*. Mumbai: Jeevan Prabhat Prakashan.

Stories from the above anthologies were re-published along with new stories in five anthologies:

1977. *Heere di Kani*.
1977. *Latiyan di Chhokri*.
1978. *Panj Varey Lambi Sadak*.
1978. *Ik Sheher di Maut*.
1978. *Teesri Aurat*.

Edited Stories

1944. *Nede*. (Anthology of True Stories)
1971. *Ajoki Punjabi Kahani*.
1973. *Naviyan Kalaman*.
1979. *Paudiyan*. (Bulgarian stories)
1990. *Mitti di Zaat*.

Edited in Hindi

1962. *Sarv Shreshtha Punjabi Sahit*.
1974. *Punjabi ki Shreshtha Kahaniyan*.
1975. *Punjabi ke Teen Upanyas*.
1975. *Urdu ke Teen Upanyas*.
1975. *Vishva ki Shreshtha Kahaniyan*.

285

1977. *Aur diya Jalta Raha.* (Punjabi stories)
1978. *Main aur Main.* (Self-Interviews / Meetings)
1979. *Aur Nadi Behti Rahi.*
1979. *Aur Baat Sulagti Rahi.*
1980. *Mera Kamra.*
1982. *Akshar Bolte Hain.* (Interviews). Delhi: Saraswati Vihar.

Prose

1958. *Bharat de Usariye.*
1960. *Mombattiyan da Bhed.*
1965. *Kiramchi Lakeerein.* Delhi: Navyug Publishers.
1973. *Safarnama: Sahit te Sahit de Adeerban da.* 2013. rpt. Delhi: Shilalekh Publishers.
1975. *Aurat: Ik Drishtikon.* 2010. rpt. Delhi: Shilalekh Publishers.
1976. *Ik Udas Kitab.* 2013. rpt. Delhi: Shri Prakashan.
1978. *Apne Char Varey.* rpt. 2013. Delhi: Shilalekh Publishers.
1979. *Kehdi Zindagi? Kehda Sahit?* Delhi: Nagmani Prakashan.
1979. *Kachche Akkhar.* rpt. 2011. Delhi: Shilalekh Publishers.
1980. *Ik Hatth Mehndi, ik Hatth Chhaala.*
1980. *Mohabbat: Ik Drishtikon.*
1980. *Mere Kaal Mukt Samkali.* 2017. rpt. Delhi: Shri Prakashan.
1981. *Shok Surahi.*
1982. *Kadi Dhoop ka Safar.* Delhi: Rajpal and Sons. (in Hindi)
1986. *Ashak Bhaur Fakir te Naag Kaale.* Delhi: Arsi Publishers.
1989. *Laal Dhage da Rishta.* 2013. rpt. Delhi: Shilalekh Publishers.
1990. *Chonvein Pattarey.* Delhi: Sahitya Akademi.
1991. *Hujre di Mitti.* Delhi: Nagmani Prakashan.
1993. *Prateek Vigyan.* Delhi: Shilalekh Publishers.
1994. *Kaal Chetna.* Delhi: Nagmani Prakashan.
1994. *Trik Bhawan di Gatha. Amrita Pritam and Pandit Krishan Ashant.* Delhi: Shilalekh Publishers.
1995. *Satt Musafir.* Delhi: Arsi Publishers.
1995. *Bure Siyalaan de Maamley.* Delhi: Shilalekh Publishers.
1996. *Darveshan di Mehndi.* 2017. Delhi: Shilalekh. Poetry + prose.
1997. *Prashan Leela.* Delhi: Shilalekh Publishers.
1997. *Anant Naam Jigyasa.* Delhi: Kitabghar.
1998. *Utth ni Sahibaan Suttiye.* 2012. Delhi: Shilalekh. Poetry + prose.
2000. *Hare Dhaage da Rishta.* Delhi: Shri Prakashan.
2001. *Ishq Allah! Haq Allah!* Delhi: Shri Prakashan.
2002. *Bal Deevdiya.* Delhi: Shri Prakashan.
2002. *Thaari Vikat Nagariya.* Delhi: Shilalekh Publishers.
2002. *Ik Takiya Tere Naam Da.* Delhi: Shri Prakashan.
2003. *Varjit Bagh di Gaatha.* Delhi: Shilalekh Publishers.
2003. *Adan Bagh de Yogi.* Delhi: Shri Prakashan.
2004. *Dekh Kabira.* Delhi: Shilalekh Publishers.
2008. *Aap Beetiyan.* Delhi: Shilalekh Publishers.
2010. *Soorajvanshi Chandarvanshi.* Delhi: Shilalekh Publishers.

2010, 2011. *Satt Kirnaan*. Delhi: Shri Prakash.
2011, 2014. *Ik si Sara*. Delhi: Shilalekh Publishers.
2011. *Raataan Jaagdiyan*. Delhi: Shri Prakashan.
2011. *Ashiq Bhor Faqir te Naag Kaale*. Delhi: Shilalekh Publishers.
2012. *Utth ni Sahiban Sutiye*. Delhi: Shilalekh Publishers.
2013. *Chiragaan di Raat*. Delhi: Shri Prakash.
2016. *Osho Rang Majithada*. Delhi: Shilalekh Publishers.
Daachi diyan Talliyan. Delhi: Shilalekh Publishers. undated

Translations

1955. *Tyag Pattar*. Trans. of Jainendra Kumar's novel.
1958. *Atmakatha*. Trans. of Dr. Rajendra Prasad's autobiography.
1960. *Vaptsarov de Geet: Nikola Vaptsarov: Bulgaria da Mahan Inkalabi Kavi.* Delhi: Navyug Publishers.
1963. *Satt Tehniyan Sattar Patte.* (Poems from the world)
1963. Panna Lal Patel's *Jeevi: Gujarati Bhasha da Elakai Novel*. Delhi: Sahitya Akademi through Navyug Publishers.
1969. *Jang ton Pichhon*. (17 German stories)
1971. *Tamil Kahaniyan*.
1973. *German Sahit di Parampara*.

Travelogues

1961. *Baariyan Jharokhe*.
1969. *Agg diyan Leekaan*. (Travel to Yugoslavia)
1973. *Ikki Pattiyan da Gulab*. (Travel to Europe)

Editing Literary Magazines / Journals

Navin Duniya. Monthly 1937–38.
Hitkari. Quarterly. January 1947.
Nagmani. Monthly. May 1966 to April 2002.
Also edited Samdarshi for some time.

Films

1975. Daaku. Basu Bhattacharya
1976. Kadambari. Directed by H.K. Verma.
2003. Pinjar. Chandraprakash Dwivedi.
[Like the proverbial kuber dhan, the revelations of texts by Amrita Pritam are ever-emerging, and this list may not be exhaustive by any means.]

CONTRIBUTORS

Salim Arif is an illustrious alumnus of the National School of Drama, New Delhi, and a very well-known name in the field of Indian theatre, television and films. Innovative in approach, Salim Arif has directed several notable stage plays and has scripted and presented *Ghalibnaama*, *Gulon Mein Rang Bharo* and *Main Tumhe Phir Miloongi* from letters of Ghalib, Faiz Ahmad Faiz-Alys and Amrita Pritam-Imroz, respectively. Shyam Benegal's *Bharat Ek Khoj*, Gulzar's *Mirza Ghalib*, and Dr Chandraprakash Dwivedi's *Chanakya* TV Series got him recognition as a Period Film Designer of repute. Nirja Guleri's *Chandrakanta*, Ketan Mehta's *Sardar Patel*, Gulzar's *Maachis & Hu-Tu-Tu*, Govind Nihalani's *Takshak* and Anil Sharma's *Ab Tumhare Hawale Watan Saathiyo* are his other films as a Designer.

Bharti Arora is a faculty member of the Department of English, Tagore Government Arts and Science College, Pondicherry University. Previously, she worked as an Assistant Professor (ad-hoc) at the Department of English, Janki Devi Memorial College, University of Delhi. She has recently completed her PhD (English) from Jamia Millia Islamia, New Delhi. She has also published a book, based on her PhD thesis, titled *Writing Gender, Writing Nation: Women's Fiction in Post-independence India* (Routledge 2019).

Hartej Kaur Bal teaches English at Government College for Girls, Patiala. She has contributed translations from Punjabi to English for Sahitya Akademi. She has also translated a collection of Punjabi short stories by Sukhwant Kaur Mann into English for the Department of Development of Punjabi Language, Punjabi University, Patiala, that is under publication.

Mohan Bhandari was a well-known Punjabi writer and won the Sahitya Akademi award in 1998. He had worked in the Punjab Education department. He wrote prolifically and has published 15 short story collections. He was also a translator from Hindi and Urdu. He is counted among the progressive writers in Punjabi.

Jasbir Bhullar, a Lt. Col. and an army veteran, has a Master's degree in Punjabi literature. He is a prolific writer and translator and has authored over 40 collections of short stories and novels, including a large number for children. His works have been translated into several other languages; Sahitya Akademi has selected his book *Jungle Tapu* as a children's classic to be translated into 21 languages. Among his numerous awards is the Sahitya Akademi 'best writer of children's literature award' in 2010 for his novel *Pataal de Githmuthe (The Midgets of the Underworld)*. He has also directed and produced several documentary films.

Charles Brasch (27 July 1909-20 May 1973) a New Zealand poet. His ambition was to start a literary quarterly journal which he did in 1947 and called it Landfall. He was passionate about his home country and wrote extensively about it. He collaborated with Amrita Pritam to translate her poems into English and this was published as *The Black Rose* in 1967.

Madhuri Chawla teaches English at Dyal Singh Evening College, University of Delhi. She translates from Punjabi to English and has participated in several workshops organized by Sahitya Akademi, Punjabi Academy, British Council and others, and her translations have been published in various anthologies and journals. She has published several research articles in journals and books and articles of general interest in leading national dailies. She has also presented papers at several national and international conferences. Her areas of interest are Gender Studies and Diaspora Studies.

Nirupama Dutt is a Punjabi poet and translator and has worked as a journalist for over four decades. She was awarded the Punjabi Academy Award in 2000 for *Ik Nadi Sanwali Jahi (A Stream Somewhat Dark)* and has several translations to her credit. She has also edited a book of fiction by Pakistani women writers called *Half the Sky* and one of resistance literature of Pakistan called *Children of the Night*. She is a convener of a women's study group called 'Hamshira'.

Jung Bahadur Goyal, a former civil servant, is an eminent writer and translator. He writes with ease and fluency in Punjabi, Hindi and English. He has authored about 20 books. His book *Vishav Sahit de Shahkar Novel (Classics of World Literature)* in four volumes is considered his magnum opus.

Harmeet Kaur Jhajj is Assistant Professor of English at SCD Government College, Ludhiana. Born and raised in Kolkata, West Bengal, she combines the ethos of Bengal with the ethnic identity of Punjab. Her areas of interest are Literature of the Diaspora, Partition, Dalit, Indian Literature in English, Hindi and Punjabi, Eco-critical literature, 20th-century English Literature and, recently, translation. She has presented research papers in national and international seminars and conferences and published them in books.

Anupama Jaidev Karir teaches English at Maharaja Agrasen College, University of Delhi. Her research areas include Romani studies, narratives of the Indian Emergency of 1975, narratives of witch-hunts, popular reading and cultural historiography of itinerant communities in the subcontinent. She writes and translates from Hindi to English. She has presented papers in national and international conferences and published work in journals and a book chapter, 'Myth, Misogyny and Marginalisation: A Reading of Mahasweta Devi's *Bayen*' in *Re-storying the Indigenous and the Popular Imaginary* (2017), Authorspress, New Delhi.

Paul Kaur is a Punjabi poet, scholar and critic who taught Punjabi language and literature at S.A. Jain College, Ambala. Known for her philosophical and feminist stance, she has published seven anthologies of poetry, one on criticism, one non-fiction book and two edited books. She has been given several awards by the Punjab Government and the Haryana Government among which is the Bhai Santokh Singh Puruskar for her overall contribution to Punjabi literature.

Rupinder Kaur Waraich is a Birmingham-based Punjabi writer and performer. Her work explores womanhood, language and history. Her debut poetry book *Rooh* (2018) was published with Verve Poetry Press. She is currently working on her second poetry collection.

Sukrita Paul Kumar is a noted poet, academic and critic. She was an invited poet and Fellow at the prestigious International Writing Program, Iowa, USA. A former Fellow of the Indian Institute of Advanced Study, Shimla, she has several collections of poetry, translations and critical works to her credit.

Amia Kunwar is the pen name given by Amrita Pritam herself to Dr Amarjeet Kaur, a poet in her own right. She retired as Associate Professor, Department of Punjabi, SGTB Khalsa College, University of Delhi. She has written four books in Punjabi and two in Hindi on criticism and prose and has edited eight books, among which are three on Amrita. She has also translated extensively from Punjabi to Hindi for Amrita. She has won several awards from Sahit Kala Sangam, Delhi, Punjabi Academy, etc.

Aman Kwatra is a Counselling Psychologist and Research Associate at Spectrum.Life. His main professional and research interests are in leveraging digital technologies for the provision and advancement of mental health services and in recovery from complex trauma. Aman completed his MSc in Psychology at the University of St. Andrews, Scotland, and obtained his Doctorate in Counselling Psychology at Trinity College Dublin, Ireland. He has previously worked with the Irish Prison Service and has a background in Post-War Recovery Studies (University of York) and International Relations (University of Bristol).

Arti Minocha teaches English at Lady Shri Ram College, University of Delhi. She has taught various courses in Indian Literature, Modern British Literature, World Literature and Women's Writing. Her doctoral project on gender and print cultures of colonial Punjab sought to re-inscribe women into histories of print and literary cultures and language debates in 19th-century Punjab. She has worked extensively on archival collections housed in India and the United Kingdom, some of which she is currently translating. She has published in the areas of Indian Theatre, Print Culture Studies and Gendered Histories of Colonial Punjab.

Hina Nandrajog is an academic, scholar, critic, teacher and translator. Her areas of interest are the Partition of India in 1947 and translation. She translates from Punjabi and Hindi into English and has won several awards and has been a part of several translation projects. She has also been actively involved in creating e-content for the Institute of Life Long Learning, University of Delhi. She is one of the editors of this volume.

Deepti Naval is an acclaimed actress, director, theatre artist, poet, writer, painter and photographer. Her directorial debut won the Best Screenplay Award at the NY Indian Film Festival (2009). She published her first selection of poems in Hindi, *Lamha* in 1983, followed by *Black Wind and Other Poems* in 2004. She also authored a collection of short stories, *The Mad Tibetan*, published in 2011. She runs the Vinod Pandit Charitable Trust, set up in memory of her late companion for the education of the girl child. She has won several accolades and awards for her sensitive acting in films and stage plays.

Sutinder Singh Noor was former Professor at the Department of Punjabi, University of Delhi, and has also served as the Vice President of Sahitya Akademi, New Delhi. He was a reputed critic, poet and translator and has several books to his credit. He served as the editor of *Samdarshi*, a Punjabi Academy journal.

Anjali Gera Roy is Professor at the Department of Humanities and Social Sciences at IIT Kharagpur. Her research interests span postcolonial fiction and theory, media, cultural and performance studies, Punjab and Sikh Studies, diaspora, migration and mixed race. Her published works include *Memories and Postmemories of the Partition of India* (Routledge, 2019) and *Cinema of Enchantment: Perso-Arabic Genealogies of the Hindi Masala Film* (Orient BlackSwan, 2015). Recently, she has coedited

291

(with Robyn Andrews) *Beyond the Metros: Anglo-Indians in India's Smaller Towns and Cities* (Primus Books, 2021).

Tanvir Sachdev is Principal, Govt. College, Ludhiana, Punjab University and previously worked on deputation at College of Engineering, Jawaharlal Nehru Technology University, Hyderabad, as well as School of Planning and Architecture, Jawaharlal Nehru Architecture and Fine Arts University, Hyderabad, India. Her special areas of interest are gender and post-colonial studies. She has published several articles in national and international journals and has presented several papers at national and international fora.

Rekha Sethi is a Professor and the Acting Principal at Indraprastha College for Women, University of Delhi. She has authored five books, edited eight and translated a poetry collection from English to Hindi. She has also published extensively in leading literary journals and presented her work at international and national fora. She recently co-organised a web-lecture series on 'Women Writings in India' with Dr Fauzia Farooqui, South Asian Studies Program, Princeton University.

Khushwant Singh (2 February 1915-20 March 2014) trained as a lawyer who won acclaim as an author and editor. He joined the Indian foreign service after migrating to newly independent India from his native land. In 1951, he joined All India Radio as a journalist, a career in which he flourished. He is known for his English novel on Partition, *Train to Pakistan*. He served as a member of the Rajya Sabha and has been awarded with the Padma Bhushan in 1974 which he returned after the Operation Blue Star in 1984. In 2007, he was awarded the Padma Vibhushan.

Manjinder Singh is Associate Professor and current Head at the School of Punjabi Studies, Guru Nanak Dev University (GNDU), Amritsar. His interests are grammar and semantics of Punjabi language and literature, Musicology of Gurbani and Indian classical music and Subaltern Studies. He has numerous presentations and publications, including three books. He has been awarded a research project by Punjabi Academy, Delhi, on 'Bharti Sahit de Nirmata, Dr. Prem Parkash Singh'. Among his administrative duties are Chairman, Board of Control and Board of Studies, School of Punjabi Studies, GNDU. He is also the coordinator for S. Nanak Singh Literary Foundation in GNDU.

Yadwinder Singh is faculty at the Department of Punjabi, University of Delhi. His publications include a book, *Poorabwad: Siddhant te Vihar*, and several articles. He has translated Amandeep Sandhu's book, *Panjab: Journeys through Fault Lines*. Currently he is writing a monograph on the American Palestinian thinker, Edward W. Said.

Prem Kumari Srivastava is Professor of English at the University of Delhi at Maharaja Agrasen College. Widely published, her research displays an overarching focus on the 'other': the popular, the indigenous, the non-urban and gender within Cultural Studies. Some of her seminal works are *Leslie Fiedler: Critic, Provocateur, Pop Culture Guru* (2014), McFarland & Inc. Publishers, North Carolina, USA; three-volume series (co-edited) on Literatures, Languages and Cultures of the Indigenous (2014 and 2017), Authorspress publishers, Delhi, *Tribal Literature and Oral Expressions in India*, Sahitya Akademi, New Delhi (2021) and *Indian Popular Fiction: New Genres, Novel Spaces* (co-edited), Aakar Books, New Delhi (2021), Routledge, UK (2022). Prem is one of the editors of this volume.

Guntasha K. Tulsi teaches at Maharaja Agrasen College, University of Delhi, specialising in Language and Communication, Indian regional writings, colonial historiography, and sub-altern and post-colonial discourses. With a PG Certificate Course in ELT and a PG Diploma in Teaching English from the School of Distance Education, EFL-U, Hyderabad, she has worked as a Corporate Communication Trainer and conducted workshops across MNCs and universities. She has recently edited a volume titled *Media and Communication: A Handbook for Students* (forthcoming), Worldview Publishers (Delhi), and her translations of two Punjabi short stories into English are forthcoming in the book *Medical Maladies: Stories of Disease and Cure from Indian Languages* (ed. by Haris Qadeer), Niyogi Books (Delhi).

Vanita is a poet, academic, translator and critic. A post-graduate in Music and Punjabi, her area of research is postmodernism and Punjabi poetry. She has a large number of publications – translations, newspaper and journal articles, edited books and magazines, as well as critical and creative publications, among which are a book on feminism and Punjabi literature. In addition, she has also presented around 70 radio programmes on All India Radio, as well as about sixty television programmes for Jalandhar and Delhi Doordarshan. She has been a member of several prestigious bodies and has served as a jury member for the Sahitya Akademi. At present, she is the Convenor of Punjabi Language in Sahitya Akademi and the K.K. Birla Foundation.

Ritika Verma is a PhD research scholar at the Department of Humanities and Social Sciences, IIT Kharagpur, India. Her research interests include Partition studies, South-Asian literature and trauma theory.

INDEX

(Note: page locators in italics denote figures)